Beautiful Practice

A Whole-Life Approach to Health,
Performance and the Human Predicament

Frank Forencich

ISBN: 978-0-9851263-0-8

For information, contact Exuberant Animal:
www.exuberantanimal.com

AN EXUBERANT ANIMAL® PUBLICATION

To my favorite dance partners.

Contents

Keep the faculty of effort alive in you by a little gratuitous exercise every day. That is, be systematically ascetic or heroic in little unnecessary points, do every day or two something for no other reason than that you would rather not do it, so that when the hour of dire need draws nigh, it may find you not unnerved and untrained to stand the test.

William James

Beautiful seeds will bear beautiful fruit.

Jack Kornfield

Predicament, promise, potential

We are continually faced with a series of
great opportunities brilliantly disguised
as insoluble problems.

John Gardener

Something is seriously amiss.

Things just aren't right.

Life feels stressful, confusing and threatening.

Distorted, unhealthy, unsustainable.

Even a superficial reflection tells us that things in this modern world simply aren't working very well. We feel it in our guts, in our minds and in our spirits. We worry about the future, we worry about our health, we worry about terrorism, economic collapse and the fate of the biosphere. These anxieties keep us up at night and haunt us during the day.

We are right to feel this way. Our dilemma, after all, is unprecedented and intimidating. On one hand, we seem to know a great deal about how the world works. We're awash in knowledge and educational opportunity, surrounded by schools and teachers of every description. Over the course of the last several hundred years, we've made discoveries that would stagger the imagination of ancient scholars.

At the same time, it's not at all clear that this educational affluence is doing us much good. We're surrounded by possibility and opportunity, but many of us are mired in ill-health, anxiety, stress, anger and depression. We know more about the world than ever before and yet we seem exceedingly uncomfortable with actually living in it.

Of course, the story of suffering is as old as humanity itself. Ever since our earliest ancestors developed big brains and big questions to go along with them, we've been struck by the perplexing and sometimes terrifying nature of life. We've struggled to live this mysterious reality, desperately seeking security and permanence in a highly dynamic and impermanent world.

This was the historic insight of Siddhartha Gautama, later called the Buddha, ("the awakened one") some 2,500 years ago. All is temporary, he taught. Our bodies come and go, our health waxes and wanes, our friends and families pass into and out of our lives. Pain, injury and loss are commonplace and even our most cherished pleasures are transient. And thus the first Noble Truth of Buddhism: "All life is suffering." Or, to put it a slightly more modern way, "All life is stressful."

But wise as he was, even the Buddha would have been shocked by the magnitude, breadth and urgency of suffering in the modern world. Not only do we experience the primal challenges of a fragile, temporary personal existence, we also face a host of new maladies that challenge us in entirely novel ways.

In the first place, we are living in what may well be described as an "alien environment." In recent years, biological scientists have described the profound disconnect between the deep history of the human body and the reality of life in the modern world. This is often described as the "mismatch" hypothesis. All animals, including humans, are best suited to a certain range of environmental conditions. When there's a match between an animal's genetic heritage and its environment, that animal is likely to remain healthy. But if the organism is forced to live outside of its normal range, in an "alien" environment, it will suffer stress and ill-health.

In our case, the mismatch is profound. Our bodies evolved in the wild, natural, forests and grasslands of Africa; this was our ancestral environment. But today, we live in a radically unfamiliar world that is often hostile to our health and happiness: Vehicles and dwellings forces us into sedentary occupations and prolonged sitting. Ancient cycles of light and darkness are now disrupted by artificial light and jet travel. Our food supply now consists in large measure of "edible food-like substances." Even worse, we now live in an alien cognitive environment, one that forces us to exercise our brain's executive powers more or less continuously throughout each day; modern life has become a relentless grind of planning, sorting, listing, researching and prioritizing.

Clearly, this mismatch is having a profound effect on the state of our bodies, minds and spirits. Over the course of the last several decades, humanity has experienced a rapid and ominous increase in so-called non-communicable diseases. Also referred to as "lifestyle diseases," these are medical conditions such as obesity, diabetes, heart disease, cancer, depression and respiratory disease. The World Health Organization reports NCDs to be the leading cause of mortality in the world, representing over 60% of all deaths. Currently, NCDs kills 36 million people a year, a number that is expected to rise by 17–24% within the next decade. The NCD Alliance, an advocacy and outreach organization, describes NCDs as "a global emergency." In many corners of the modern world, disease is rapidly becoming "the new normal."

Primal relationships

Even more distressing, we have nearly lost contact our most vital life-support systems; our primal relationships have been stretched almost to the breaking point. The body, once a source of incredible power and resiliency, has diminished in significance to a mere shadow. The body has now become, to use Sir Ken Robinson's famous description, "a mere locomotor device for the head." Our disembodied, "brain on a stick" style of working and living leaves us with only a tenuous connection with the power and intelligence of our native physicality.

Habitat, our primary life-support system, has been largely exiled from human experience. No longer do we live on or even near the land that supports us. We are largely divorced from the earth, living in isolation from the natural processes that sustain us. Environmental destruction now looms as a constant threat. Even as we try to keep our minds focused on our work, our families and the brighter side of modern living, the threat of planetary-scale challenges creeps into our bodies and minds. We try to keep our stress and anxiety at bay, but there is really no place to hide. Our bodies know full well that something is desperately wrong. We live, as Aldo Leopold famously put it in *A Sand County Almanac*, "in a world of wounds."

Finally, we have seriously distorted our tribal experience, both shrinking and expanding our circles of connection with one another. Our brains are wired for a moderate number of human relationships, but today our social circles have shrunk to almost nothing and simultaneously expanded to include vast numbers of faceless individuals. To make matter worse, human communication is being degraded at a ferocious pace by electronic devices. The human brain and body evolved for social contact and communication in real time. In a normal, face-to-face human relationship, the entire mind-body participates in communication; posture, gesture and tone are vital for complete understanding. The actual words represent only a fraction of the total meaning. By disembodying the communication process, we make promote anxiety, confusion and alienation.

Unfortunately, most of us have no idea how to respond to any of these challenges. When faced with the ancient challenge of impermanence and the modern problems of habitat destruction, social chaos and stress, most of us tend to fall back on our primitive behaviors. Sometimes we panic and run with the ever-popular "fight, flight or freeze" response. Sometimes we hide inside the comfort of habit or retreat into a state of passivity and sleep living.

Other times we turn to compulsive activity. Unable to sit still in the ambiguous present, we whip ourselves into a frenzy of doing. Likewise, many of us seek escape through attachment and addiction. We attach ourselves to substances and sensations, to power and control, to work, to ideas and explanations, thinking and analysis, distraction and possessions. Alternately, some of us lunge for hyper-stimulation in the form of high risk sports, drinking or sex.

Naturally, many of us become absorbed in drama. As stress and uncertainty escalate, we begin to feel powerless and in turn, cast ourselves as victims. We blame and complain. We attribute our problems to perceived perpetrators. We point our fingers at people, ideas or organizations that are abusing us. If that fails, we seek out rescue from people, substances or ideas, hoping that these agents can make our woes disappear.

Some of us turn radically inward. Terrified that our social systems, environments and institutions will collapse, we retreat into our own private worlds of self-interest and narcissism. We focus obsessively on our careers, our sports, our bodies or our wealth, leaving the rest of the human family to fend for itself.

That's not the end of it. Many of us defend ourselves from the prospect of suffering by living a life of irony and cynicism. Instead of risking our lives with sincere and authentic engagement, we take refuge in cognitive and spiritual distance. We claim not to care, we toss off our challenges with black humor and pretend that it's all meaningless anyway.

Finally, many of us resort to watered-down living. Unable or unwilling to take on the challenge of the present, we dilute our experience with all manner of distractions and diversions. We stall, we procrastinate and chase the latest trivia. We entertain ourselves away from robust life experience, adopting a lifestyle that cultural critic Neil Postman once described as "amusing ourselves to death." And when all else fails, we simply hang on in quiet desperation, keeping up a brave front, but wishing for some kind of "out."

We need a practice

To one degree or another, we all engage in these primitive responses to stress and suffering. We all fight and flee, we all attach and fixate, we all hide out in disguise, we all craft clever ruses to protect ourselves from unhappiness. And we do it now more than ever.

Sadly, our compulsive and reactive attempts to deal with our predicament always seem to exhaust themselves into depression, calamity, injury and confusion. Our habitual responses sometimes buy us a bit of time or an illusion of satisfaction, but ultimately, they wrap us ever tighter in a wicked spiral of anxiety, stress and unhappiness. Even worse, they're contagious.

Not only that, our primitive responses also close us off to the wonders of life. By compulsively defending, attaching, isolating and withdrawing, we cut ourselves off from the beauty, power and magnificence of life. Sleep living, mindlessness, attachment, addiction; none of it works. None of it provides real safety and even worse, it takes us out of touch with the beautiful adventure.

Unfortunately, we have no curriculum for dealing directly with the challenges of human suffering in the modern world or for learning how to live this beautiful adventure. Most of our health and educational models are based on old challenges; our institutions are always fighting the last wars. We are adept at dealing with exposure, infection, invasions, food shortages and other urgencies, but we have nothing that deals directly with our suffering or our planetary predicament.

Even worse, we have built a system that actively promotes reactivity, not intelligence or wisdom. Most modern organizations are constructed on a foundation of behavior modification: evaluation, incentives and promotion, tracking and manipulation. In other words, a culture of carrots and sticks. We see this approach in almost every modern setting, from schools to business and government. Educational critic Alfie Kohn describes the prevailing message of this culture as "do this and you'll get that." Follow the rules and you'll get the carrot; play the game and you'll get ahead.

Naturally, this kind of culture leaves us unsatisfied and depressed. As Kohn put it, we are "punished by rewards."

So what are we to do? Naturally, many of us will go in search of understanding. We want to know the nature of our predicament. We want to know how the brain and body work, the forces that shape our behavior and the path to transformation. This knowledge exists, but most of us are already overwhelmed with information. Every day brings new research reports, findings and discoveries; many are fascinating and worthy of exploration, but how are we supposed to integrate them into our lives? Our heads are ready to burst with cognitive overload as it is. What are we to do with it all?

Education is always the answer, but what we need more than anything else is a unifying, whole-life experience, a focal point for meaning in our lives. We need engagement and discipline, a time and a place to draw our energies together into a powerful and coherent whole. We need a renewed culture of learning, one in which the process and experience of education is valued for its own sake. Most importantly, we need to put our lives up against the world and find out what we're really capable of. And we need to do it often, with regularity, with discipline, with commitment and with resolve. Mere knowledge is not enough. There must also be a doing, a consistent, engaging, risky and powerful doing.

In other words, we need a practice.

What's a practice?

Our need for engaged experience is clear, but what exactly *is* a practice? Is it like an athletic training program? Is it like school? Or is it like an apprenticeship? Is it something we do together or is it something we do on our own?

The short answer is that practice may be all of these things. It can be a traditional discipline such as yoga or martial art. It can be a professional practice such as law or medicine. It can be the training we do for music or dance. It can be something organized, or it can be profoundly personal, something that we do in the familiar moments of everyday living.

Most of us are familiar with the verb *to practice*, the deliberate and intentional repetition of some activity or skill that we'd like to develop. We've all been told to practice our music, our reading and our sports and of course, we've all heard that such practice "makes perfect."

But practice can also be a noun, as in a discipline, a profession or a craft. Used this way, the word refers to a broader experience, one that goes beyond simple repetitions and skill development towards some greater purpose. Naturally, people use the word practice in many ways and in many different contexts, but here we will use the word to refer to any artistic, educational or professional discipline, especially those with a comprehensive or holistic approach to the art of living.

For some of us, this notion of practice is familiar and obvious. If you've done the rounds of meditation, yoga or the martial arts, practice is something you've talked about thousands of times. If you've done intensive training in music, athletics or the arts, practice is a daily reality. If you're in a professional field, you're comfortable with the idea of a legal, medical, therapeutic or accounting practice. All of these forms share similar qualities of engagement, focus, discipline and experience. In this respect, there are many beautiful practices, both formal and personal.

But for many, this notion of practice is an unfamiliar, even foreign concept. Sadly, many of us have never experienced the full immersion and consistent engagement that characterizes a true practice. Conventional schooling fails spectacularly in this regard; competing objectives and distractions lead to watered-down learning experiences that are fragmented, weak and sometimes meaningless. On graduation, many students wander away, never having experienced the joys that deep engagement can bring. Similarly, our sense of practice often disappears in adulthood as concentrated training in athletics, music and dance gives way to the chaotic and fragmented realities of making a living.

A new golden age

Fortunately, this is an exciting time to be involved in education, training and practice. We may well be challenged by biological mismatch, lifestyle disease, environmental destruction and other forms of suffering, but there's a powerful new narrative that's pulsing through the modern world, a highly optimistic story of growth and performance. Now, for the first time in human history, we have a solid understanding of how the nervous system works, how people learn and how to train ourselves for health, happiness and engagement with the beautiful adventure. We are entering a new golden age of training and practice, an era that promises to rewrite everything we thought we knew about human performance and potential.

Our story begins with the realization that neuro-fatalism, the dogma of a static, unchanging nervous system, is officially dead. Starting in the late 20th century, a series of ground-breaking discoveries demonstrated conclusively that the human brain is a highly dynamic, "plastic" organ that changes itself constantly throughout life. Synapses are continuously remodeling themselves into new patterns of activity and new neurons are even being created from stem cells.

This new view, now known as "neuro-optimism," has taken the scientific and popular imagination by storm and this time, the implicit message is deeply empowering. We now know that we can take control of our learning and development. We can learn new arts, skills and disciplines throughout life. We can transform our brains, our bodies and our spirits. Through training, we can develop almost any quality we desire.

Lessons from modern athletic training, combined with discoveries in neuroscience and epigenetics, have demonstrated that the potential for human development is far greater than previously imagined. In fact, one of the greatest and least-appreciated discoveries of the 20th century is the almost unlimited trainability of the human mind-body-spirit. As it turns out, inborn traits are far less important than we thought; it's training that makes the real difference in performance and in life.

Books such as *The Talent Code* by Daniel Coyle and *Talent is Overrated* by Geoff Colvin have laid to rest the notion that talent is something that we're either born with, or not. Using a combination of case studies and lessons from neuroscience and psychology, researchers have shown that the field for human development and performance is effectively wide open. Even so-called "prodigies" such as Mozart, Ted Williams and Tiger Woods turn out to have been rigorously trained, beginning at a very young age.

In 2006, a special edition of *Scientific American*, "Secrets of the Expert Mind" concluded that "The preponderance of psychological evidence indicates that experts are made, not born." Many writers in the world of business management have come to similar conclusions; it's what you do with what you've got that makes the difference. Nature will always be important, but nurture is what's really hot.

Here we see an exciting synthesis of old and new, East and West. Beginning with the Buddha's legendary experience under the Bodhi tree in the 4th or 5th century BCE, Eastern culture has developed an incredibly sophisticated approach to mind-body practice, skill development and training. More recently, we have witnessed a landmark collaboration between cognitive scientists and the Dali Lama, beginning in the late 1980's. Training, as it turns out, is far more powerful than we thought. Researchers began to realize that regular practice can transform the very circuitry of the brain, as well as subtle human qualities such as kindness, compassion and empathy. Taken together, these ancient and modern discoveries are completely re-writing our assumptions about who we are and what we might become.

We are witnessing nothing less than the emergence of a new educational paradigm, one that's Copernican in scope and influence; the field of training and education has been blown wide open. When we couple the discoveries of modern neuroscience with the transformative practices of Eastern tradition, we come to the conclusion that almost any quality of mind, body or spirit can be sculpted by practice. We may not be able to change our hair color, but when it comes to the really important qualities of our bodies and life experience, it's all there waiting for us, open to modification and refinement through beautiful training and practice.

In this sense, we might even say that, when it comes to the important qualities that define our mind, bodies, spirits and lives, "it's all muscle." We know that we can make our muscles bigger and stronger with a regular program of sets and reps, but that's just the beginning; almost every system in the body behaves similarly. Bones get dense with vigorous use, nerve cell circuits get faster and metabolism becomes more efficient. And, since the mind, body and spirit are intimately interconnected, it's safe to say that the entire system will have similar characteristics. Whether it's our ability to lift a heavy weight or produce a state of compassion, kindness, happiness, resilience, courage, love, willpower or present-moment attention, it's all trainable.

Naturally, we will have to engage in the rigors of sustained and disciplined practice, but we have far more control over the trajectory of our life experience that we might suppose. Given enough time, repetitions and focused concentration, there is no practical limit on how much we can grow. Yes, our lifespans are limited and choices must be made, but still, the opportunity for training, growth and development is vast. All we need is a doing.

About Beautiful Practice

Beautiful Practice is a guide to creating and enhancing your training in whatever form it might happen to take, in your community, your organization and your life. This book is for trainers, coaches, classroom teachers, yoga teachers, martial artists, professionals, managers and parents. If you're so inclined, you might want to create a new program from scratch in your school, organization or community. Maybe you'd like to open a studio and start training people full time. Perhaps you'd like to base your practice on meditation, athletic training, sports, music, dance, art, scholarship or a profession. Maybe you'd like to create a hybrid or simply refine what you're already doing. The possibilities are endless.

No matter your path, your training will consist of a series of lessons, each marked by a gradual darkening of your training belt as you progress. The shade of your belt will serve as a reminder of your experience, your developing knowledge and your all-important "time on the mat."

Along the way, you'll learn the fundamentals of practice as you develop a new sense of possibility and potential. You'll learn about health, training, habits of mind, relationship and imagination. As your training belt darkens, you'll begin to look at your body, your health and the routine moments of your life in an entirely new way.

No matter your specific discipline or art, you'll discover new ideas that will improve your skills, sharpen your performance and increase the depth of your engagement. By the time your belt turns black, you'll have a deep appreciation for the process and you'll be ready to put your understanding into action. Finally, when your belt begins to fray around the edges and turns back to white, you will become a sensei and a leader.

Welcome to Practice

A beginning is the time for taking the most
delicate care that the balances are correct.

Frank Herbert

Dune

The future begins today.

Wayne Gerard Trotman

Welcome, grasshopper. Today is the first day of your apprenticeship, your journey into a new life of health and possibility. This will be the start of a beautiful adventure.

Take a look at your belt. It probably feels stiff and unwieldy in your hands. It's difficult to tie around your waist, the knot won't hold its shape and the ends stick out like flags, advertising your status as a raw beginner. The color is stark white, symbolizing your beginner's mind and body to everyone around you.

You may well feel awkward at this point, but this is actually a special time, an ideal state, one to remember as you progress through higher levels of training and mastery. As a beginner, you can see many possibilities for creativity and skill. You have yet to develop any burdensome assumptions, expectations or beliefs about what your creative process should look and feel like.

This is no time for self-imposed limitations. What would you like to become? How far would you like to go? Practice is more powerful than you might suppose; it's like receiving a grain of rice that doubles every few months. In the beginning, you won't be aware of much change or transformation in your life, but after a few years, your health, power and insight will have grown dramatically. Your mind-body-spirit is capable of incredible things; this is a good time to dream big. You are going to go a long way.

What makes a beautiful practice?

Before you begin your training in earnest, it's essential that to reflect on the nature of practice and consider the qualities that are common to beautiful practices around the world. Naturally, there are myriad ways that human beings have trained and practiced throughout history. Ever since the advent of stone tools, we've set up methods, programs, organizations and culture to teach each other our various arts. Details vary widely, but the most successful practices share a common set of qualities:

Above all, a beautiful practice is *authentic*. It is sincere, engaging and risk-taking. Teachers and students have a shared sense that the art is something worth doing and worth doing well. This is no mere pastime or hobby. We are engaged in practice, not simply to secure a credential or a position, but to transform our lives and the lives of others.

Those who are engaged in a beautiful practice believe that, in some very real sense, "this is something worth dying for." This is not hyperbole. After all, when we commit to a sustained engagement with any art, sport, skill or discipline, we are in fact spending a substantial portion of our lives training, practicing and performing. We are literally giving our lives to what we do. Anything else is just dabbling.

When we engage in a beautiful practice, we act courageously, exposing ourselves to the challenges of learning and the world at large. By making ourselves vulnerable to the process, with its inevitable risk and real possibilities of failure, we choose a path with heart. This becomes a journey of substance and authenticity. As screenwriter Robert McKee put it in his landmark book *Story*, "Life teaches that the measure of the value of any human desire is in direct proportion to the risk involved in its pursuit. To live meaningfully is to be at perpetual risk."

A beautiful practice is also *physical*. Our skill, knowledge and expertise is built upon the vitality and wisdom of the body. The body is source of everything we choose to do in our lives, our careers and our professions. The body contributes, not just vitality, but to cognitive performance, emotional regulation and creativity. Our bodies process vast amounts of sensation, regulate our activity and manage our relationships with the world. Even in professions that are not overtly physical, it is our whole bodies, not just our brains, that make us who we are.

A beautiful practice is *integrative*. No matter the form or specific details, our practice strives to bring disparate elements together into a single whole. In this respect, every beautiful practice is a form of yoga. The word *yoga* is taken from the Sanskrit meaning to "add," "join," "unite," or "yoke." Here we bring the knowledge and skills of our particular art together with character development and non-cognitive skills such as courage, patience, resilience and grit. Above all, we seek to embody and live the things that we have learned in practice. Our goal is to develop the whole person.

A beautiful practice is also *disciplined*. There's a method, a sequence, a form and a curriculum. Intuition, freedom and creativity are vital, but there must also be a solid framework and foundation for learning, a core experience that's consistent, intentional and deliberate. As we'll see, highly disciplined reps are the raw material for learning and skill development. Whether it's weight training, dancing or playing a musical instrument, the same principle applies; do a thing over and over again and the nervous system adapts. Nerve cells that fire together begin to wire together.

At the same time, a beautiful practice is also *playful*. It's animated by wonder and curiosity. A sense of play helps us engage with our task, complete our reps and create new combinations of knowledge, movement and experience. Play is our original learning, a proven method that is probably tens of millions of years old. Thus, a beautiful practice is marked by both gravity and levity, both discipline and freedom.

A beautiful practice is *social*. Human learning thrives in teams and tribes, families and communities. Occasional periods of solitude may well be fruitful, but in general, a shared social experience is the ideal. We learn and train together; everyone works with everyone else. We are all practitioners. We are all creators.

A beautiful practice is also *mindful*. It is intentional, deliberate, conscious and awake. This is where we bring all our powers of mind-body-spirit together into a single, concentrated effort. Beautiful practice is an island of mindfulness in an otherwise chaotic, reactive and often unconscious world.

Finally, a beautiful practice is *alive*. Far from being a formula or recipe that's administered over and over to faceless students, clients or colleagues, beautiful practices are always revising themselves, adjusting and changing. As a living, breathing organism, a beautiful practice is fundamentally open-ended. This is a quest and an adventure. There will be no final end point, no arrival at perfection, no ultimate destination. It's all process. It's all journey.

The power of beauty

Practice is obviously beneficial to our lives and a path to transformation, but why this focus on beauty? Isn't it enough to simply put in the time and the reps? If success is simply a matter of training, why not just do the necessary exercises and move on?

In fact, there's a lot more to practice than mere repetition of motor skills. You're about to immerse yourself in a whole-life process that will span years, even decades. Along this journey, reps will be necessary, but they are far from sufficient. Our bodies and spirits want to engage on many levels and here, a sense of aesthetics is essential. Beauty guides us and integrates our efforts into a single coherent whole.

For some, this focus on beauty might seem to be an afterthought or a luxury that we add to our art once the work of skill development is complete. But in fact, this orientation forms a central organizing principle for everything we do. Not only does it nourish our spirits, it's also inherently practical; beauty makes our training more effective.

If beauty was a substance, it would be powerfully therapeutic; the effects would be both broad and deep. The simple, but often overlooked fact is that beauty is good for the entire human organism. Beauty stimulates the parasympathetic branch of the autonomic nervous system, which directs tissue healing and the essential "feed and breed" response. In this way, beauty can serve as an antidote to stress, depression and anxiety. Beauty also offers the promise of depth, meaning and sustainability in the learning process. It promotes positive emotion and helps to solidify our attention and concentration.

Beauty captures our attention and pulls us deeper into experience. It stimulates our curiosity and engagement; it brings life to the process and gives us the enthusiasm for long hours of repetitive practice. Without a sense of beauty, we become mired in endless repetition; our performance may improve to some degree, but the whole person is left wanting.

The beauty of beauty is that it's also highly functional. Beauty can serve as a practical solution to some of our most wicked problems. Obviously, this is an urgent necessity in today's world. Every day is a wicked balancing act of competing demands, shifting priorities and razor-thin judgment calls, overlapping dilemmas and excruciating choices. There are hundreds of ways to look at personal health, lifestyle and most especially, stress. And if personal health is a wicked problem, public health can only be described as hyper-wicked. Epidemics of obesity, diabetes and heart disease bring us face-to-face with dilemmas of free will, public good, social class, equity and responsibility.

Even worse, our 21st century presents us with an avalanche of wicked problems: education, environment, human relations, child rearing, technology and criminal justice to name a few. Increasing complexity, ripple effects and dynamic relationships are everywhere; we are embedded in a world of wicked problems.

This is where beauty can help lead us in the right direction. Beauty has the potential to balance impossible choices and turn them into something that's life-promoting and sustainable. When systems and predicaments become hyper-complex and rational analysis becomes impossible, aesthetics often provide a solution. We may not always get the "correct" answer to our dilemmas, but we may well create something even better. We may not be able to reason out the competing demands within our personal lives or in large-scale systems like public health and environmental protection, but we can almost always create something that's more proportional, balanced and pleasing to our senses. In this respect, beauty works.

The path

Before we begin our training in earnest, it's essential that we reflect on where we're going and what we're doing. What, we may well ask, is the ultimate point of this enterprise?

The easy answer is to say that the prime objective of our training is skill development and mastery. We're practicing our reps because we want to perform at a higher level; we want to be better at what we do. We want to be more skillful athletes or more adept musicians. We want to be more knowledgeable experts or accomplished professionals.

This all sounds sensible enough, but in fact, we're often vague about what we're really after. Or maybe we're driven by competing needs and desires. Maybe we're not really sure what we want. It could be anything. Maybe we want to improve our times, win a medal, become photogenic or live forever. Maybe we want to get skinny or win the respect and attention of our peers. Maybe if we get our picture on the cover of a magazine, we'll be there. Maybe a yellow jersey or a championship will do the trick. Maybe an Olympic gold medal or acceptance into the Hall of Fame. Maybe a trophy spouse and a pile of money. Maybe we just want to be "great."

But these are dubious dreams. In general, they're distractions and side-shows. Even if we do achieve them, they fail to bring lasting satisfaction. Our skills may become extraordinary and we might even look great and impress our friends, but all this fades away in short order and we're still left wondering, "What's the point?"

Spiritual teachers through the ages have given us good answer on this score. No matter the culture or tradition, they all say pretty much the same thing. That is, the ultimate point of our practice is to live the journey of life more completely. The goal is to experience the Beautiful Adventure of life in all its richness and wonder, to develop an intimate relationship with the totality of the world, the universe, the cosmos.

This is where we find the classic rookie mistake. That is, we confuse achievement and process. At the beginning, we are quick to focus on externals, especially the carrots that are dangled before us as incentives. If we practice long and train hard, we'll get the award, the attention, the recognition, the bonus, the lifestyle or the security. But as we mature, we find ourselves wondering if maybe we had it all wrong. The thing that really satisfied us was not the incentive, but the engagement. The reward may have well been pleasing, but it was the striving and the participation that really nourished us. Or, to put it another way, the real carrot is to be found in the living itself, not any particular achievement.

This may seem obvious, even trivial, but in fact, the art is long and the challenges are immense. Complete immersion in life requires dedication, commitment, discipline and courage. It's easy to get distracted along the way. The Beautiful Adventure is rich beyond our imagination but it also exposes us to ambiguity, uncertainty, mystery and impermanence. On this path, suffering, stress and grief are not uncommon. It would be foolish to suppose that everything we see, touch and feel is magical and wonderful.

The challenges are quiet real and yet, it is a beautiful journey. The beauty lies in the way that life keeps us poised on the cusp of mystery and uncertainty. We are always on the brink of wonder, living a beautiful riddle of impermanence, joy, loss and mystery. Even our most astonishing scientific explanations seem to expand before our eyes, incredible discoveries leading to yet more wonder, more questions and a deeper curiosity. No matter which direction we look, we find ourselves in the middle of an immensely rich, unfolding universe. Science puts us squarely in the center of Big Space, Big Time and Big History, while spirituality puts us in contact with vast oceans of human passion and wonder.

Our problem is that we forget the nature of the quest. We treat life as a problem to be solved, a challenge to be endured or a set of conditions to be mastered. We forget to be amazed by the immensity and magnificence of our situation. And then, we craft responses and behaviors that are awkward, unskillful, destructive and dangerous. Obviously, we need both reminders and training.

So what is the path to experiencing the beautiful adventure? It starts, of course, with attention. Keep getting back to the point of engagement, over and over. Embrace the risk that comes with growth and participation. Play a bigger game. Open your heart to the ambiguity and the beauty of the adventure.

To live this beautiful adventure most completely, you must develop a well-rounded capability that's comprehensive, holistic and multi-disciplinary. Specialization will only take you so far. Train yourself across the range of human capability; develop a repertoire of skills. Most importantly, you must learn to embody the lessons that you learn along the way. Knowledge is vital, but the true mark of mastery will lie in the way that you bring that knowledge to the ground, into the actual living of your life.

Dojo rules

Before we begin our practice, it's essential that we review some basic guidelines for participation. In the world of martial art, these guidelines are often presented as "dojo rules," but we see a similar emphasis on discipline in most high performance training environments around the world. No matter the art form, experienced coaches, trainers and teachers know that a sense of order is essential for learning to occur. Some typical guidelines:

- Show respect for people, process and place.

- Exercise responsibility and mindful attention.

- Be on time.

- Participate fully and stay for the duration of the session.

- Everyone works with everyone.

The beauty of such guidelines is that they make expectations clear at the outset. Students are not required to guess about appropriate behavior and teachers don't need to waste time enforcing training sessions. When expectations are clear, everyone involved can focus their energies and perform at a higher level.

Rules and guidelines also promote safety and in turn, set the tone for a robust training process. Clear guidelines plus challenge create a "safe emergency," an optimal stress environment that encourages intensity while simultaneously offering support. This is the ideal formula for growth and transformation.

Explicit rules also help us establish and maintain a sense of contrast between practice and our routine, daily lives. Without contrast, all of our experience feels homogeneous; our days merge into a single amorphous stream of reactivity. Without contrast, life becomes one long string of tasks to be performed. With our attention spread out equally over our days, weeks and months, we end up flat-lining our way through life. The beauty of contrast is that it gives our minds the space and time to enter into periods of deep engagement; this is where we can bring our maximum possible concentration to bear on the matter at hand.

Likewise, rules and discipline also give us a sense of sacred place and time. The implicit message is one of respect: This place is special, this practice is valuable. This is an experience worth protecting and worth doing right. We're establishing guidelines because we respect the process and the people involved.

Clear rules also set a policy of on-time performance and fully-present behavior. Obviously, there will be push-back on this score; in a world of near-universal impulsivity, many people feel entitled to come and go as they please. But this must not be permitted in a beautiful practice. It is a disastrous slippery-slope. Laxity and lateness send the implicit message that this practice is not particularly special or valuable. It's better to hold a strong line on this score than to allow the erosion of quality.

Bow to the mat, sweep the dojo, empty your cup

As you begin your first practice session, now is the time to focus your energy. Begin with a pause, a moment for mindful reflection. Step outside of your routine activity and bring our full attention to the process at hand.

In the world of martial art, we create this pause by bowing to the mat. Take a moment to focus our concentration and show our respect, then cross the threshold into a fresh world of experience, effort and engagement. Your dojo of course, is your training and practice area, whatever it may happen be. It may be a classroom, an office, a presentation room or even a special room in your home.

An actual bow is not necessary, but some sort of mindful pause will make for a richer, more effective practice session. A short meditation, a ritual cleaning of your desk, or even a pre-briefing before the day's challenges: all of these forms integrate the mind-body-spirit into a complete whole. No matter your art, treat it with the respect it deserves.

Likewise, this is also be a good time to "sweep the dojo." By cleaning your training area or work space, you will simultaneously open your minds to new experience; clearing the way for bare attention. In this process, you will begin to see, as Rumi says, "with first eyes." The act of sweeping is ideal for this purpose. It's physical but also soothing and rhythmic. If you have an actual dojo, studio or similar training space, sweep it. If you have an office or a classroom, set it in order. Establish a ritual that is both purposeful but with a deeper meaning. Prepare your mind-body for a fresh experience and engagement.

Finally, this is an ideal time to "empty your cup." Many of us are familiar with the classic Zen story of the beginner who shows up for practice with a head full of assumptions about his powers and knowledge. The master, sensing trouble from a student who is insufficiently humble, pours tea into his cup until it overflows, thus making the point that the student assumes too much. Better that he should discard his presumptions before embarking on this new journey.

It's sound advice, but it's even more powerful than we might suppose. "Empty cup" is now recognized in mindfulness studies as a powerful metaphor for releasing expectations and judgments, thus clearing the way for direct experience of the here and now. The "cup" contains our categories, our expectations, our beliefs, predictions and past experience, all of which add up to some pretty tight constraints on what we're able to sense, feel and learn. These habitual preconceptions can severely limit what we can become.

And so, the practice of emptying your cup is far more than a single, one-off action to be performed by the entry-level student at the beginning of a new career. Rather, it's the basis for a lifetime of mindfulness, something to be repeated thousands of times. By emptying your cup again and again, you'll open yourself to immediate experience and in turn, all the benefits of mindfulness training and experience. So pour it out now, then do it again, then again.

Lesson 1

Begin with the body

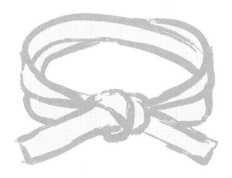

Unless you have been thoroughly drenched in perspiration
you cannot expect to see a palace of pearls on a blade of grass.

Blue Cliff Record, a collection of Buddhist koans

There is more wisdom in your body than in your
deepest philosophy.

Nietzsche

We start with physicality. We begin by moving our bodies deeply and often, pushing the boundaries of what we think is possible. In this practice, we experience fatigue, muscle soreness and an incredible rush of supercompensation as our bodies generate new tissue and new pathways for energy and function. We learn our capabilities; we become good animals.

Physical experience is the groundwork for our journey. There is nothing sophisticated about this; the challenge is raw and primal. This is the basis for all of our arts and disciplines, all of our knowledge and our skill. No matter your profession or place in life, your body is your primary source for your everything you might want to do in life. This is where it all begins.

And so we immerse ourselves in a robust physical apprenticeship, a sustained, multi-year period of intense physical striving, followed by regular physical refreshers. In this experience, we learn what it feels like to push and be pushed to the far edge of our physical and psychological comfort zone. We feel the deep fatigue when our breath comes in gasps and our muscles quiver with exhaustion. We experience doubt and the desire to quit. And, we learn how to sustain our effort.

The particular discipline for this engagement is largely irrelevant; most sports and movement arts offer this experience in one form or another. But no matter the form, your effort must be intense and sustained. Dabbling doesn't work. Nor does leapfrogging. We can't simply bypass the body and move on to the cognitive, professional or aesthetic arts. If we do, our practice will never be powerful or complete.

Remembering the physical

Beginning our practice with a deep physical immersion might well seem obvious, but then again, many of us have missed the call. The body has fallen through the cracks of modern culture and many of us have forgotten its power, its value and necessity. Our "neck-up" style of engagement, so common in schools, professions and business, treats the body as a distant afterthought, even a nuisance. The body becomes an object of concern only when it breaks down into epidemics of obesity, diabetes, heart disease, low back pain, absenteeism and presenteeism. But this Cartesian style of living and working is not only ineffective and expensive, it's also contradicted by an avalanche of modern research that proves the deep interconnections between the body and cognition, social intelligence, decision-making and happiness. Without a healthy body, there can be no skill, no learning and no performance. No body, no adventure, no art.

The power of the body is being brought into ever-sharper focus by modern science, most particularly neuroscience. Several key insights have emerged over the last several decades: In the first place, Cartesian dualism is officially dead. The long-standing assumption that mind and body are separate entities has been thoroughly discredited and now belongs on the trash heap of history. In its place, a new understanding of mind-body interdependence has emerged. As neuroscientist Antonio Damasio put it in *Descartes' Error*, "the human brain and the rest of the body constitute an indissociable organism…" Psychologist Carl Jung made a similar observation: "The separation of psychology from the premises of biology is purely artificial, because the human psyche lives in indissoluble union with the body."

It sounds absurd, but finally, after several hundred years of confusion and misplaced efforts, we have at last come to realize that yes, the body and the head are connected. And even more to the point, we have come to realize that the body is far more than a locomotor device for the brain; the body makes powerful contributions to our emotions, our cognitive performance and our ability to engage with the world. Without the body, the head would be not just lifeless, but also stupid.

We now know that learning itself is a profoundly physical act. We know that "cells that fire together, wire together." Synaptic membranes adapt and become more permeable as they're used, in a process called "long-term potentiation." All learning, in other words, involves a change to the tissue of the body. Anything we aspire to learn, from aikido to zoology, involves a transformation of tissue. In this respect, all education is physical education; all teachers are physical educators. The facts are clear on this score: healthy bodies learn better.

Your body is your brain

This new, unitary understanding of mind and body is now being described with the phrase *embodied cognition*. Intelligence, we now realize, is not concentrated in the mind or the brain, but is distributed across the entire mind-body system. Information flows top-down to be sure, but it also flows bottom-up. Our guts, our muscles and our endocrine systems have a voice in every decision we make. Even the bacteria in our digestive tract produce informational substances that influence the ways we think and behave.

The artist Auguste Rodin captured the essence of embodied cognition in his description of his famous sculpture *The Thinker*:

> *What makes my Thinker think is that he thinks not only with his brain, with his knitted brow, his distended nostrils, and compressed lips, but with every muscle of his arms, back and legs, with his clenched fist and gripping toes.*

In other words, we "think" with the whole body. Or, to put it yet another way, your body is your brain.

Movement first

Given this intimate relationship between mind and body, it comes as absolutely no surprise to learn that vigorous physical movement has profound effects on cognitive performance. As John Ratey put it in *Spark: The Revolutionary New Science of Exercise and the Brain*, "There is a direct biological connection between movement and cognitive function…exercise is the single most powerful tool you have to optimize your brain function."

Of course, just about everyone now knows about the health-promoting effects of exercise. We know that vigorous physical engagement benefits every system of the body and that the effects are both broad and deep. Without question, exercise is the most powerful medicine we know; side effects are minimal and there are very few if any contraindications.

So clearly, it's time to get up and start moving. But before we begin our physical quest, it's essential that we understand the difference between *exercise* and *movement*. This may well sound like a case of technical hair-splitting, but in fact, it will make a big difference in the quality of your experience and the trajectory of your life.

To put it simply, exercise is a repetitive, stereotyped pattern of human movement. We choose a particular activity and do it over and over again for a prescribed period of time, or until bored or exhausted. Movement, on the other hand, is a much broader category that includes any kind of physical activity. In this sense, movement includes a great many behaviors that lie outside the realm of exercise, things like dance, gardening, physical labor and sex.

There's an important history here. Prior to the modern industrial age, there was no such thing as exercise. Primal humans gathered, hunted, played and danced; they got plenty of movement simply staying alive. In contrast, exercise has been part of our experience for a only few hundred years at most. Yoga, martial art and dance may well be thousands of years old, but these early forms were holistic endeavors, not exercise.

We see a similar distinction in non-human animals. With the possible exception of laboratory rats on running wheels, we never observe non-human animals doing anything resembling exercise. They hunt, gather, graze, mate, play, fight and flee, but never do they perform repetitive movements for the sake of "staying in shape." They move their bodies for pleasure, to explore or stay alive, but otherwise, they rest.

Today we know that it's movement, not exercise, that keeps us healthy. Across the board, research shows that all forms of physical movement are health promoting and that exercise is only one possibility among many. This realization leads us to a powerful general principle. That is, when it comes to maintaining health, *exercise* *is optional, but movement is essentia*l. No one ever died from lack of exercise, but a lack of physical movement is absolutely dangerous to health. As long as we're getting vigorous movement during the course of our days, we can even skip the exercise altogether. Instead of setting aside big chunks of time to perform stereotyped exercise in specialized facilities, our challenge is to weave movement back into the fabric of our daily lives. If we can make our lives more vigorous in some way, our health will take care of itself.

There's another big advantage in choosing movement over exercise. When we exercise, we engage in a human-specific specialization, but when we move, we put ourselves back into community with every other animal that has ever lived. Instead of isolating in specialized facilities with specialized disciplines, we're sharing in common experience with every primate and every mammal, a deep heritage that goes back some 500 million years, all the way to the Cambrian explosion. When we move our bodies, we celebrate our shared kinship with the natural world and make ourselves part of something much, much larger than ourselves.

Focus on function

Movement is obviously the way to go, but many of us are inclined to wonder what kind of discipline is best for our bodies and our health. With hundreds of options to choose from, it's easy to get confused.

The short answer is that it's all good. Every movement discipline, from the most meditative tai chi practice to the most explosive gymnastics, tends to promote health. Almost everything "works" to some degree. Personality and preference have a lot to do with our choices and our success, but ultimately, it comes down to the actual doing. That's why more and more public health specialists advise us to "Do the thing that you'll actually do" and "Do something that you love." Try a bunch of disciplines and when something turns you on, stick with it.

That said, there's more to physical training than simply following our muse and doing what feels right. All the movement arts are good, but for best results, we need to keep our eyes on function.

Functional training is a concept that's emerged from the athletic training and physical therapy community over the last several decades. In contrast to common appearance-based disciplines such as bodybuilding, the focus is on our ability to execute practical movement. Superficial appearance, muscle tone and body-fat percentages are largely irrelevant for the functional coach; it's our ability to move powerfully, gracefully and effectively that counts.

Of course, we all want to look good; the desire to be attractive is a human universal. But the mistake we make is to put the appearance cart in front of the functional horse. If we start by emphasizing cosmetics, we may never make it to full athletic function. Even worse, we set ourselves up for biomechanical inefficiency and increase the potential for injury. We may look pretty good for a time, but once we're injured, we're out of the game. But if we start by emphasizing function, we can have it all. We'll get the athletic efficiency that we're after and over time, our bodies will look better too. Even better, we'll have longer careers without injury. This means more fun and better looks.

The functional training process can be quite sophisticated, but in general, the focus is always on integration of the entire body in movement. In contrast to single-joint, single-plane exercises often seen in bodybuilding, functional trainers seek to spread the load across the long kinetic chains of neuromuscle; the movements are "multi-joint and multi-plane." In this respect, functional training has a great deal in common with dance, martial arts and other traditional disciplines. The emphasis is always on whole-body performance, not isolation; as legendary athletic coach Vern Gambetta put it, "Work movement, not muscles."

In the functional approach, trainers and coaches take a holistic, systemic view of the body. When training the abdominal muscles for example, functional trainers don't really make a distinction between the abdominal core and the rest of the muscular system. "Toenails to fingernails" they say. It's all core. Use your core in every movement. As coach Gambetta teaches, "Make every exercise an abdominal exercise."

Naturally, it's about more than just muscle. Functional trainers put a lot of emphasis on the nervous system, especially proprioception and sensory-motor integration. In fact, when you get right down to it, it's all skill training. Even endurance sports and strength events depend on our ability to sense our bodies in space and apply the appropriate motor commands. Muscle is great, but it's only one element in the total system.

The beauty of functional training is that it prepares us to thrive in conditions that we are most likely to encounter in the real world. For example, most of the objects that we encounter are free weights of one kind or another: Boxes and buckets, luggage and lumber, tools and furniture, grocery bags and infants; all of these objects are "free." This suggests that our training ought to be conducted, not on exercise machines, but with free weights. The goal is to mimic and train ourselves for actual conditions. In short, train for the way you want to live. Figure out what you want to do with your body in the future and train yourself to do exactly that.

Make it specific

No matter what sort of movement discipline you choose, it's essential to remember the principle of specificity; this is one of the most powerful concepts in the world of athletic training and human learning in general.

In short, the body sculpts itself to meet the demands that are imposed upon it. We become what we do; we get precisely what we train for. If you train for strength, you'll get strength. If you train for agility, you'll get agility. If you train for compassion and kindness, you'll get compassion and kindness. That's it; everything you need to know about training in a nutshell.

In the body, the precision of this adaptive process is astonishing. The slightest variations in intensity, duration, repetition and emphasis are all reflected in actual tissue changes in every system, right down to the molecular level. To the body, three sets of ten is completely different than ten sets of three. Running one mile 5 times a week is completely different than running 5 miles once a week. If we examined our tissue closely enough and tracked the changes that took place, we'd see the difference.

Vascular tissue adapts to the specific challenge of endurance training. Muscle tissue adapts to the specific challenges of strength work. The nervous system adapts to challenges of speed, agility, balance. Not only does synaptic connectivity change, but the actual membranes of nerve cells change as well, allowing greater or lesser sensitivity to message conduction. Changes take place in the nucleus as well, with genes switching on and off (expression), changing the process of protein synthesis, hormone production and tissue repair. Every tissue and every organelle gets into the act of adaptation.

The beauty of functional training is that it goes beyond sports and athletics, deep into the real-world conditions we are likely to encounter in daily life. When we train functionally, we prepare ourselves for the way we want to live. The lesson here is clear: Instead of choosing a training program at random, decide in advance what you want your body to become, then start practicing that thing. Focus on you functional objectives, not appearance. What kind of capability do you want to develop? What do you want your body to do? Vague objectives will give you vague results. Instead, write down exactly what you want to do with your body in the future. This will give you the direction you need.

Make it vigorous

When it comes to movement and physical activity, there's one more thing that everyone wants to know. That is, "What's the right amount? Big health institutions have been asking this question for decades, with dozens of large scale studies looking at the question "How much exercise do people need for health?" This issue has been hashed and rehashed from all directions, with the consensus finally coming to rest with the recommendation "vigorous activity on most days of the week."

This recommendation may not be precise enough for everyone, but it's actually pretty helpful; most of us can readily understand the meaning of "vigorous activity" and "most days of the week." Nevertheless, it's also important to understand our efforts in a larger context of the dose-response curve, the famous bell-shaped, inverse-U that appears so often in the world of physiology and health. Using this curve will help us understand and adjust the frequency and intensity of our physical efforts.

The basic idea is quite simple. At the extreme left end of the curve is sloth and sedentary living. At the extreme right end is radical over-training and life-threatening exertion. Somewhere in the middle is the optimal level of effort. In study after study, research has found that the greatest improvements in health come on the left side of the curve, when people make the transition from being sedentary to "moderately active." In other words, getting off the couch into "vigorous activity on most days of the week" will give us a tremendous payoff in health and vitality. On this side of the curve, we can safely say that for most Americans and in fact most people in the modern world, more effort is almost certainly better.

As we move our bodies more frequently and more vigorously, we climb higher on the curve and enter the sweet spot of mind, body and spirit. In this zone, we get a powerful reward; by extending ourselves and pushing our limits, we actually increase our energies and our payoff. We experience the physiological magic of "supercompensation." The body responds to challenge by creating a higher level of capability; we become stronger, faster and more endurant.

So far so good; if we can get ourselves into the sweet spot of exertion on most days, we'll feel better. But it's the top of the curve where things get really interesting. As we train harder, we learn to love the feelings of exertion and payoff of supercompensation, so we redouble our efforts. But then, as we cross the tipping point, we find ourselves in the realm of over-training and wasted effort. Now, everything changes and the body begins to break down; further efforts become wasteful, counter-productive and even destructive. Tissue begins to degenerate, systems go out of balance and our even our spirits begin to fade.

This is why it's so essential that to pay attention to our physical experience. Dig in to your movement practice and feel the rush of improvement. Train harder, then harder still, but remember that a tipping point is coming. Feel the sensations that course through your body. Once you feel the onset of depletion and diminishing returns, back off on the volume. Rest more. Ease back into the sweet spot. You'll have a lot more fun if you do.

Movement snacks

Obviously, the modern world presents our bodies with an excruciating dilemma. In order to make a living, many of us are forced to sit at our desks for long periods of time; computer work has become the standard of the day. But prolonged sitting has also been shown to be a distinct threat to health. Studies show that even short periods of inactivity have negative effects on insulin response, DNA repair mechanisms, oxidative stress and gene expression. In the *New York Times*, fitness writer Gretchen Reynolds described the health consequences of sitting as "swift, pervasive and punishing." In fact, several researchers now have come to the conclusion that "sitting is an independent pathology." In other words, sitting is bad for our bodies, no matter what we do in the rest of our lives.

Given this occupational and health predicament, we may want to re-think our current habits of physical movement. That is, we're accustomed to thinking that exercise must be experienced in a "workout" that is roughly one hour long. We get dressed in the proper clothes, enter the appointed space, do some sort of warmup, build the intensity, do a cool-down, shower and go home or more likely, back to work. Some sessions are longer, some shorter, but this is the basic unit of physical exertion in the modern world.

This kind of exercise is obviously valuable, but in many settings, it's not even close to being practical. Many people can't afford the time or the sweat-shower-clothing challenges that go along with it. Many workplaces don't have the necessary facilities and many people can't afford a gym membership.

What we really need is a way to refresh our physicality at more frequent intervals. This means finding more ways to get out of our chairs. It means moving in unlikely places: in our offices, our workplaces, our homes–anywhere that sitting is imposed on our bodies. What we need are *movement snacks*, short but frequent periods of movement scattered throughout the day.

Instead of doing a one or two hour session a few times a week, imagine doing several short sessions of movement every day of your life. These micro-workouts won't add up to any heroic training effect and they won't be enough to develop your athletic potential, but for maintaining health, they may well be ideal. Movement snacks will keep your energy levels high, sharpen your cognition and keep your spirits up.

Of course, to make it work, you've got to take responsibility for your body and your health. You can't rely on designated, formal workout times and routines. You've got to take matters into your own hands and move when you need to move. This means paying attention to your moment-to-moment physicality. Listen to your body and heed the urge for movement. Be mindful of your physicality, your sedentary predicament, and your body's inherent desire to move. Don't park your body on the back burner of consciousness. When you feel the itch, take action.

When crafting a movement snack, follow these guidelines:

- Be an opportunist: Keep your eyes open for gaps in time and place where you can move your body. Seize the moment.

- Make stuff up: You don't need to know specific routines, traditional postures or biomechanically-correct exercises. Start with some reaches, some pushes, pulls and steps. The right way is the way that feels good.

- Bend your knees: Your legs are powerful pumps. Use them to promote circulation of fluid throughout your body. Do some squats, take the stairs. Bending your knees helps to integrate the entire system.

- Reverse gravity: Many hours at a desk and in the car will deform your posture and pull your upper body towards the earth. This wreaks havoc on your upper back and neck. Counteract this tendency with intentional anti-gravity movements: stretch, reach and move toward the sky. Extend your back and adopt a posture of exuberance and vitality.

Above all, take a chance. Public displays of physical movement are healthy, adaptive, intelligent and pleasurable. Don't worry about the public exposure. You are the normal one. Your body is beautiful, especially when it's in motion.

The motivation is in the movement

Embedded in every discussion of exercise, health and the body is the nagging question of motivation. For many, this is seen as a problem of epic, even insurmountable proportions; many people seem incapable of voluntarily moving their bodies in any vigorous way. Even worse, many experts in the world of public health have simply given up on the notion that people will ever find the motivation to move, turning instead to second-tier options such as drugs and bariatric surgery. This is called throwing in the towel.

Sadly, the conventional "wisdom" holds that exercise is inherently unpleasant and that participants must be motivated with various "carrots," incentives and hyper-normal stimuli such as loud music and TV. But obviously, something is wrong with this picture. If the activity is unpleasant, maybe it's the activity, not the people, that's the problem. If we crafted more enjoyable movement practices in more beautiful settings, maybe people would be more inclined to participate.

Carrots and distraction devices demean and dilute the quality of an experience that's inherently meaningful, engaging and uplifting, even sacred. People are tired of being manipulated with rewards for every behavior, every action and every rep. People are tired of being distracted at every turn. When modern gyms add TVs and loud music, they're simply taking attention away from the body itself. How are we supposed to feel anything when we're being "motivated" by hyper-normal stimuli? Isn't our physical experience rich and rewarding enough as it is?

So where shall our motivation come from? What will get us off the couch? The answer is the same thing that gets every artist, musician, scientist and creator moving: the anticipation of a quality experience. The motivation is in the content, the material and the living. We will move our bodies when we have a pleasant and meaningful experience of moving our bodies. Beautiful movement will move us. If it's boring, painful or meaningless, no amount of external reward or audio-visual stimuli will make a difference. The body knows what it wants. Go out and find it. Find those movements that feel wonderful. And if you can't find them, create them.

Lesson 2

Embrace the animal

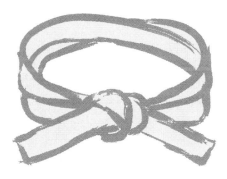

When health is absent, wisdom cannot reveal itself, art cannot manifest, strength cannot fight, wealth becomes useless, and intelligence cannot be applied.

Herophilus

Each patient carries his own doctor inside him.

Norman Cousins

Anatomy of an Illness

In conventional conversations about our bodies, many of us describe health as a state of being. It's something that can be measured, tracked and tweaked. It's something we can achieve, something we can lose. But when we take a deeper look, we're likely to discover that health really isn't a thing at all. More to the point, health is a kind of relationship. It's a relationship we create, not just with our bodies, but with the totality of our life experience. It's a relationship that we create in every moment of our lives.

Sadly, this relationship has become radically distorted in recent years; our primal alliance with the body has become stretched almost to the breaking point. Today, many of us experience a profound sense of duality. The body is a vast, dark and mysterious unknown. It's not to be trusted; it's treacherous, traitorous and unpredictable. Anything could bring us down: a genetic wild card, an environmental toxin, a renegade organ, hormone or neurotransmitter. According to this view, we are mere victims of our physiology; things can go wrong without warning and we have no control.

For others, the relationship with the body is adversarial. The body must be beaten into shape, tamed and brought to heel. We exercise like demons, living the belief that the body must be pounded into condition with endless sweating, suffering and pain. If we let up our efforts for a day or a week, we'll degenerate into obesity, sloth and disease. Alternately, we abuse our bodies with all manner of substances and behaviors, trying to punish it for sensations, emotions and motives that we don't understand or know what to do with.

For still others, the primal relationship is marked by apathy and ignorance. The body is something far away; it's a foreign land. We don't know what it's capable of and we don't much care. As long as it gets us to work and back home at the end of the day, we're content to leave it to its own devices. If something goes wrong, we'll just take it in to the shop and all will be well. We're not even curious about what it is or what it might become.

These relationships are exceedingly common, but none are sustainable, pleasing or beautiful. In short, they are not healthy. Even if we follow all the recommended health and lifestyle practices prescribed by today's experts, we still won't be in the sweet spot of our life experience. Your body might even pass a routine health screening with good biomedical results, but if your primary relationship is out of harmony, you're going to feel it somewhere in your life. Even worse, you'll miss out on all the pleasure and exuberance that comes with an integrated physical alliance.

Wild health

What we need is a renewed sense of intimacy, harmony and trust in the body. To re-discover this intimacy, we need to remember our deep biological history. Here we come to a startling realization. That is, for the vast majority of our time on this planet, we have been wild animals. Our history as primates goes back perhaps 60 millions years. Our history as hominids or human-like creatures, goes back some 6 million years. And for the vast, overwhelming majority of this time, we were clever, modestly successful animals, with a strong sense of integration. There was no duality between self and body. That would only come much later, with consciousness, language and domestication.

For wild animals, both human and non-human, there could be no fragmentation of the primal physical alliance. The relationship between self and body was indivisible. There could be no mistrust, no apathy and no need to punish the body as an adversary. The body was the ultimate ally, the most intimate partner in the quest for survival. In short, the body was all.

Given this history of integrated experience, many of us are likely to conclude that wildness is the very essence of health. Forget the details of biochemistry, biomechanics and all our other recipes for proper eating and moving; our most vital objective is to put ourselves in touch with the wild nature that animates our bodies and spirit. We may even conclude that domesticated health is something of an oxymoron. That is, the more domesticated we become, the less healthy we are. We might eat a perfect diet, do a precisely periodized program on the treadmill and take the perfect combination of supplements, but if we give up our wildness, we give up our very lives.

Of course, this presents a practical challenge. It's essential that we heed the call of the wild. It's vital that we maintain contact with our history, our deep bodies and our experience of living in nature. It's crucial that we learn to trust our bodies and build a better relationship with our most intimate ally. It's important to be a good animal. But still, there's simply no going back to the Paleo. Like it or not, we have to live in this world as it exists. We have to respect certain civilizing constraints. And while many of us might dream of living naked in the bush, it's a tough lifestyle to manage. There's not many places we can go to live such a life, and there aren't many people who'd be willing to go along. We have to make due with the opportunities that present themselves.

Care and feeding

So how do we best promote our wild health in this modern world? How do we care for an exuberant and vigorous human animal?

Naturally, we start with the basics. Simply put, the human animal needs to eat real food and drink clean water. There's no mystery here: When you eat high-quality food, you provide your body with the vital raw materials and fuels it needs to rebuild tissue, fight disease, and perform at a high level. And of course, since our minds, body and spirit are so tightly interconnected, you'll become happier as well.

Sadly, food is a major source of stress in the modern world, a veritable feast of anxiety that afflicts millions of people. We study and suffer, we analyze, argue and agonize, we consult experts. We worry about where our food comes from, what's in it, how it's prepared and most of all, what it will do to our bodies. Behind it all, many of us hate our bodies and wish that somehow, if we eat or avoid the right things, our bodies and our lives will be happy once again.

The solution is to put ourselves back into a right relationship. Here we look to feed our intimate ally in a way that's consistent with our heritage and our history. Strictly speaking, humans are omnivores. In the world of biology, this means that we are opportunistic feeders; we can survive on both animal protein and vegetation. Clearly this ability to eat a wide range of food has contributed to our success as a species; in a natural environment, an omnivorous feeding style worked in our favor. But in a world that's saturated with new and often toxic food-like substances, our natural abilities and inclinations actually put our health in danger.

The solution is actually quite simple. Stop thinking in term of "diet" and "nutrition" and instead, start thinking about real food. Get back to the fundamentals. Stop worrying about biochemistry and the therapeutic effects of specific nutrients; concentrate instead on eating whole foods from natural sources.

This practice begins with the understanding that humans have co-evolved with real food for millions of years, and that our bodies are intimately, microscopically adapted to whole, natural foods. Every detail of our digestion and biochemistry is the way it is because of our history in wild habitat. It simply makes sense to assume that real, Paleolithic foods would be ideal for keeping us strong and healthy.

The lesson here is clear: Learn to distinguish between real food and the so-called "edible food-like substances." When in doubt, choose the simple options. Real foods have few ingredients; faux foods have many. Real food are unrefined or minimally refined; faux foods are highly refined. Real foods are colorful; faux foods tend to be white. Real foods are tasty and satisfying; faux foods are hyper-flavorful, exaggerated caricatures of older, more authentic forms. Real foods are perishable; faux foods are almost indestructible. Real foods would be recognizable to our ancient ancestors; faux foods are only recognizable when preceded by a large-scale media campaign.

In the world of food and eating, the art lies in exercising two complementary orientations. On the one hand, we look to avoid the negative. Be on the alert for the toxic ingredients and products that infect our food supply, reject refined and adulterated food products, especially those that are loaded with high levels of sugar, salt and mystery ingredients.

This is good practice, but by itself, "avoiding the poisons" is not enough to keep us healthy. In fact, it can even backfire. By focusing exclusively on the negative, we begin to see toxins and pathogens all around us. The supermarket becomes a place, not of life, but of disease. In the extreme, this focus on the negative actually contributes to stress and fuels a nocebo effect.

So, we must also focus on the positive. Reject the "glow in the dark" foods, of course, but seek out those foods that are rich and flavorful. Turn the process into a positive experience. The modern supermarket may well be stocked with an astonishing amount of disease-promoting substances, but it's also bursting with good stuff, foods that will make our bodies healthier. This focus on abundance, by itself, will tend to be health promoting. When you see yourself living in a world of nutritional plenty, you can celebrate at every meal.

With real food as a starting point, the next step is to recognize the importance of vegetables as a primary food source. Vegetables are so important in fact, we would do well to associate the word "food" with the word "vegetable." Many nutritionists believe that vegetables ought to be our first choice at every meal; more is almost certainly better. If you like to count, do so. Or, you can simply strive for maximum possible color at every meal.

As for protein, it's clearly essential and we need to seek it out. Meat is obviously a personal judgment call. If you're carnivorous, stick with grass-fed meats and cold water fish such as salmon. In any case, avoid highly-refined foods, especially those containing high-fructose corn syrup and trans-fats. Start by eliminating soft drinks, which are best described as "liquid candy." Limit your intake of "carbage," the highly-refined, high-carbohydrate baked goods and other so-called "white foods." These goodies do little more than spike our blood sugar levels and contribute to diabetes, metabolic disorders and quite possibly, neurological damage as well.

But no matter the details of your diet, remember that food has meanings that go beyond the chemistry of the food itself. Placebo and nocebo effects are everywhere. Culture and personal history play vital roles in our experience and our biochemistry. Be mindful of what you're eating, but don't fall into the trap of zealotry or fundamentalism. People can thrive on radically different diets. Find one that works for you and enjoy it.

Sweet are the uses of adversity

The animal's need for authentic food and water are obvious enough, but there's another need that must be met if we are to remain healthy. This is our need for exposure and adversity. Coming as we do from a culture that prizes comfort and ease, this suggestion may will come as a surprise. After all, we have spent the last few thousand years actively insulating ourselves from adversity and doing our best to promote our physical comfort.

Nevertheless, the value of adversity has been well-validated by an immense body of research and personal experience. Exercise scientists, ancestral health experts, psychologists and an increasing number of physicians are united in the understanding that challenge in almost any form makes us stronger. If we're going to remain healthy, we're going to have to expose our bodies to outdoor conditions and the adversity of psychophysical striving. In a sense, adversity is a kind of food, even a kind of medicine.

The idea that adversity has therapeutic potential is a familiar theme in popular culture. When we're faced with a challenge, many of us are likely to quote Nietzsche: "Whatever doesn't kill you makes you stronger." Our adversity may be unpleasant, but in the long run we'll be better off.

This is precisely what we see in the realm of physical training. As we've seen, it's a good practice to stay on the left side of the dose-response curve; stick with moderate intensity and avoid going past the tipping point into over-training. Nevertheless, there is something extremely valuable to be learned on the right side of the curve. That is, while you may waste some energy, you'll also reap a valuable payoff in knowledge and experience. With occasional encounters with over-the-top adversity, you'll gain an understanding of what you're truly capable of. Now you know; you've been to world of extreme stress and survived. Yes, you may well have wasted some training hours, suffered some unnecessary injuries and compromised your immune system, but you eventually came back into health and balance. The experience may have hurt you temporarily, but it also showed you something essential:

if pushed into circumstances beyond your control, your body will survive. You can tap your deeper reserves; you are resilient.

This is the value of intense psychophysical challenge. At some point in your life you'll probably be pushed beyond what you think you're capable of. Circumstances may force you over the top of the curve, into the realm of over-training, over-stress or overwhelm. So learn your body, find out what you're capable of, then settle back into the sweet spot of vigorous activity on most days of the week. Your physical education will not be complete until you've made this journey.

Just as adversity strengthens us, so too does exposure, especially when we put our bodies in contact with natural elements and habitat. Most obviously, exposure to sunlight stimulates the production of vitamin D. But that's just the beginning. A growing body of evidence suggests that exposure to dirt and animals, may actually be protective against a range of diseases. Encounters between the immune system and micro-organisms such as bacteria and parasites are part of human evolution and may therefore protect against the development of auto-immunity. Similarly, some studies have found that children raised in relatively sterile suburban environments have higher rates of asthma than those raised with exposure to farm animals. Dirt, in other words, can be medicine.

Of course, this calls our entire modern lifestyle into question. As a people, we're suffering from a deficit of physical challenge, exposure and adversity. Modern life simply isn't hard enough to promote health. We sit too much, drive too much and lay around too much. We spend too much time indoors. Our lives are easy and therefore dangerous.

Clearly, this calls for a counter-intuitive approach. Promote your health by exposing yourself to nature, frequently. Risk your body and leave your comforts behind, whenever you can manage it. Make yourself vulnerable to the elements. Go further into the mountains than you think you can. Stay out longer. Rub your body up against the world and see what it does for your health and happiness.

Sweet are the uses of sweetness

Just as adversity and exposure nourish us, so too do our favorite physical pleasures and comforts. Every animal appreciates the simple sensations of warmth in the winter, shade in the summer, water when thirsty and touch when anxious. These things speak directly to the body, whispering the message that "the world is friendly." It's no wonder that we go to such great lengths to pamper ourselves whenever possible.

Pampering is an expression of the loving relationship that we seek to create with our most intimate ally. We expose our animal bodies to adversity, then give them the pleasures that we crave. We get out of the wind and the rain, out of the sun. We wash and shower, we rub sweet oils on our skin. We dress in clean clothes and lounge on soft carpets. We celebrate with fine food and great friends and then, when all our energy comes together in a flood of oxytocin and warmth, we seek out sweet darkness for sex and slumber.

All of these behaviors are essential and powerfully health-promoting; you must never feel guilty about pampering yourself in these ways. In fact, we might well make the case that we need *more* of this kind of sweetness in our lives and with our bodies. Adversity and exposure are essential, but it's the contrast that really promotes our health. The body loves it all. Take care of yourself by being active at both ends of the spectrum. We need more adversity *and* more pampering.

A case in point is sleep. As we all know, this is one of the sweetest of all the animal pleasures. But sadly, our culture has long held a negative attitude about this fundamental aspect of human life. As compulsive workaholics, we treat sleep as an adversary, an obstacle to be overcome by the force of will or if necessary, drugs. People who sleep are considered slackers, a point of view voiced most notably by Thomas Edison who declared that "Sleep is a criminal waste of time."

In recent years, sleep advocates have become increasingly outspoken about the crucial importance of sleep across every dimension of our physiology and performance. Perhaps the leading sleep advocate of our day is circadian neuroscientist Russell Foster. In a notable TED talk, Foster urges us to take sleep more seriously, pointing out the fact most of us are desperately sleep deprived. The consequences are no laughing matter: poor memory, increased impulsiveness, poor judgment, decreased creativity, weight gain, suppressed immunity and increased stress.

Good sleep turns this all around: certain restorative genes are turned only turned on during sleep, brain function and memory consolidation is enhanced, genes promoting myelin formation are turned on during sleep, creativity is increased and synapses are strengthened. Furthermore, sleep and mental well being are tightly linked.

As for the practice of sleep promotion, the basics are clear: taper your activity and light exposure gradually throughout the evening, limit your alcohol consumption to early evening, make your room as dark as possible, and avoid caffeine after lunch. And remember, sleep is not an indulgence; it is absolutely vital for health and performance. Stop bragging about how little sleep you're getting; it's not something to be proud of.

Likewise, deepen your practice in the restorative arts. Get a massage table and learn how to use it. Set up your dwelling for physical comfort and rejuvenation. Nurture your body and the bodies around you; give them the message that "the world is safe." Prioritize these practices and give them the attention that they deserve.

Ultimately, it's all about crafting the right relationship with our bodies and giving ourselves permission to rest, permission to sleep, permission to enjoy the creature comforts that come on the heels of exposure and adversity. As Tony Schwartz, author of *The Power of Full Engagement* put it, "In a world of rising demand, rest should no longer be demonized but celebrated for its intimate connection to sustainable high performance."

Your body is your most powerful and most intimate ally. Stop treating it like an alien or an adversary. The animal wants to be happy, so give it what it needs: adversity and exposure and then, when the time is right, outrageous pampering. Then repeat.

One breath away

The fundamentals of health are all worth knowing and practicing, but we also need to keep our practice in perspective. This is where we so often fool ourselves. We forget the ultimate nature of our predicament. That is, no matter how hard we train, no matter how perfect our diets, we're still only one breath away from death.

There's simply no way around it. No matter how sophisticated and powerful our knowledge might be, our bodies are still subject to the ultimate constraints of physics and biology. We may know every last detail of nutrition, biomechanics and training, but we're still living smack in the center of the human predicament. We can analyze, measure and study until we're blue in the face, but we are still vulnerable, fragile organisms living in a highly dynamic, fundamentally impermanent world.

This realization makes us wonder what exactly it is that we're trying to do in the world of health. Are we trying to celebrate life in all its mystery and ambiguity, through vigorous physical movement and a sensible diet? Or are we trying to escape from our earthly predicament? Are we going towards something or away from something?

When we look at the magazine rack, the popular health and fitness industry comes across as one vast, fear-based effort to protect and defend ourselves from the impermanence of the world. "Before and after" photo spreads sell promises of instant sex appeal and immortality. We hear preposterous claims about "turning back the clock" and "age-proofing" our skin and bodies. We read about "injury proofing," and "stress proofing" as if we might somehow insulate ourselves from the realities of biology.

But these efforts are destined to fail: When we try to death-proof our bodies, we simultaneously take ourselves out of the natural flow of life. In other words, death-proofing actually becomes a form of "life-proofing." In turn, this only makes our suffering worse. By insulating ourselves from the primal flux, flow and ambiguity of life, we actually increase our stress, our delusion of separateness and even our susceptibility of disease.

Make no mistake. Foundational health practices make good sense and will probably extend our "health span" as well as our life span. Vigorous movement and a real-food diet will promote our vitality and probably protect us from some diseases. But no level of fitness dietary perfection will insulate us from the ravages of time and the cumulative traumas of life. Even the most vigorous wild animals, living in pristine natural conditions, eating perfect food and moving their bodies in perfectly natural ways, eventually loose their vigor and perish. Are we really expecting something more?

No matter how sophisticated our knowledge, there are certain inevitabilities that we cannot escape: Our bodies are constantly being injured in daily activity–cancer cells are proliferating, mutations are being generated, pathogens are constantly attacking our tissue. Cellular repair mechanisms and immune defenses keep most of this damage in check, but the fact remains: we are constantly falling apart, always on the cusp, always poised precariously between life and death.

So what is health? Is it the ability to insulate ourselves from the flux and flow of life? Is our goal to become impervious to the natural biological decay that takes place in every organism on earth? If that's the case then we are clearly on the wrong path. Maybe we need to re-evaluate our vision. Maybe it's time to suspend our war on injury, aging and death. Maybe it's time to look squarely at the impermanence of our incredible, beautiful, fragile and highly temporary lives.

Yes, health is a noble pursuit. With just a little more education, training and behavioral change, we could save millions of people from immense amounts of suffering. We could help reduce the levels of diabetes, heart disease, depression and neurological disorders. But let's not delude ourselves; aging, illness, injury and death are part of who we are. Life is a package deal, one that includes loss, injury, disease and suffering. Rather of fleeing from it, perhaps we'd do better to embrace it in its entirety. Once we give up our attachment, we can live life more completely, in health and happiness.

Lesson 3

Do it yourself

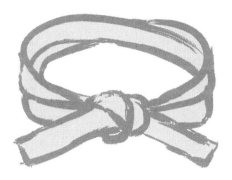

One of the weaknesses of the Western medical approach is that we have made the physician the only authority, with the patient too often a mere recipient of the treatment or cure.

Gabor Maté

When the Body Says No: The Cost of Hidden Stress

Waking up is ultimately something that each one of us can only
do for ourselves.

Jon Kabat-Zinn

Wherever You Go, There You Are

As we go deeper into our explorations of the body and health, it won't be long before we find ourselves wondering about the nature of healing and medicine. Our bodies get injured or diseased and we go in search of the best therapeutic methods we can find.

This is a rich and exciting area of inquiry, but our beliefs tend to polarize pretty quickly. Many of us divide the medical landscape into two groups: On one hand are conventional, Western medical practices such as surgery, pharmaceuticals, chemotherapy and the like. These practices are reductionistic, highly technological and often impersonal. On the other hand are the so-called alternative or Eastern practices such as massage, homeopathy, chiropractic and acupuncture. These methods are often described as holistic. And of course, there are the hybrids, often described as "complementary" or "integrative."

Most of us hold strong opinions about the merits and values of each approach. Arguments rage. People tell stories about the "evils" of Western medicine, while others tell counter-stories of spectacular technological successes, especially in surgery and trauma care. Accusations of quackery, malpractice and poor-quality research fly in both directions. As a consequence, we're left wringing our hands, trying to sort out the questions of genuine effectiveness and the problems posed by placebos.

But after all the shouting and hyperbole dies down, the question remains: Does this East-West, conventional-alternative, reductionist-holistic classification system do us any good? Or is it simply a child's cartoon, drawn with a blunt crayon? How are we to make sense of it all? What can we really say about the various styles of medicine and health practices?

Many clinicians and medical philosophers have decided that the only sensible solution is to evaluate medical arts and practices strictly in terms of effectiveness, judged by hard evidence. Under this model, we make our distinctions, not on the basis of personal anecdote or cultural origin, but on the measured outcomes of laboratory tests, coherent theory and double-blind clinical trials. When we look at it this way, the whole field of medicine suddenly breaks down into two entirely different categories: methods that work and those that don't. In this light, we have no interest in where a practice comes from or what it looks and feels like. All we care about is whether or not it actually has a genuine therapeutic effect on the human organism.

This would seem to be a move in the right direction, but even here, things are not as straightforward as we would like to think. That's because there are two huge monkeywrenches in the works. The first is the placebo effect, the power of suggestion and belief to promote pain-relief, tissue healing and performance. Placebo and nocebo effects lurk in every health and fitness environment, modifying the effectiveness and outcomes of every modality, for better or for worse. To make matters even more complex, culture gives us expectations and beliefs about the body that can radically alter the course of the healing process; practices that are effective in one culture may be spectacularly ineffective in another. (See *The Spirit Catches You and You Fall Down* by Anne Fadiman.) Consequently, it is often hard to tell who or what is really working in a health, fitness or medical setting.

The power of agency

So maybe there's another way to group health and medical practices. Perhaps we can throw some light on the problem by looking at medical practices, not in terms of origins or even in terms of effectiveness, but in terms of agency. In this model, we ask a very simple question of health and medical practices: Is it something done *to you* or is it something done *by you*?

This distinction was first suggested by Dr. Herbert Benson in his landmark 1979 book *The Relaxation Response*. As a professor at Harvard Medical School and a pioneer in mind-body medicine, Benson was forced to wrestle with the typical East-West, conventional-alternative classification system. Wisely, he resisted being pigeon-holed one way or the other. His research demonstrated conclusively that meditation and similar practices produce measurable and substantial benefits, but these practices were not something administered by outsiders. Rather, they were something done by individuals themselves. This led him to the realization that self-authored health behaviors were an immensely powerful, but largely uncharted area of medical practice.

This *to us-by us* distinction provides us with a completely new picture of health and medical practices. Things done *to us* include surgery, drugs, acupuncture, massage, rolfing, chiropractic, herbal treatments, nutritional supplements and homeopathy. In contrast, things done *by us* include exercise, meditation and related stress-relief practices, cognitive training, personal food choice and lifestyle modifications such as changes to social life, time and work management. (And yes, there are some practices such as physical therapy that include a mix of both *to us* and *by us* methods.)

This distinction is exciting because it generates a host of surprises and strange bedfellows. Suddenly, our minds are forced out of traditional ruts and new ideas are free to emerge. For example, when we think about things done *to us*, we find that surgery, acupuncture, root canals, crystal healing and craniosacral bodywork all belong in the same category. If someone applies a treatment to us, no matter its nature, history or cultural tradition, it belongs in this category. Even shamanism–if it involves an intervention, spell or potion applied by a trained expert–may very well be lumped into this category as something done *to us*.

On the other hand, if you change your behavior with exercise, food, ideas, meditation, social affiliation or environment, you are the author of your treatment and your process. Even if that behavior is inspired or informed by a coach, therapist, trainer or teacher, the operative agent is you. This is what Jon Kabat-Zinn refers to as "participatory medicine."

This *to us-by us* distinction is immensely valuable because it gets us away from tired, unproductive polarities of East-West, conventional-alternative. Conventional distinctions suddenly lose their power to tyrannize our thinking. This forces us to look at the roles being played by patient and healer. This not only scrambles our standard world-view on medical practices, it also generate some fascinating and powerful conclusions.

This takes us right to the heart of our relationship with medicine and the way we live. Throughout history, we have always hoped and prayed that healers, shamans and physicians could heal our injuries and diseases with procedures and substances, but sadly, the vast majority of those early efforts were ineffective, even dangerous. Many things were done *to us*, but the actual healing came, when it came at all, from the power of the placebo.

Finally, in the early 20th century, we began to experience a new medical reality. We learned about germ theory, vaccines and antibiotics. We came to the conclusion that real medicine was something done *to us*. Our parents and grandparents were awed by the powers of antibiotics and vaccines. Many people still remember their early childhood experience, going to the local high school to receive the precious sugar cube laced with polio vaccine. The prospect of preventing and curing a dread disease with a simple sugar cube convinced many people that procedures and substances done *to us* were the very essence of medicine.

This experience has been passed from generation to generation. Today, many of us approach doctors, trainers and other health professionals with a clear expectation: this person is going to do something *to me*. It might be a procedure, a program or a prescription, but in any case, the locus of agency and action lies outside of ourselves. We have little or nothing to do with the process. All we have to do is report our symptoms, comply with the procedure and we'll be healed. Medicine, whether it be surgery, pharmaceuticals, radiation or physical manipulation, is something done *to us*.

A new challenge

But today, a new paradigm is emerging and with it a new appreciation for the power of individual action. While things done *to us* remain important, things done *by us* are getting a lot more attention. Exercise and diet are the most obvious examples: Every day we hear about new research documenting the immense power of movement and nutritional choice to improve the health and performance of every system in the body, including the brain.

Every day brings fresh evidence for the power of individual action in health. In his more recent book, *Relaxation Revolution*, Dr. Benson shared the startling discovery that sustained meditation practice can have profoundly beneficial effects on gene expression. A consistent practice of focused relaxation affects hundred of genes that in turn, have powerful effects on the health of the body. This simply cannot be done *to us*. It must be done *by us*.

The entire field of stress medicine sends much the same message. We now know that most of today's lifestyle diseases–heart disease, high blood pressure, obesity, diabetes, depression and neurological disorders–are exacerbated by stress. But stress is all about our relationship with the world. In this context, it is things done *by us* –interpretation, narrative, attitude and perspective–that will have the greatest impact.

Of course, this realization comes with a challenge. No longer can we passively sit back and swallow the sugar pill or sit still for an injection; we have to put our bodies directly into the path of risk, engagement and action. It also forces us to come to grips with personal responsibility in matters of health. Who is in control of your life and your body? Would you prefer to have the locus of responsibility inside or outside yourself?

We can be sure that many patients and clients are attracted to things done *to us* precisely because they remove any sense of accountability or responsibility: We can simply lie back and submit to whatever procedure the expert decides to administer. If the surgery fails, it's the surgeon's fault. If your knee still hurts, it's the physical therapist's fault. If your back still hurts, you can always blame your bodyworker. The onus of success or failure lies squarely on the shoulders of the person doing the treatment.

This is why we absolutely love things like antibiotics. Penicillin works wonders most of the time, and almost no personal effort is required. Just show up at the doctor's office, state your complaint, fill the prescription and swallow. Beyond the basic mechanics of showing up and paying your bill, there's scarcely any participation required. Once the pills are in your system, the deed is done and you're off the hook.

On the other hand, things done by us issue a direct challenge and put us right on the crux of personal responsibility. There's no place to hide. Once we choose to take control of our lives through exercise, food choice, meditation and other *by us* means, we suddenly find ourselves naked before the world. Here we are, with our habits, our genes, our bodies, our personalities, our families and our lives. There's simply no place to hide. What kind of life and health do you want to create? Suddenly, there is no one else to blame.

The challenge is stark, but the payoff is potentially immense. By taking on the responsibility of *by us* methods, you'll position yourself for personal, physical and spiritual empowerment. This is something that is simply unavailable with *to us* methods. Medical procedures that are done to us may very well be effective, but they do not empower us; they merely fix us. In contrast, things done *by us* have the potential to be profoundly empowering. When you participate fully and engage completely with life, you take action and accept risk. When you create change in your life and in your world, you will feel a sense of satisfaction and control. This is inherently health-promoting.

When you're successful with things done by you, you'll move from being a victim to being a creator, a shift of potentially enormous proportions. Not only do you heal your body through self-authored programs of exercise, food choice, stress management and meditation, you also position yourself for an entirely new experience of life. The changes that you create will ripple throughout your life in ways that are simply impossible with any things done to you. Even more to the point, success at things done by you opens up enormous new vistas of possibility. If you can succeed in these domains of lifestyle transformation, what else might be possible?

Lesson 4

Find your meaning

The least of things with a meaning is worth more
in life than the greatest of things without it.

Carl Jung

Meaninglessness inhibits fullness of life and is therefore equivalent to illness. Meaning makes a great many things endurable-perhaps everything.

C.G. Jung

Memories, Dreams, Reflections

How would you feel if someone asked you to roll a large boulder up a steep hill, over and over again? For no reason? Until the end of time?

Chances are you'd get pretty demoralized. The raw physical labor would be bad enough, but even worse would be your feelings of futility and worthlessness. It's one thing to sweat and suffer under the weight of sustained effort, but it's an entirely different thing to do it without promise or purpose.

This, of course, is classic Greek tale of Sisyphus. Zeus, "the father of gods and men," chose to punish Sisyphus by forcing him to roll a huge boulder up a steep hill. Before he could reach the top, the massive stone would always roll back down, forcing him to begin all over again. In the process, Zeus consigned Sisyphus to an eternity of useless efforts and unending frustration.

If this sounds like an accurate description of your job and your life, take note. Something is probably missing and that something is probably a sense of meaning. What's lacking is the sense that your efforts count for something. You may not mind pushing a few boulders up a hill, but you want that effort to count. You want to make a difference.

This need for meaning is a human universal, but it becomes particularly vital when taking up the challenge of an art, discipline or profession. Today's coaches and trainers often tell us that it takes 10,000 hours of practice to reach mastery. This figure is a matter of some dispute, but no matter the actual number of hours, we know full well that proficiency and skill require immense numbers of repetitions and highly-focused attention over the course of years, even decades. There are no short cuts; the process is going to take a long time.

But how will this experience feel? Will your practice amount to 10,000 hours of boulder-pushing? If so, your results will be weak and uninspired. You may well survive and you may even succeed in some sense, but you'll expend more energy than necessary and you'll probably get injured or burned out along the way. The boulder will feel heavier with every passing day and even if you do manage to master the skills you desire, your spirit will feel fatigued, even depressed. Even worse, you might well become cynical and conclude that there's no meaning to be found anywhere. You may even quit your practice entirely.

Build a better why

Clearly, the challenge before us is to build a better why. Why struggle to learn? Why do a million reps? Meaning won't make the boulder go away, but it will replace the effort with a sense of possibility. The more meaning we can bring to the process, the more powerful we will become. And so, the question before us: What makes something meaningful?

Unfortunately, many of us begin, not with any particular meaning or larger purpose, but with simple desires. We want to have fun, we want to win a championship and enjoy the attention that goes with it. We want to earn money, we want to achieve security. All of these wants are valid and may well be important, but they are not powerful enough to sustain us. Fun is not enough, pleasure is not enough. Money, fame and victory are not enough. Hedonistic desires are seductive and temporarily motivating, but are simply inadequate to keep the boulder moving up the hill.

Modern happiness research is absolutely clear on this score; once people have achieved a basic level of material, social and educational wealth, they have the raw material of contentment and happiness. Further increases in hedonic pleasure do little or nothing for our life satisfaction. Our immediate pleasure, while important and worthy of attention, does not carry us very far. For meaning to really move us, there's got to be some greater significance that goes beyond the self. There has to be an effect upon the world, a consequence and an influence. Our effort has to change something, some relationship, some process, some dimension of culture or someone's life.

Of course, many of us find meaning in the basic quest for physical mastery. Skill development just feels good; it gives us a sense of power and efficacy in the world. Our training gives us greater physical power or endurance, greater dexterity or agility, deeper knowledge or sensitivity. This mastery can go a long way towards building resilience and moving us forward through life, but even here, we search for larger meanings. Skill development, after all, is achievable. Then what?

For many of us, it's a simple sense of love. We love the content, the process, the culture and the people who practice our art form. We feel a sense of wonder and enchantment with every detail of the art. We are intensely curious; driven by passion and the need know everything about our arts, crafts and disciplines. Every day generates new questions about where our arts might lead. The possibilities feel rich and expansive.

And of course, many of us derive meaning from the contributions we make to the welfare and happiness of those around us, to our families and to the world at large. These are some of our most powerful motivators; altruism can take us far beyond anything we might do on our own account. The desire to make a difference in other peoples lives, to share our knowledge and our energy; this is what animates many of our most beautiful practices.

Having a larger sense of purpose can drive the entire creative system. Psychologist Ellis Paul Torrance followed the lives of several hundred creative high achievers from high school through middle age. Among them were academics, writers, inventors, teachers, consultants and business executives. In his research, Torrance noticed that it wasn't scholastic or technical abilities or achievements at school that set them apart, but characteristics such as having a sense of purpose and the courage to be creative. Most important, he concluded, was to "fall in love with a dream." Torrance called his group "beyonders."

Story

The meanings that we bring to practice are often found in the stories that we tell about what we do. Stories tell us why we're striving, why we're working so hard to master our discipline and why we care about the process. Without story, our training would simply be a bunch of lifeless reps. The boulder would be nothing more than a large, heavy rock.

But with the right story, the boulder becomes part of a larger drama and a human creation. We're not just pushing with our bodies, we're playing a role. We're participating in a process that extends human knowledge, explores human emotion, lifts spirits, makes new discoveries or connects people in some new way. It's not just labor, it's a quest and an adventure.

If the story is not explicit, it's implicit. If it's not expressed literally, then it finds its way in through the cracks and around the edges. People demand a story and if it's not offered up by the teacher, parent, coach or trainer, then students will simply adopt whatever's handy, whatever story is closest at hand, served up by the culture at large. Even the most technological, rational and neutral program will still be colored, even dominated by prevailing cultural narratives.

So ask yourself: Does your personal story fit inside a larger narrative of history, culture or tradition? Are you simply reacting to circumstance or are you participating in an epic human drama? Dream big. Will your effort help to right a great wrong in the name of justice? Will it give back to the world? Will it save the biosphere from destruction? Will it reduce human suffering? Will it increase the levels of health, vitality and compassion in the world? Will it push the limits of human imagination? Will it inspire others to great things? Will you feel as if you're participating in an timeless quest of discovery?

The specific story line is up to you. If you choose, you can simply remain reactive and deal with each moment as it comes. But when you merge your efforts with some larger narrative, you will gain power and resilience. Now you're part of something much larger than yourself; the story and its meanings will carry you along. Even when the boulder threatens to crush you to dust, you'll find a way to redouble your efforts, even in the face of stress, tragedy and suffering. As Frederich Nietzsche famously put it, "He who has a why to live can endure almost any how."

Practice

For some, the primal meaning of our lives and practice is obvious; we discovered a powerful purpose early in life and we never looked back. But for most of us, it's an ongoing hunt and a practice. We focus on one narrative for a time and see how well it serves us; we start with simple desires or hedonism and discover that we need something more substantive. We live by one purpose only to find that life has changed; our original sense of meaning no longer gets the boulder up the hill.

As we grow, we try new story lines, looking for meanings that ring true to who we are and what we seek. The vital thing is to keep looking and questioning. Your purpose and meaning might be revealed in a dramatic flash of insight, but it might just as well be revealed in the minute and mundane details of familiar life. Each moment holds the possibility of purpose. "Why am I doing this?" The more you search, the sharper your attention will become. As Dr. Rachel Naomi Remen, an early pioneer in the mind/body holistic health movement put it, "Seeing meaning is a muscle."

Once you discover a meaning that resonates, remain mindful and true to it. When your attention wanders, bring it back to your focal point. Do it again and again. Write down your purpose with radical clarity, then revisit the process every now and then. Talk to others about your meaning; this will help solidify your story. And when the boulder threatens to crush you, reach out for your narrative and your meaning. It will take you a lot further than you might suppose.

Lesson 5

Do your reps

That which is used develops.
That which is not used wastes away.

Hippocrates

You are what you practice most.

Richard Carlson

As we dig deeper into our beautiful practice, it soon becomes obvious that skill development is an essential part of the process. We seek proficiency, expertise and grace in our movements, relationships and behaviors; we seek mastery in complex forms. Skill is not only useful and satisfying, it's also incredibly beautiful. We love to watch skillful performances, but even more to the point, we love to experience them.

It starts with a membrane

For many, the word *skill* suggests a mysterious and ineffable process, some rare alchemy of inborn talent, attention and dedication. But we can also describe skill as the coordinated activity of the human nervous system; it's simply an orchestration of sensation and motor commands. When we get the organism functioning together as a unitary whole and prime it with sufficient practice, skill is the result. But how does this process work? How do we learn new skills and integrate them into our performance?

The long answer would take us on a grand tour of the nervous system, but the short answer is easy to grasp. That is, it all starts with a membrane, specifically, the post-synaptic membrane in a typical nerve cell or neuron. The process is called LTP for "long term potentiation." In a nutshell, this is the process by which post-synaptic membranes become increasingly sensitive to repeated stimulation.

The brain is home to billions of nerve cells that connect to one another at junctions called synapses; together these structures form circuits that control everything that we think, say and do. But synapses are not just dumb gaps between neurons; the membranes at these sites are amazingly intricate structures, packed with thousands of receptor molecules that respond and adapt to the chemical influence of upstream or pre-synaptic neurons. Repeated stimulation sets in motion a cascading set of changes in the post-synaptic membrane that make subsequent communication between the two neurons far more likely.

When a circuit is stimulated frequently, the information flow in that circuit is facilitated; the flow becomes faster and more efficient. With repeated use, the neurons fuse together in a functional embrace. This is why neuroscientists say "cells that fire together, wire together." This is the cellular basis for learning, skill and memory. In turn, it suggests a general principle: if we want to learn a new skill, we need to perform the desired action over and over again until the circuit takes hold. In other words, we need to perform reps.

The post-synaptic membrane is a marvel of structure and function, but not all the action is at the synapse. There's also myelin, a living form of insulation that wraps long nerve cell fibers, increasing their speed dramatically. Like LTP, the process is also "use-dependent." That is, the more we fire a particular neural fiber, the thicker the insulating wrappings become. And, just as with LTP, the action happens in just the right places: if we fire the circuit that helps us play a particular chord on the guitar, and do it repeatedly, those exact nerve fiber wrappings will begin to grow. More practice equals more insulation equals more speed and more skill.

All about reps

The discovery of long-term potentiation and myelination confirms what coaches, teachers and trainers have know for thousands of years. That is, learning is all about reps. Reps are the raw material of human learning and skill development. Cells that repeatedly fire together form a stronger connection and in turn, the circuits in question become faster. The more we repeat an idea, an action or a behavior, the greater the probability that it will stick.

Repetition has long been a familiar theme in education, but the new research tells us something more. That is, the process of neuroplastic change is incredibly fast. The brain is constantly at work, seeking out patterns and rewiring its circuitry, second by second; our plasticity, in other words, is constant. This brings us to a surprising and challenging conclusion. That is, *every moment of human life is a rep.* We are always practicing something. Whatever you are doing at this moment is your practice, for better or for worse. You might be practicing something as simple as sitting with a particular posture, observing the world in a particular way or exercising a particular belief. But whatever it is, you are setting yourself up to do and become more of that very thing. We are always etching grooves in our brains and nervous systems.

And it's not just the body. Given the tight interconnection between body, mind and spirit, we can safely assume that the process goes further. We tend to think of reps as motor behaviors such as athletic movements and musical passages, but we can just as well talk about cognitive reps, emotional reps and even spiritual reps. We don't just practice movements, we also practice meanings. The processes that shape the human body also shape the totality of our life experience.

Going further, we also begin to see that human nature itself is also plastic. Individual changes in neurophysiology don't remain locked within the bounds of our skin. We may well feel like individuals but in fact, our attention and behavior is highly contagious. As we transform our bodies and minds through training and practice, we inevitably change the way those around us attend to the world. Multiplied by billions of people and spread over the span of generations, this contagion can make very real changes in human behavior, values and culture. Each one of us is changing humanity, in every moment.

Smart reps

Reps are the raw material of learning, adaptation and development, but not all reps are created equal. If we're really serious about improving our performance, we'll need to perform high quality reps. But what makes for a smart, high-quality repetition?

Here we turn to the vast experience of coaches, teachers and trainers, backed up by the discoveries of neuroscience. No matter the sport, art or discipline, a similar formula emerges again and again: That is, a high-quality rep is characterized by precision, attentional density and motivation. Together, these qualities form the core of high-performance training.

The need for precision is obvious. As we've seen, it's vital to make our reps relevant to the desired outcome; we attempt to perform each rep exactly the way it needs to be done. We might play around the edges with variations on a theme, but when the time comes for serious learning, it's essential that we focus all of our available resources and energy on perfect execution. This establishes the "neural groove" in the just right place and makes everything that comes after it that much easier.

In this process, specificity is crucial. If you want to develop a particular aptitude, skill or trait, you must begin by practicing that very aptitude, skill or trait; if you want carrots, you must plant carrots. If you want a skill or capability, you must give your brain and body the specific reps it needs to develop that very skill or capability.

This, of course, is where many of us go astray. We want carrots, but we plant beets instead. We want to be strong, powerful, happy and successful, but we plant seeds of procrastination, distraction and impulsivity. We pin our hopes on some future change of life circumstance, oblivious to the fact that we are creating our futures in every moment, right now.

Of course, you can't be precise or specific about a training objective unless you know exactly what it is that you're trying to create. That's why it's essential to know your target as intimately as possible. Study. Watch your chosen role models. Listen to examples. Describe exactly what it is you want. What does it look like? Feel like? Know it backwards and forwards, inside and out. Then, start focusing your reps on the desired outcome.

This will be a good start, but precision alone is not enough. You will also need to pay highly focused attention to what you're doing. Coaches know this by experience and neuroscience proves it conclusively. Drawing on research with both human and non-human animals, neuroscientists have discovered that the actual structure and function of the brain can be altered by the way we pay attention.

Attention may seem like an intangible product of mind, but it has real physical consequences for synapses and neurons, and in turn, the informational substances that circulate throughout our bodies. The old cliché tells us "That which you focus on, grows." To update it, we might well say "That which we focus on grows neurons, synapses and networks."

Smart reps develop high quality skills, adaptive behaviors, grace and beauty. They are fast and effective in creating the desired circuits and the desired outcome. In contrast, stupid reps are ineffective and wasteful. They reinforce actions, movements and behaviors that we don't really want; they take us away from skill, grace and beauty. They sap our energy because it takes us longer to reach our goals; even worse, we may not reach them at all.

Sadly, many of us persist in practicing mindless, ineffective and wasteful reps. Even worse, some coaches use reps for punishment and "character building" a process that develops neither skill nor character. Others fail to consider long-term goals and choose reps that have no particular relevance to anyone's objectives. And of course, reps that are too hard or too easy might also be described as stupid. Too hard and we fail early, before any nervous system adaptation can occur; too easy and the student or athlete quickly becomes bored and looks for other forms of stimulation.

Today we know that the stronger our attention, the more profound the effect on tissue and performance. Neuroscience confirms common sense; the harder we try to learn something new, the more completely the body responds. The buzz phrase of the day is "attentional density." In other words, if you want to make progress in some field or discipline, you've got to bring maximum attentional resources to bear on it. The more passionate and intense your concentration, the better.

Naturally, high attentional density is driven by desire and motivation. Loving what we do is vital. High-performance training can be extremely challenging at times, as we struggle to create brand-new capabilities from what feels like thin air. The skill lies just out of reach, a promise that we can sense, but not quite execute. If we can drive our attentional density with passion and motivation, we can push ourselves into this new domain. And if we can do it repeatedly, we can develop real skill.

Raw effort is essential. Concentrate your psychophysical energies on skill, endurance, sensitivity or execution, whatever your chosen target. Gather your resources, concentrate them in one direction and push the effort to the maximum possible level. Philip Toshio Sudo gives us a perfect example of this approach in *Zen Guitar*: "Here is where you start: Play one note on one string and pour in *every ounce of your heart and soul*. Then repeat."

Quality before quantity

No matter the specific details of your art or discipline, the primary goal is to keep your attention focused on smart reps. Forget training harder; train smarter. Design your reps with a purpose and an intention. Visualize and describe the performance goal that lies just outside of your reach, then create reps that will lead you in that direction.

Remember, a small number of highly-focused reps is far superior to a large number of half-hearted efforts. High quality reps, even in small numbers, carve the grooves in the right place and ease the path for subsequent efforts. But large numbers of weak efforts simply lead to mediocrity.

Above all, strive to do one thing really, really well. Even if it's just a single high-quality, beautiful rep, that one effort might well make all the difference.

Lesson 6

Touch the earth

One touch of nature makes the whole world kin.

William Shakespeare

Knowing who you are is impossible without knowing where you are.

Paul Shepherd

As we think more deeply about our bodies and our experience in the world, we naturally begin to wonder our habitat, the living earth that surrounds us. Habitat is not only our home on earth, it is also the ultimate source of everything that sustains us. It makes us who we are.

Sadly, it has now become obvious that something is desperately wrong with this primal relationship. Not only do we destroy our habitat with all manner of bad behavior, we also fail to experience it in a truly meaningful way. We isolate and insulate ourselves from the very processes that give life to our bodies and our spirits.

In his landmark *Last Child in the Woods*, author Richard Louv tells us that today's children are suffering from "nature-deficit disorder" and speaks of our "atrophied awareness" and "place blindness." He points to a host of afflictions that may well be caused by isolation from the natural world: attention disorders, anxiety and depression. "Our children," he says, "are the first generation to be raised without meaningful contact with the natural world."

But it's not just kids that are suffering from a nature deficit. Our entire culture is profoundly dislocated from land and habitat. We go where the jobs are, we live where the housing prices are tolerable. We spend our days in digital isolation, manipulating abstract symbols that have little or no relationship to anything living. Pixels flash before our eyes and we react. In the meantime, nature is out there somewhere, we hope. In a very real sense, we are effectively living in space. This is an unprecedented and exceedingly dangerous way to live.

We are embedded

Unfortunately, many of us are caught in the grip of a powerful illusion. Not only do we think of our bodies as isolated objects, we also imagine that "the environment" is something "out there" and separate from ourselves. We strive to be green, but most of us experience the environment as something external to our bodies, if we experience it at all.

Indigenous cultures would find our view disturbing and delusional. Native people have always respected the relational nature of life and the interdependence between people and habitat. Today, this ancient knowledge has been fully validated by modern science. As Charles Darwin and thousands of biologists have shown, there is a deep and ancient continuity between human beings and the rest of life on earth. Like it or not, we are living smack dab in the middle of the natural world, poised between the microbiome and the macrobiome. We are literally immersed in life, with life-support systems both inside and outside our bodies. The relationship is intimate. As the French philosopher Maurice Merleau-Ponty put it, "Our body is in the world as the heart is in the organism...it forms with it a system."

The inside story is simply mind-blowing. Our bodies are hosts to trillions of microorganisms that live on us and in us, primarily in our guts. And we are massively outnumbered: our bodies are home to 10 times as many microbial cells as body cells. (Microbial cells are much smaller.) Even more striking is the fact that our human genes are outnumbered 100 to 1 by microbial genes. We are home to a vast ecosystem that we are only just beginning to understand.

The microorganisms in and on our bodies participate in our physiology at every level. They contribute to digestion, development, immunity and even produce neurotransmitters and other informational substances that in turn, affect our cognition. Mark Lyte of the Texas Tech University Health Sciences Center in Abilene, studies how microbes affect the endocrine system. As he puts it, "These bacteria are, in effect, mind-altering microorganisms." In other words, we don't just think with our brains, we think with our microbiome, which is to say, our guts.

In 2006 a team of scientists surveying human gut bacteria published a paper in the journal *Science*, writing that "Humans are superorganisms, whose metabolism represents an amalgamation of microbial and human attributes." Nathanael Johnson put it even more graphically in *All Natural*: "We are great walking bags of primordial muck. We contain multitudes."

Moving from the small to the big, we find ourselves embedded in the large scale dimensions of habitat. We are literally living inside the body of the earth. Here we are reminded of the physiologist Claude Bernard and his famous description of the *milieu intérieur* or "internal milieu" (the environment within). This is the extra-cellular fluid environment, an internal "habitat" that provides protective stability and life-support for the cells, tissues and organs of the body. Bernard used the phrase in several works from 1854 until his death in 1878.

Likewise, physicians and environmental scientists are beginning to talk about the *milieu extérieur* or what we might call the *external milieu*. This is our habitat, described in physiological terms. Just as with tissues of the body, our external milieu provides essential, life-giving support and protection. Far from being a passive container for the human body, the external milieu literally keeps us alive. The dimensions and details of interior and exterior physiology are of course different, but the principles are precisely the same: extract a cell from its body or a species from its environment and health is bound to suffer.

Zen philosopher Alan Watts described an *external milieu* perspective in his 1970 book *Does it Matter?*

> *...civilized human beings are alarmingly ignorant of the fact that they are continuous with their natural surroundings. It is as necessary to have air, water, plants, insects, birds, fish and mammals as it is to have brains, hearts, lungs and stomachs. The former are our external organs in the same way the latter are our internal organs.*

John Muir would have agreed. So too the Spanish philosopher and essayist Jose Ortega y Gasset. He captured the totality of our position perfectly when he wrote "I am I plus my surroundings." We are embedded. We are part of something much larger than ourselves.

Earthly cognition

Throughout history, human cognition has been intimately connected to habitat. Contrary to our modern, Cartesian assumptions, the thoughts and ideas that we experience don't just come from our disembodied minds, they also come from our bodies operating in an environmental context. We think, in other words, not just with our brains and bodies, but also with the earth itself.

Even a casual understanding of human evolution would be enough to suggest that this is the case. After all, if you're living in a dangerous, wild environment, you're naturally inclined to pay extremely close attention to the most subtle features of habitat and place. Whenever you find food or encounter danger, you're likely to form an extremely vivid memory of that place. Likewise, that location will carry an intense meaning, one that will shape your thoughts and even your imagination for years to come. You won't just think *about* the land, you literally think *with* the land. In this way, our cognition becomes embedded in habitat.

It comes as no surprise to learn that scientists have begun to uncover the neural correlates of this mind-habitat association. In 2013, researchers reported the discovery of special cells in the brain's hippocampus that "geotag" events in our lives. That is, we have a neurological inclination to associate memories and experiences with particular places in habitat.

We should have seen this coming. In ancient Greece, scholars and orators memorized and practiced their speeches by walking through the city and anchoring their points of argument to particular locations. Their phrasing, "In the first place…" "In the second place…" was a literal reference to their environment, to habitat. We have always done this sort of thing, but today, we have effectively cut the cord that binds us to the world. People now live anywhere they can, anywhere the money is, regardless of the features of habitat.

In the process, our cognition and culture have become ungrounded. Our thoughts and imaginations are now free-floating, divorced from their earthy origins. Today, we live very much like the notorious sci-fi "brain in a vat" experiment; our cognition runs like a computer simulation with no connection to anything natural or real. It is no wonder that we experience such epic levels of anxiety, depression and other psycho-spiritual afflictions. Our minds are literally built to connect to the natural world, but when that connection is broken, we have nowhere to turn.

This uncoupling of human cognition from the natural world has given some of access to astonishing levels of creativity and imagination, but this has come with a terrible cost. Today our minds are almost entirely free to choose whatever sensory experience we can imagine; we can and do innovate to our heart's content. But the price we pay is excruciating. For those who suffer with crippling anxiety, depression and disordered attention, living apart from habitat will never be a path to health, performance or spiritual happiness. We need our habitat to make us whole.

The power of the outdoors

Given our massively embedded nature and our deep historical continuity with the natural world, it comes as no surprise to find that contact with natural surroundings enhances human health. In fact, studies of biophilia (literally "love of life) and landscape preference are highly suggestive. A commonly-cited study by Roger Ulrich in 1984 demonstrated that a simple view from a hospital window enhances recovery from surgery. Patients with a view of nature had shorter postoperative hospital stays and took fewer analgesics than matched patients in similar rooms without such a view. Similarly, the new field of "green exercise" shows precisely what we would expect– intimate and vigorous contact with the natural world is strongly health promoting.

Naturally, this tight association between outdoor experience and human health leads us to speculate about informational substances that flow through the body and the brain. We may well imagine that the natural environment stimulates the production of powerful brain chemicals known as *outdorphins*. This, of course, is a play on the word *endorphins*, the famous opioid peptides notable for the "runner's high," pain-suppression and other feel-good effects. This comparison is only partly in jest; given the incredible subtlety and sophistication of the mind-body system, it would not be far-fetched to suppose the existence of neuro-hormonal messengers that signaled contact with the natural world.

If such *outdorphins* did in fact exist, they would surely have long-lasting salutary and anabolic effects on the entire mind-body-spirit complex. They would boost cognition, mood, immune function, cardiovascular function, metabolic efficiency, digestion and growth. They would also have a neurotrophic effect, stimulating neurogenesis, synaptogenesis and brain plasticity.

Likewise, we might well speculate about the existence of *indorphins*. These substances, produced by the brain and body in indoor environments, would have their own effect on cognition, mental function and spirit. In small doses, they would sharpen our ability to focus on individual objects, especially abstract symbols. They would probably enhance the function of the brain's left hemisphere, promoting the development of analytical thought, logic and reason. However, *indorphins* are almost certainly poisonous in large doses. Sustained exposure will produce anxiety, depression and a marked inability to see relationships.

Just as we speculate about *indorphins* and *outdorphins* in the body, the time has come to speculate about the difference between indoor and outdoor cognition. Incredibly, this is largely unexplored territory; a quick Internet search returns only a handful of results. But how can this be? Given the incredible sophistication of the human organism and the massive influence of environment on our minds and bodies, it's safe to assume that there would be a significant, even radical difference between "indoor thinking" and "outdoor thinking."

After all, we know that cognitive activity is far more than simply the processing done by the brain; the entire organism is involved. And there can be no question that the body senses, behaves and responds differently when it's outdoors. It would be truly bizarre if there wasn't a difference in the form and content of our thoughts.

Consider our experience of vision. When we're outdoors, the body naturally scans a wider range of territory. As hunter-gatherers, we naturally rely on our peripheral vision and in turn, our cognition almost certainly goes along for the ride. When we're outdoors, we're more likely to adopt big-picture perspectives and to explore the world with a comprehensive, wide-angle scan. If you focus in one place for too long, you become vulnerable to attack from some other direction.

But when we move indoors, our vision shifts from panorama to narrowrama and our visual-cognitive field shrinks. This is precisely what we experience in the modern world, where many of us are committed to a single-point visual focus through most of our waking hours. As we spend our days reading, scrolling, focusing and clicking, our peripheral vision becomes increasingly irrelevant and atrophied. In turn, our panoramic view of life and relationships also begins to fade.

We might well wonder about the cognitive and health consequences of such chronically-focused vision. Center-focus vision has its advantages, but it's also a form of peripheral deprivation. For the human animal, this is significant. In a primal, natural setting, anything that would have interfered with our wide-angle view would immediately lead to anxiety, an increase in stress hormones and of course, a shift in cognition.

Indoor cognition is more about depth of inquiry, but outdoor cognition is more about breadth. Indoor living allows us to specialize, but outdoor living opens up our experience and our minds to greater cognitive vistas. Can it be any wonder that humanity's great move indoors, beginning some 10,000 years ago, resulted in a concentration of highly focused intelligence, resulting in the spectacular development of modern science and hyper-specialization?

At the same time, we are forced to wonder about our loss of panoramic cognition. As more and more people live their entire lives indoors, our sensitivity to context, environment and relationship declines, just when we need it most. And this, of course, is just one more reason to get out of the office, get out of the house, get out of the car, and go climb a mountain. We need to see the big picture while we still can.

Naturally, many people have begun looking deeper into this habitat-health connection and many are promoting "nature therapy" as a solution. This approach is supported by several lines of research. For example, Louv cites a study presented to the American Psychological Society in 1993. Stephen and Richard Kaplan surveyed more than 1,200 corporate and state office workers. Those with a view of trees, bushes, or large lawns experienced significantly less frustration and more work enthusiasm than employees without such views.

In another study, researchers compared groups on proof-reading performance. The group who backpacked in a wilderness area showed better performance than those who traveled to an urban area or who took no vacation. Other studies show additional benefits to "green" exposure: better motor coordination, increased ability to concentrate, less impulsivity and improved ability to delay gratification. The same effect applies to mammals, primates and rodents across the board: environmental enrichment increases brain activity, just as environmental deprivation actually shrinks the brain. The effect is well understood by neuroscience: environmental stimulation leads to thicker myelin sheaths, which allow neurons to fire more efficiently.

None of this comes as any great surprise. The brain, like the body, evolved over the course of millions of years, nearly all of that time in natural environments. It makes sense that our brains and sensory systems would be highly attentive to natural shapes, sounds, colors, textures and forms. After all, our lives depended on it. Brains that failed to attend to natural qualities were unlikely to make it to reproductive age. But now, when we take away those natural shapes, colors, textures and forms, the brain gropes for connection. If it comes up empty, attention becomes disordered and our spirits becomes confused.

Exposure to nature reverses the ill effects. Not only does it make our bodies feel better, it also gives us wonderful raw material to think with. It provides us with primal sensations, forms, patterns and structures. It gives us a sense of dynamism, rhythm, pace and place. These lessons can in turn be applied to any form of decision making in any realm.

The effect becomes even more profound with vigorous physical movement. People who move their bodies in outdoor settings expose themselves to more of Nature's content. Natural qualities are welcomed by the senses and are absorbed more completely. In this way, the natural world teaches us not just how to move, but also how to think. People who move their bodies in outdoor settings are more likely to think organically, systemically and panoramically. They are less likely to fall into reductionistic habits of thought and are more likely to look towards integration, harmonies and connection. This organic outlook is powerful medicine for all decision makers, especially those who are forced to work in abstracted, non-natural realms of thought and action.

Deep ecology, deep health

As we immerse ourselves in conversation about human beings and their relationship in the natural world, it's essential that we explore the distinction between "shallow" and "deep" ecology. Understanding this difference will go a long ways towards improving the power of our practice.

In shallow ecology, we practice a fair-weather relationship with nature, both literally and figuratively. We use nature for recreation, amusement and escape. We keep it at arms' length; we buy nature calendars, recycle cans and bottles and make occasional donations to non-profit organizations. This, of course, is better than nothing, but there's no fundamental change in our relationship with the world; we simply go about doing what we normally do, only with slightly more intelligence.

In contrast, deep ecology makes a radical change in our perspective and relationship. It puts human beings back into an intimate relationship with the living world. In deep ecology, we no longer declare ourselves to be the alpha animal; we are simply one of many, a mammal of no particular distinction. We remain vulnerable, temporary and highly dependent on the natural world.

The phrase *deep ecology* was first coined by the Norwegian philosopher Arne Næss in 1973 and was further developed by Bill Devall and George Sessions in *Deep Ecology: Living as if Nature Mattered*. The idea has also been explored by Aldo Leopold in *A Sand County Almanac*, Daniel Quinn in *Ishmael* and of course, the writings of John Muir. Deep ecologists take issue with the notion of human supremacy and call for a more participatory, intimate relationship with the natural world. This has also been a theme across native and indigenous cultures, most notably in the 1854 speech by Chief Seattle: "The earth does not belong to man. Man belongs to the earth."

Obviously, the entire notion of deep ecology is radically disruptive and counter-cultural and there's been plenty of push-back on the idea from the very outset. Western civilization has a long history of domination. We believe that our species holds a privileged place in creation and that we're entitled to whatever riches we can extract. It's no surprise that most people prefer the safer ground of shallow ecology or "green lite."

But no matter how controversial it may be, deep ecology is perfectly consistent with the discoveries of modern biological science. Beginning with Darwin's *Origin of Species* in 1859, biology has produced a tsunami of research proving our deep, embedded affiliation with the living world. We may well be smart, innovative and technologically savvy, but we are still subject to the constraints of the natural world.

The challenge of deep ecology comes with serious implications. We would much prefer to think of ourselves as a special, gifted, even exalted species. If think of ourselves as just another life form, we lose our special status and in the process. Deep ecology feels like a step down, a drastic, even cosmic reduction in rank.

Our reaction is understandable, but in fact, we've got it completely backwards. By declaring ourselves above and separate from the rest of the natural world, we isolate ourselves from the very source of life and health. We don't become stronger or more powerful, we become weaker. Isolation is not just lonely, it's dangerous.

In the deep ecology view, we lose our privileged position, but we gain a sense of integration and participation in something much larger than ourselves. Arne Naess captured this sense perfectly when he wrote "The smaller we come to feel ourselves compared to the mountain, the nearer we come to participating in its greatness." We may well be very small fish in an immensely large pond, but that pond is throbbing and pulsing with life and energy. As intimate participants, we get to share in that energy, mystery and beauty. There is both power and health in this humility.

Never one thing

Ecology teaches us in many ways. Not only does it instruct us by drawing our attention to the vast web of inter-relationship in the natural world, it also offers inspirations for how we might live our personal lives. Consider the work of ecologist Garrett Hardin (1915-2003). Hardin was famous for his 1968 description of "the tragedy of the commons," the notion that community spaces such as pastures, oceans and atmospheres make convenient dumping grounds for all sorts of unwanted rubbish, toxins and waste products. Hardin also coined one of the most powerful phrases ever to come out of the ecology movement. Struck by the incredible interdependence he observed at every level of ecosystem functioning, he remarked "We can never do merely one thing."

This phrase surely ranks as one of the most profound statements ever spoken. Not only does it accurately describe our large-scale impacts on forests, wetlands and

80

oceans, it also shocks us into a new appreciation for the power and potential of personal behavior. It reminds us of a deep primal truth: everything we do in this world and our personal lives has consequences. Everything we touch, say or think impacts the whole, sometimes in surprisingly powerful ways.

This principle of far-reaching consequences is about more than our effects on external ecosystems. After all, it's easy to understand that building a dam is "not one thing." A massive concrete structure that chokes a river is certain to have a multitude of destructive consequences that ripple across space and time. But the same principle also applies to the seemingly trivial acts of our everyday lives, behaviors that we rarely think of as "green" or "ecological." A word, a gesture, a kindness or an extra effort; all of these behaviors ripple and cascade through our lives and the lives of the people around us. No matter how insignificant they may seem at the moment, they are never "just one thing."

Of course, most of us understand the fact that our large-scale behaviors will have consequences: Steal from your neighbor and you'll poison the community trust; misuse antibiotics and you'll increase the virulence of bacteria for all of us. But it's not just gross physical actions that cascade through the flux and flow of our lives. Neuroscience tells us that the subtle activity of the mind actually shapes neural connections. In other words, our thoughts have tissue-level consequences. And when brain tissue changes, so does our attention, cognition, memory, learning and behavior. And when behavior changes, so do social relationships and habitats. Ultimately, no thought is without consequence; no thought is merely one thing.

This is where ecology and the art of personal living intersect with the field of chaos theory. Few of us understand the detailed science behind hyper-complex systems, but most of us have heard of the "butterfly effect." In the classic example, scientists tell us that the atmosphere of the earth is so interconnected and sensitive to initial conditions that "the flap of a butterfly's wings in Texas can set off a thunderstorm on the other side of the world."

This is a wonderful and enchanting image, but it's also an accurate description of how non-linear, complex systems change and grow. When systems become hyper-complex (atmospheres, habitats, human brains and social relationships), minute disturbances can trigger immense, large-scale transformations; the subtle can be extremely powerful. In other words, little things aren't always so little. As

Beautiful Practice

the French philosopher Blaise Pascal put it: "The least movement is of importance to all nature. The entire ocean is affected by a pebble."

As we learn to appreciate the ecological nature of our personal lives and the systemic effect of our actions, a host of implications become clear. In the first place, we realize that there can be no isolation in this world. When everything is interconnected, there can be no place to hide, no alternative but to be involved. Escapism is impossible; even passivity has consequences. Nothing is truly neutral.

Of course, most of us recognize that some moments are special. We feel the power of these "butterfly moments" in new beginnings: the first day of school, the first day of music practice or the start of a new athletic season. It's a fresh start and most everyone is willing, even eager for new insights, skills, challenges and discoveries. Intuitively, we feel that these special moments are likely to have profound consequences that will go far beyond this particular place and time. And of course, these are the times for rapt attention, discipline, clarity and mindfulness. This is when we give and receive inspiration; this is when we step up for a larger purpose.

But in fact, all of us are acting on the world in every moment; we are all intrinsically powerful. And in this process, no effort is wasted. Every act of courage, no matter how small, has consequences. Every time we make a move towards health, knowledge, mindfulness or compassion, we make such qualities more likely, not only in our own bodies and experience, but in our families and communities. Every time we exercise, eat right, meditate, say a kind word or open our hearts, not only do we benefit personally, but so do others, both near and far.

Once we begin to appreciate the reach of our most subtle attitudes and behaviors, we are simultaneously challenged and inspired. The things that you do matter. Know it or not, like it or not, you will make a difference. Every moment is a call to step up, an opportunity to transform, not only your own life, but the wider world as well. In the end, we realize that the ecologists were right all along, not just about forests and farms and oceans, but also about the way we live in every day. Every moment touches the web of life. And who knows? That seemingly minor act of courage you create today may very well set off an inspirational cycle of transformation in someone else's life, community and habitat.

Lesson 7

Feel the world

I don't want to be the one who says life is beautiful.
I want to be the one who feels it.

Marty Rubin

Here's a "what if?" scenario for you:

What if you woke up one day and discovered that the sensations you were experiencing in your eyes, ears, nose and skin didn't match up with the physical reality around you? Wouldn't you find that experience disorienting and disturbing? And what if that disconnected experience continued for a long period of time? Wouldn't you begin to feel alienated? And ultimately, wouldn't that disconnection begin to make you, quite literally, crazy?

And to come at it from the other direction, isn't it true that one of the primary goals of performance training is to make our movements and behaviors congruent with the sensations that we're experiencing in the world? Don't athletes and other high performers spend years, even decades trying to fine tune their nervous systems to the subtle qualities of their environments? Isn't it essential that we sense and perceive the world as it truly is?

So what then are we to make of the fact that millions of people now spend a considerable portion of their lives in a state of profound sensory disconnect with the world around them? What are we to make of the epidemic of sensory distortion and isolation brought about by portable music players and devices, now in widespread, almost universal use by exercisers and non-exercisers alike? This is no trivial matter—we are talking about billions of hours of human attention each year, directed away from the world as it is. What if those billions of hours were spent in direct sensory connection with the world? How would our consciousness and behavior change?

Some observers have looked at this audio-electronic disconnect between sensation and reality and dubbed it *schizophonia*. This, of course, is a play on the word schizophrenia, that notorious mental illness marked by a distorted sense of reality, disintegration of thought, bizarre delusions and auditory hallucinations. Of course, it would be foolish to suggest a causal connection between *schizophonia* (the act of wearing an music player) and schizophrenia (the mental illness), but the parallels are just a little too close for comfort. After all, if you've been wearing an device consistently for months or years, you already are, in a very real sense, disconnected from reality and your body. You may not yet be experiencing the symptoms of delusion and hallucination that characterize full-blown schizophrenia, but you are clearly out of contact with the world.

The power of sensation

Sadly, many of us fail to take sensation seriously. We like to see things and hear things and touch things, but our everyday abilities are familiar and we take them for granted. Rarely do we attempt to improve the performance of our senses or explore the subtle capabilities of vision, taste, hearing or touch. Most of us are content merely to experience the coarsest, most obvious qualities of the world we live in.

The folly of this lifestyle becomes apparent as soon as we imagine our natural history and our experience in a wild, natural environment. Suppose that you're a Paleolithic hunter-gatherer, walking through the bush in search of food. Your environment is "predator-rich," which is to say, it's dangerous and unpredictable. If your sensitivity is deficient or mismatched with conditions on the ground, you are likely to wind up in the belly of a hungry carnivore. Obviously, you'll be highly motivated to pay attention to the subtleties of sensation; even a whisper of sight, sound or touch might make the difference in staying alive.

The same question goes for *any* creature in a natural environment. Animals have a 500 million year history of sensation, a capability that is absolutely essential to survival. Would any wild animal voluntarily wear a device that pumped substitute sensory information into its nervous system? Not a chance. Wild animals are smart enough to know that survival depends on tight integration between sensory experience and reality. That, after all, is one of the primary reasons we–both human and non-human animals–have a nervous system in the first place. When we flood our senses with artificial stimuli or fail to use them wisely, we pay disrespect to an incredibly elegant system that has been hundreds of millions of years in the making.

High quality sensation is the foundation for anything that we might choose to do with our bodies, minds and spirits. If you're going to act in the world, you've got to know the world. Sensation is the foundation for skill, speed, strength and posture, as well as practical intelligence, activism and leadership. When sensation fails or becomes distorted, effectiveness is invariably compromised. Without an accurate and timely sense of the world, we can merely grope our way through life; we become little more than chimps in a china shop.

There's more here than meets the eye, ear and nose. We are accustomed to thinking of sensation in terms of our primary senses, but sensation is everywhere in the body and many of these capabilities lie below the threshold of consciousness. Chemoreceptors and interoceptors collect and communicate information about metabolism, pheromones, blood pressure, pH levels and gas concentrations. Muscles, tendons, ligaments and connective tissue are littered with proprioceptors, mechanical sensory receptors that constantly send information to the spinal cord and brain about joint position and motion. The skin itself is one massive sensory system. The foot is a sensory organ, the hand is a sensory organ. For all practical purposes, the entire body is a sensory organ.

Hyper-normal blues

In a natural, ancestral environment, the human sensory system provides fast, subtle and accurate information about the qualities of the world; we are literally wired for natural habitat. But today we live in an alien sensory environment; our modern world is saturated with hyper-normal stimuli, sensory information that goes beyond the evolutionary status quo.

Examples are everywhere. In the supermarket, food products are saturated with extra salt, sugar, fat and other "flavor enhancers," intentionally engineered to be "hyperpalatable." These foods are known to trigger our reward systems by boosting dopamine levels, much as addictive drugs do. In the world of vision, we are flooded with "special effects" and CGI, combinations of hyper-normal speed and color that appear on our electronic devices. In the world of sound, we have an entire industry devoted to artificial, electronic, synthesized stimulation. And in the exercise world, we routinely flood our senses with loud music, flashing lights and mirrors, none of which are remotely natural or normal.

In the short term, the flood of hyper-normal stimuli is a wild, high-energy party, a sensory joy ride. It stimulates our enthusiasm and maybe even our creativity. So we turn up the volume, pass around the food products and fire up the panoramic flat screen TV. In our frenzy, we live like rock stars, gorging on exaggerated, hyperbolic stimuli in almost every minute of the day. In this hyper-normal world, too much is never enough. And for awhile, it feels great.

But as a steady diet, our hyper-normal binge begins to wreak havoc on the entire mind-body-spirit system; chronic exposure begins to have significant, even catastrophic consequences to our nervous systems, performance and quality of life. Most obviously, hyper-normal stimuli leads to addiction and adaptation. The hyper-normal addict requires ever-greater forms of stimulation to maintain a sense of interest and excitement. Over time, this leads to dopamine depletion, stress, anhedonia, exhaustion and depression.

Even more worrying are the consequences for human attention and our relationships with the natural world and each other. For example, an increasing number of young people report that "nature is boring." Similarly, many people prefer texting and electronic messaging to authentic meetings with real people. This is exactly what we would expect; when you're addicted to hyper-normal stimuli, anything that's less than hyperbolic seems bland and dull: natural conversation is boring, real people are boring, unadulterated food is boring. Most of normal human life in fact–walking, reading, cooking, eating, sleeping–all boring. As hyper-normal stimulation increases its grip on our attention, our most basic human behaviors begin to fade from view; if it's not rad, it might as well not even exist. In the process, we are increasingly pulled away from the very things that would improve our health and our happiness in the world. In the end, hyper-normal makes us hypo-happy.

Sensation is a muscle

In a beautiful practice, we naturally take a keen interest in developing our sensory capability. Sadly, many of us lapse back into habitual ways of thinking. That is, we think of sensitivity as just another talent or gift that's bestowed upon us by an accident of birth; we've either got good sensory capability or we don't. But given what we know about the sophistication and plasticity of the body, it's safe to assume that all our sensitivities are tunable and trainable. In this respect, all sensation is "muscular;" we can improve our capabilities through engagement and smart reps.

Similarly, there can be no doubt that sensation is a use-it-or-lose-it capability. If we stop using some sensory range, the corresponding circuits in the sensory cortex will be taken over by other functions. The brain simply assumes that the unused capability is no longer important and responds by turning its energy to other uses. If you don't use your visual, olfactory or tactile acuity, you'll tend to lose it. Just as sedentary living makes our muscles weak, sensory disuse contracts our ability to see, hear, taste and feel the world.

The solution, as always, is practice. Follow these guidelines:

First, slow down. Speed is a sensation killer. Busyness makes us blind to nuance and subtlety. The harder we push into the future, the more we abandon the sensory experience of the present. Hurrying forces our body into a sort of sensory triage; we only pay attention to those qualities that are essential to the task at hand. In a sense, the faster we go, the dumber we get.

By taking ample time for the tasks in our lives, we allow ourselves to savor sensation, subtlety and nuance; we bring more attentional density to the process. By doing less and feeling more, we allow the body to gather more information. Clearly, relaxation is vital to the process. Fear and stress tend to skew our sensation, making us hyper-attentive to some things while becoming blind to others. Similarly, excessive cognition, worry and analysis tends to obscure our attention to the body; the more we think, the less we feel. Even if we do manage to think our way out of our predicament, we loose contact with the intelligence of the body, our most valuable ally.

Similarly, we would do well to talk less and listen more. Practice "noble silence." Exercise your ears, your skin and your sense of touch. Listen mindfully; your mouth is already strong and endurant enough as it is.

Whenever possible, swing your attention back to nature, back to the kind of sensations that humans have experienced for millions of years. Avoid hyper-normal stimuli, or use it sparingly. Concentrate your attention on the primal sensations: the feel of your bare feet on the earth, the touch of the wind, the sound of the birds and the play of light and shadow on the land. These qualities may strike you as dull or boring at the beginning, but that is simply your conditioning at work. With effort over time, you will see and feel more depth and breadth in familiar qualities.

As you reach for subtlety and nuance of sensation, lead with your imagination. Curiosity is vital. What would it feel like if you body was more sensitive to the natural world? Can you imagine hearing the distant sound of a wolf in the wild? What would it be like to see just a little better on a dark night? Your imagination will prime your body for actual changes in capability.

Remember too that just as with muscle, it's a matter of effort and repetition. No one ever developed their sensory capability by accident. A couple of easy reps won't do it. There has to be a sustained and vigorous reaching for the small differences that add up to big changes.

Above all, focus. Increased sensitivity can only take place in the here and now. The more you dwell in the land of past and future, the more your sensation will be compromised. The more you practice mindfulness and attentional stability, the more you will see, hear and feel.

A glimpse of a glimpse

Just as this art calls upon us to develop and sharpen our sensitivities, it also reminds us of just how limited our capabilities really are. The world is vast beyond imagining, but our senses only reveal the smallest fraction. Even the sharpest eyes only can only detect a sliver of the electromagnetic spectrum. Even the sharpest ears can hear only a fraction of the sound waves that wash over us. In comparison with other creatures, our tactile and olfactory skills are weak at best. And of course, we only inhabit a small spot on the planet. And even more to the point, our lives are extremely short. All in all, we see only a glimpse of a glimpse of our world.

In theory, this realization should inspire a sense of wonder and humility. It would be folly beyond measure to assume that what our view of the world is complete, detailed or accurate. Even when assisted by modern scientific instruments and connected to other astute observers and researchers around the world, we are still unlikely to get anything approaching a comprehensive view of reality.

And yet we persist in our claims to knowing what's real and what's true. We thunder on about our perspectives and attack those who disagree. Our senses are barely adequate to find our way in the woods on a dark night, but we are quick to lay claim to understanding all reality. In some respects, our pets know more about the world than we do and yet, we stand ready to fight and die in defense of a glimpse.

Clearly, some humility is in order. As philosopher and historian Will Durant once put it, "We are such microscopic particles in so immense a universe that none of us is in a position to understand the world, much less dogmatize about it." Instead of arguing over the merits of our world views, perhaps we'd do better to enlist and welcome collaborators in our quest to for understanding. In this way, other people's senses can help us expand our own.

Lesson 8

Inhabit this moment

May you live every day of your life.

Jonathan Swift

With mindfulness there is more to unlearn than there is to learn.

Michael H. Brooks
This. Only This

Have you ever paid attention to the way you pay attention? Have you ever observed the way you're observing the world? If you have, you're off to a good start because you're using your mind in a special kind of way, a way that promises to bring substantial benefits to yourself and the people around you. In short, you're practicing a kind of mindfulness.

Being a mindful sort of person, you've no doubt noticed that mindfulness itself is all the rage these days. Teachers, coaches, artists and scientists across a broad swath of modern culture have been speaking and writing about the benefits of focusing our attention. According to the latest research, mindfulness training can reduce our stress, calm our anxiety, improve our relationships with the world and improve our workplace performance. Enthusiasm for this kind of practice is growing and many people report significant improvements in their health and happiness.

Mindfulness is often described as the practice of continuous, present moment attention. When we're mindfully aware, we're inhabiting the moment as it is, right now. Instead of mentally of running away to the elsewhere or elsewhen, we embrace the totality of our current circumstances and experience. We relinquish our ruminations about the past and abandon our relentless planning for the future.

More broadly, we can describe mindfulness as the ability to concentrate and sustain our attention on a chosen focal point. Classically, this focal point is our experience of the present moment, but it really could be almost anything; an art or craft, a quality or sensation, an object, person or idea. In this sense, mindfulness is all about attentional stability. This stability is something that we can learn. In other words, mindfulness is trainable.

The power of mindfulness lies in the way it unifies our energy and our experience. When we bring our attention into the here and now, we integrate our entire mind-body-spirit system. In this process, nothing gets wasted; all of our energies become come together into single acts of movement, sensation, action or stillness. This unification of experience has profound consequences, not just for our performance and our health, but also for how we experience our lives. When we integrate our experience with mindful attention, not only do we become more powerful, we also experience life more completely. Things become easier *and* more interesting.

The perils of mindlessness

Classically, mindfulness is the ability to fully experience our experience, to feel what we're feeling and become intimate our lives. But sadly, most of us spend a substantial proportion of our lives at arm's length from our experience. Driven by incessant desires, ambitions, to-do lists and stress, most of us overclock our brains in every waking moment, doing everything *but* live in the present. We dwell on our memories, we dream about the future, we strategize our next moves and get lost in our emotions. In a sense, we're not even living our living.

Mindless reactivity is commonplace, but it's also bad news. We like to think we're in control of ourselves and our circumstances, but we spend much of our time reacting to events and forces around us. We're often unconscious, lulled to sleep by the familiar. We spend much of our time sleep walking, sleep eating, sleep driving, sleep working, sleep talking, sleep exercising, and sleep listening. When we're mindless, we fall back into a kind of reptilian intelligence and begin to function as mere stimulus-response mechanisms. No longer animated by curiosity or wonder, we simply process tasks as they come into our field of experience. It's a human universal, this tendency to wander away from the here and now, but it's also a tremendous drag on our performance and our happiness.

Singing and scheming

To better understand our practice of mindfulness, consider the difference between two common behaviors: "singing in the shower" and "scheming in the shower." In the first case, we're complete immersed in the present moment; we're singing for joy in the here and now. The soap and water just feel great and we're celebrating the experience. Our animal bodies love this experience.

But in the other case, we're not really experiencing the shower at all. We're planning, previewing and reviewing, mentally preparing for our upcoming challenges, refining our to-do lists, crunching some numbers and trying to decide among competing options. Cognition is working hard, but it's all about the elsewhere and elsewhen. We don't even feel the water running over our skin.

Similarly, there are times in our lives when we're just "singing in the rain." We're overcome with passion for the moment, and we're lovin' the here and the now. Who cares if we get wet? In contrast, many of us spend our days "scheming in the rain." The sky is painted with glorious colors and the clouds are swirling in timeless natural cycles, but we could care less. We're lost in planning and rumination, our minds far away in a neuro-simulated reality. This kind of behavior is becoming increasingly common in our wired world; lost in our prefrontal world of abstraction, the environment is becoming increasingly irrelevant.

But what is the practice here? In the world of mindfulness education, many teachers tell us that present moment living is the path to high performance and happiness; if we just keep "singing in the shower" and "singing the rain," we'll live our lives to the fullest. This kind of engagement sounds appealing and is clearly worth practicing, but there is a flip side too. No matter the wonders of the present moment, the fact remains that we've got to do some scheming at some time or other. Previewing and reviewing are essential elements of functional living, especially in the modern world. Without abstract planning, speculation and executive function, we'd never get anything done. And in fact, the shower might well be an ideal place to preview our actions and prepare to meet the world. After all, this is one place in the world where we can be free from distraction for a few precious moments.

There is no right answer to this conundrum, of course. We'll always be faced with a choice between the present and the elsewhen. No one can or should tell us how to take a shower or what to do in the rain. Of course, if we were monstrously, robotically disciplined, we would only do our scheming, previewing and reviewing at designated times, when sitting at our desks. We'd put firewalls around our present-moment mindfulness and protect it from intrusion and distraction; we would never scheme in the shower or the rain. But such a draconian limitation feels forced and almost inhuman; only a 50-year monk could pull it off. And besides, a healthy, creative mind needs some freedom to roam; a complete disciplining of the mind would be stifling and ultimately sterile. And we can be certain that many scientists, artists and professionals have reached some powerful realizations and insights, just when the warm water hits their skin.

As usual, the answer comes down to our sense of proportion; in other words, beauty. If all we ever do is sing in the shower or the rain, we may very well be happy, for awhile. Present-moment focus might be an ideal way to live, but it fails in a world that demands strategic preview and review; just try living without a calendar for a few weeks and see how far you get. At the same time, if we *never* sing in the shower or the rain, are clearly setting ourselves up for unhappiness. By constantly living in the elsewhere and the elsewhen, we literally miss out on the adventure of our lives. We may well have our strategies and tactics all mapped out to perfection, but then what?

The answer is personal. Some of us will need a little more singing; others, a little more scheming. But whatever you need, get into it. When you're scheming, immerse yourself in the process; dig down deep into the past and future and get the job done. Explore the elsewhere and the elsewhen as completely as possible; squeeze your prefrontal brain and shine your attention on the object of your wonder. And then, let it go. When singing, sing out with every cell in your body. Sing this moment. Sing this place.

Athletic attention

Our problem with mindlessness begins with the brain and the seductions of simulation. The power of the modern human brain is that it allows us to make incredible journeys into the past and future, via our imagination and the action of the prefrontal cortex. In essence, this system functions as a simulator, allowing us to review past events or test out possibilities about how the world might be. We can do thought experiments that ask "What if?" We can speculate. We can plan, schedule, sequence, review and evaluate; we can scheme. This kind of ability is essential to our modern human experience, civilization and personal success.

The simulator is a fantastic piece of gear, but indiscriminate use can be costly. In the first place, simulation displaces real life experience; the more we live in the imaginary world of past or future, the less we live in the present moment of here and now. Used occasionally and in moderation, this is a cost worth bearing, but when used in excess, the simulator strips away vast swathes of our experience, leaving us removed, isolated and out of touch with the beautiful adventure. Even worse, compulsive and chronic use of the simulator becomes a form of addiction; many of us become obsessed with ruminations of the past or plans for our utopian futures. Finally, chronic use of the simulator is expensive. It takes a lot of psycho-physical energy to run our simulations. Over time, this leads us into exhaustion and depression.

So what's the art? Obviously we can make good use of simulation to review and plan our lives. Indeed, human life as we know it would be impossible and impoverished if all we did was live in the present. The challenge, it would seem, is to make intelligent use of this capability, to train ourselves for smart simulation.

We might well describe this capability as "athletic attention" or "athletic intelligence." Just as we seek to develop athletic bodies, with movements that are both strong and flexible, so too should we look for the ability to focus and re-focus our attention. Here we look for the ability to bring all of our focus to bear on a single point or task and then relinquish that power as we move gracefully into some other point or task.

Of course, most of us are untrained in the attentional arts and so we swing from one extreme to the other. Some of us wander off into the world of attentional instability, fragmentation and the inability to focus. In this condition, we lose our sense of coherence and integration and become vulnerable to every passing stimuli. We get swept along by events, mindlessly reacting to impulse. At best, this condition leads to incompetence and ineffectiveness; at worst it leads to addictions, dysfunctions and a life without meaning.

At the other end of the spectrum our attention becomes rigid and fixated on a single point, idea or task. This is where we find obsessions, extremist cognition and fundamentalism. Captivated by a single quality or feature of the world, we pay obsessive attention to that one thing, unable to move on. Locked into a single point of view, we become boring, inflexible and then dangerous. We alienate the people around us and destroy our ability to grow. In the extreme, our lives become irrelevant and tragic.

This is where training comes into play. We make our attention more athletic by practicing precisely this. We begin by choosing a focal point. Popular choices include the breath, a flower, a candle, a rock, or a bit of food. It could also be a sensation, a feeling or a phrase. Simply focus your attention and when your mind begins to wander, bring it back, over and over as necessary. Start simple, then try other kinds of targets as desired.

This kind of training, in one form or another, is the essence of scholarship, art, craft, music and athletic training. Coaches, trainers and teachers select a focal point, then instruct us to bring our attention back to it, over and over again until we stabilize. This is the very essence of all human training and education, the core discipline that carries us forward regardless of the specifics of any particular art. As William James famously put it, "The faculty of voluntarily bringing back a wandering attention, over and over again, is the very root of judgment, character and will... An education which should improve this faculty would be the education par excellence."

Practice the pause

We learn to increase our mindfulness through the practice of pausing, of getting outside of the stream of reactivity. Buddhist writer Jack Kornfield described the process this way: "In a moment of stopping, we break the spell between past result and automatic reaction. When we pause, we can notice the actual experience, the pain or pleasure, fear or excitement. In the stillness before our habits arise, we become free." This perspective is popular in Eastern traditions, but we find a similar orientation in many settings and cultures. Nazi prison camp survivor Viktor Frankl expressed a strikingly similar view in *Man's Search for Meaning*: "Between stimulus and response there is a space. In that space is our power to choose our response. In our response lies our growth and our freedom."

In fact, many professions feature good opportunities to practice a pause and get outside of routine, reactive action. The martial artist sweeps the mat, clearing his thoughts as he returns to his beginner's mind. The surgeon scrubs up before the operation, gathering his attention and sharpening his concentration. The musician tunes her instrument, along with her mind and spirit. Similarly, police and military teams often hold daily briefings before going into action. And in the world of sports, pre and post game meetings and in-game time outs provide a vital opportunity to review and sharpen concentration.

Such pauses give us a chance to view our lives and behavior from a mountain top. We can refresh and restabilize our attention. We can observe the way that we're observing. Similarly, we can build these mindful pauses into our daily lives, no matter what our discipline or profession. Don't wait for stress and anxiety to overwhelm you. Break the action with something different. Relinquish your reactivity and go up onto the mountain top for a panorama. Look at the totality of your action, then immerse yourself once again.

Build your mindfulness by practicing a rigorous, regular pattern of preview-execute-review. Acknowledge your tendency to wander in the midst of the action, then set up a simple set of intentional, mindful brackets. First, preview: look ahead and declare your specific intentions: "This is what I am going to do" or "Here is what we are going to do." Describe this action or behavior in as much detail as possible.

Next, go out into the chaos of the world and attempt to do exactly that. Follow your plan as closely as possible, but remain flexible and change your movements and behaviors as necessary. Whatever happens, remain focused on your objectives.

Then, once your session has run its course, gather yourself or your team back together and review your performance. How well did you stick to the plan? Did your performance wander? How well did you deal with the inevitable surprises? How will you do better next time? This is also a time for mindfulness.

In practice, you might begin a working day with a planning session or briefing, then dive into engagement. When a natural break occurs, step back for a mindful pause, a rest or another review-preview. Then, back into the game with flow and engagement.

You can use this simple pattern across any time period you choose: an hour, a day, a week, a semester or year. In any case, maintain discipline. Avoid the tendency to lapse back into the familiar, reactive flow of events. Use the previews and reviews even in familiar activities. Pause in the before and after moments and be particularly alert for transitions. When one activity runs its course, don't simply launch into another. Use that moment for a quick review and a preview. Look back, then ahead. Engage, then repeat.

Mindfulness is a muscle

The vast experience of meditators, athletes and other professionals, coupled with discoveries in neuroscience, prove that mindfulness is just as trainable as any other human skill or aptitude. Every time we focus on the primacy of the present moment, we reinforce our attentional stability. Every time we pay attention to our breath and our body, we become more aware of what we're feeling. Every time we relinquish our attachment to the past and future, we give our executive brains a rest and allow ourselves to experience our circumstances more completely. Every time we abandon our judgmental attitude, we become more capable of seeing things as they really are. Every time we sit quietly with ourselves in meditation, we make future acts of mindfulness more likely.

This suggests that our practice must lie, not in the exotic or the spectacular, but in the familiar and the commonplace. After all, special moments are rare. If we reserve our mindful attention only for these exceptional occasions, we spend our lives missing much of what we do. Our intelligence and skill go largely unused. We may well develop extraordinary skills in unique and specialized arts, but much of our lives will remain untouched. Perhaps we need to turn our attention around. Once we focus our intelligence on the familiar, a vast new realm of opportunity opens up. Anything we you can become your art and your practice.

Lesson 9

Return to your breath

When the ocean is searching for you, don't walk
to the language-river. Listen to the ocean,
and bring your talky business to an end.

Rumi

All the principles of heaven and earth are living inside you.
Everything in heaven and earth breathes. Breath is the
thread that ties creation together.

Morihei Ueshiba, founder of aikido

It's inevitable. As soon as we start talking about training, health and performance, we eventually find ourselves coming around to the most classic of all practices, meditation. The Buddha recommended mental training as an antidote to suffering and impermanence some 2,500 years ago. Since that time, meditation has endured as a foundational practice and is now widely viewed as powerfully supportive of other arts, disciplines and professions.

In fact, meditation can well be seen as an essential model for every other form of training and skill development in the human repertoire. Since skill development ultimately depends on the power of attention, it would not be an exaggeration to say that *all* forms of art, athletic training and professional development are simply varieties of meditation, exercised in different ways.

In each case, it's a matter of focusing our attention on a target and returning our attention back to the target when it begins to waver. The target might be a particular tone on a musical scale, a certain kind of brushstroke on a canvas, a sense of physical power in a gym, a point of law in a court case or the execution of a medical procedure. It doesn't matter whether our discipline is yoga or snowboarding, aircraft mechanics or public speaking, our challenge is to put our minds in the right places at the right times. In this sense, it's all meditation.

The beauty of meditation is that gives us time to step outside the reactivity of our normal, daily lives and observe exactly what we're up to. It's a time to feel what we're feeling while allowing the chattering, judgmental mind to rest. It's a time to get intimate with our bodies and our non-verbal experience.

Meditation may appear to be an escape from the challenges of our daily experience, but in fact, it's a direct face-to-face engagement with ourselves and our life experience. This, of course, is what makes it so challenging. In normal experience, we're constantly moving about, planning and reviewing, dancing all around our experience, sometimes meeting it directly, but many times avoiding it or denying it entirely. But when we sit still in one place, these acts of disassociation and escape become impossible. This is point that we can start to work on our relationship with ourselves and experience of life.

There's something about nothing

The list of proven and probable benefits of meditation continues to grow. There are now thousands of research studies documenting beneficial effects that range across a broad range of human function and experience. As Kelly McGonigal put it *The Willpower Instinct*,

> *Neuroscientists have discovered that when you ask the brain to meditate,*
> *it get better not just at meditating, but at a wide range of self-control*
> *skills, including attention, focus, stress management, impulse control, and*
> *self-awareness.*

Meditation reduces inflammation, lowers levels of the stress hormone cortisol, reduces anxiety, depression, anger and fatigue. It also stimulates the vagus nerve, a powerful autonomic player that helps us activate metabolic processes that are vital for healing, tissue repair and psycho-physical rejuvenation. Meditation also has a powerful epigenetic effect. Work by Herbert Benson, documented in *Relaxation Revolution,* showed that a modest 6-week training program turns on clusters of beneficial genes.

Even better, meditation improves the function of the brain's prefrontal cortex by giving it some time off from chronic executive activity. In meditation, we avoid activities such as planning, sorting, selecting, organizing, editing or revising. By giving the prefrontal brain a rest, we also improve our emotional regulation and as our ability to modulate fear.

Meditation also appears to promote positive mood, approach behavior and happiness. Work by Richard Davidson at the University of Wisconsin shows a pronounced "left shift" in long term meditators. That is, neural activity becomes more pronounced in the left prefrontal cortex, an area associated with positive emotions and engagement.

The beauty of meditation is that it gives us a chance to "meet the first beginnings" of our mental activity. It's a precious opportunity to get in at the earliest instant, before your mind gets wrapped around the axle its own momentum. Clearly, many of our thoughts have a certain "stickiness" to them. The mind generates an image or idea and then attaches to it, sometimes with tenacious holding power. If left to its own devices, the process becomes self-reinforcing and difficult to reverse. But when we get in at the beginning, we can let go of our attachments while things are easy to manage.

Meditation also improves our performance by providing an essential sense of contrast. The visual artist might say that meditation is the blank space on the canvas of our lives, a content-free space that allows the rest of our actions to stand out in sharper relief. This gives us a chance to see what we do more clearly. With regular meditation, the quality of our tasks and behaviors become increasingly obvious to us, giving us the opportunity to revise and adjust our behavior.

Take a seat

So let's have a closer look at the how it's done. The fundamental practice is pure simplicity. To begin, just sit still in one place for awhile. Forget about breathing, attention, mindfulness, compassion and loving kindness for the moment. Can you just sit quietly?

You may find this surprisingly difficult. After all, many of us are addicted to activity and cognition. But sitting still is an essential first step; there can be no moving forward in this practice until you stop moving. Here it may help to imagine a glass of muddy water. If you simply sit quietly for awhile, the particles of dirt will sink to the bottom and you will become calm. This is a well-known Buddhist image, but not exclusively so. In *The Art of Worldly Wisdom*, Baltasar Gracián also pointed to the power of non-action: "To give way now is to conquer by and by. A fountain gets muddy with but little stirring up, and does not get clear by our meddling with it but by our leaving it alone."

Once you've proven to yourself that you can sit quietly for a few minutes, take a moment to attend to the details. First, make sure that your sitting posture works for you. A meditation cushion is a good choice or you can use a stack of blankets, adding or subtracting to get the right height. Make sure that your sitting position is both comfortable and attentive. Cross your legs as best you can, then sit upright in a balanced and relaxed manner. Feel for a sweet spot between being bolt upright and slumped. This will promote a sense of relaxed alertness.

At this point, its essential to decide ahead of time exactly what it is you want to do in your session. Classically, most teachers advocate some form of "aim and sustain." That is, choose an object or quality in advance, then sit down and concentrate on it. In the simplest possible terms, your objective is to maintain attentional contact with a focal point. When you loose contact, re-establish it and continue. The essence of the practice is return.

The classic focal point is the breath. The breath has a long history of significance in many traditions and is honored as the vital spirit, life force, or *prana* that animates our bodies and our lives. Most importantly, the breath lies right at the intersection of mind and body; this allows us to speak directly to the autonomic nervous system, a system that's usually below the radar of consciousness. Here we can learn to dampen the body's flight-flight response and keep ourselves in a state of relaxation. So, when in doubt, return your attention back to your breath, over and over again.

The art of return

No matter the target of our attention, the crucial issue for meditation is what happens next. If you're anything like a normal human being, your attention will begin to wander almost immediately. You begin with the best intentions, but it won't be long before your attention drifts off into the elsewhere or the elsewhen. This is the nature of the human mind.

The crucial issue is what we do at the turning point, when we suddenly realize that our minds have been wandering. How do we navigate back to our chosen focal point?

First, it's important to understand what doesn't work. Force, wrestling, strong-arming and judgment all backfire; each of these tactics tends to produce more of whatever derailed our attention in the first place. Evaluation puts us into a positive feedback loop of increased mental activity; the more we try to force our minds into position, the worse our predicament becomes.

At the other extreme, passivity also fails. If you simply allow yourself to be swept up in whatever thoughts and imagery your mind cooks up, you'll never get a training effect. You'll never learn how to stabilize your attention or increase your attentional density. You'll simply have a nice daydreaming session.

The tricky part of wandering off target is that distraction feeds on itself. We drift off our focal point, then we react to the fact that we're off target. This, of course, generates a new image, word or story line and before we know it, we're light years from our original intent. And then, to make matters worse, we leap to judgment about our performance. We judge the content of our off-target thoughts and we judge the fact that we've failed to stay on task. We beat ourselves up ("I'll never be a good meditator!") and send ourselves off on another round of thoughts, images, self-criticism, explanations and rationalizations.

The solution, as the Buddhists so often point out, is compassion and non-judgmental awareness. Every time you drift off target, you'll get another chance to practice this art. Just let it go. There's nothing to be gained by judgment. Instead, meet your off-target thoughts with kindness. Everyone drifts off target; it's a human universal. Keeping our attention on the present moment is not easy; we all struggle with this one.

The great thing about meditation is that it's bursting with opportunity for practicing self-compassion at the turn-around point. In the course of a short session, your attention is likely to drift off dozens or even hundreds of times. And with each drift, you'll get a chance to accept your wanderings, and nudge our attention back on target.

Imps, jokers and dragons

To the casual observer, meditation may well seem like the easiest thing in the world, but when we actually attempt it, it soon becomes obvious that our minds are nearly so quiet or peaceful as we would like. We begin with a few easy breaths, thinking "How hard could this possibly be?" We are competent, successful people after all; meditation should be as easy as breathing itself.

But before long, our session will be interrupted by the internal imp, that chattering, opinionated, relentless narrator of well, everything. As our own personal life commentator, the imp is forever going on about every subject in the universe. He wants to run the show. He has an opinion about everything and isn't shy about interrupting the silence. True to his name, the imp is perfectly impulsive.

Likewise the joker. This character loves to play tricks and subvert the process. Never satisfied with peace and calm, he's determined to be the monkeywrench at every gathering. He's a comic and a clown, sometimes funny, but also annoying. Much as we try to keep our attention focused, he's always plotting some subversion to keep us off balance.

Imps and jokers are bad enough, but even more troubling are the dragons that sometimes appear out of the shadows, disturbing our peace with their dark moods and malevolent disposition. They frighten us and revolt us. We try to fight them off, but it feels like a losing battle; the more we push them away, the stronger they become.

Unfortunately, many of us give up when we encounter these distracting creatures. "I must be a really lousy meditator," we shrug as we head back to our normal, non-meditative lives. "And besides, I'm really too busy to meditate." But this is no time for resignation. The appearance of commentators, imps, jokers, tyrants, rebels and dragons is not a sign of failure. Rather, it is the sign of a normal human mind doing what normal human minds do. In fact, our minds are a virtual zoo of characters, each with its own voice and inclinations. Trying to silence all of the critics, editors and hecklers will inevitably end in frustration; the more we try to shut them up, the noisier they become.

The solution lies, as it so often does, in relationship. The imps, jokers and dragons will have their voice. Like all of us, they like to be heard; they don't respond well to rejection. So when the imp speaks up, don't evaluate or talk back. Remain non-judgmental, both to the content of his opinions and the fact that he is interrupting. The same holds true for all the other voices. Relax. Observe. Take note. "That's the imp," "That's a dragon," "That's a critic," and go back to your breath. Above all, maintain compassion for yourself and all the voices that appear in your session. They are a part of you. They are a part of us.

Not all of our interruptions are bad news of course. Almost as distracting as the imps, jokers and dragons, are the juicy, creative ideas that seem to pop up out of nowhere. Sit quietly for a few minutes, watching your breath, and it won't be long before some solution to a nagging problem comes to mind. This is similar to the problem-solving effect of sleep and exercise. You've been grinding away on a complex task for hours or days, but you're not getting anywhere, so you give up and sit down to meditate. Then, after a few minutes of relaxed breathing, an ideal solution materializes, seemingly out of nowhere.

This fresh insight is welcome, but it also presents a dilemma; you may be tempted to jump up and get back to work. Or you may get lost in processing the new solution, excited about the new possibilities. "I've solved it!" you want to shout. But don't go there. Simply take note: "Good idea," then get back to your breath. Your precious solution will still be there after your session. You won't forget.

Soften and stay

When we're feeling good, meditation is pretty simple. We sit, stabilize our attention on a chosen focal point and get to work. After awhile, we start to feel pretty good, maybe even wonderful. But if we're in pain of any kind, things can become exceedingly difficult. The greater our pain, the more it distracts us from our creative focal point.

Our typical response is to push back against the sensation and the experience, to force it "out of mind." Unfortunately, this approach tends to intensifies our suffering, which destabilizes our attention even more. Traditional teachers have a helpful insight on this score; the problem is not simply the pain itself, but our resistance to the experience of being in pain. In fact, our condition might well be expressed in a simple formula: suffering equals pain plus resistance. The more we resist, the greater our suffering.

This calls for a reversed effort, a practice of non-resistance. Allow the pain to have its place; give it room to breathe. Curiously, this often gives us what we seek. By yielding, we actually gain a sense of control over the experience. The pain still hurts, of course, but we prove to the deep body and the autonomic nervous system that all will be well. The world is safe; it's all going to be OK. As our resistance begins to fade, so too does our suffering. And as our suffering begins to fade, so too does the pain.

The practice is to stick with it. When pain or distraction intrudes on your experience, relax. As Pema Chodron, author of *When Things Fall Apart: Heart Advice for Difficult Times* advises, "soften and stay." Relinquish effort, but maintain focus. Note the pain, note the distraction, then return to your breath.

Throughout the process, maintain the role of a compassionate, curious, non-judgmental observer. Observe the way your mind goes on long journeys into the past and the future. Observe the chatter and the commentary. Observe the random images and that appear as if from nowhere. Observe all this, and return your attention to your breath.

Don't attempt to block sensations from your body. Feel the weather within, the storms of anger, the fog of uncertainty and depression, the heat of anxiety, the cold of rejection and isolation or the fair weather of happiness and contentment. Welcome whatever experience you're having. It's all a part of who you are.

In fact, traditional teachers have suggested that we adopt the perspective of the wise and gracious host. You're simply holding a dinner party. Your job is to make your guests feel at home, no matter what their demeanor. Some will be friendly and respectful, others will be drunken louts, but no matter their nature, welcome them into your home and in the process, become one.

Rumi described this perfectly:

This being human is a guest house.

Every morning an new arrival.
A joy, a depression, a meanness,
some momentary awareness comes
as an unexpected visitor.
Welcome and entertain them all!
Even if they're a crowd of sorrows,
who violently sweep your house
empty of its furniture,
still, treat each guest honorably.
He may be clearing you out
for some new delight.
The dark thought, the shame, the malice,
meet them at the door laughing,
and invite them in.

There's no need to be a bouncer. Welcome the activity of your mind, your body and your gut. Welcome your history, your stories, your memories and your sufferings. Let your guests come in and serve them as best you can.

Relinquish to reveal

Meditation works well as a solo activity, but guided meditation can also be a powerful experience. In this practice, everyone sits comfortably and the teacher reads the following meditation, repeating as desired. Begin as usual, in a comfortable posture and concentrate your attention on your breath for a minute or so. Take your time and repeat the series as desired:

Relax your entire body, every cell, every system, every joint, every limb, every organ, every vessel...

Reverse your effort, your striving and your ambition...

Release your expectations and your predictions. *Release* your calculations and your commentary. *Release* your ruminations about the past, your anger, your bitterness and your grievances. *Release* your anxieties about the future and your need to control the outcome…

Relinquish your attachment to thoughts, ideas, beliefs and points of view. *Relinquish* your defenses and your judgments. *Relinquish* your explanations and your narrative…

Receive your experience of this present moment, and all that comes with it. Feel what you're feeling. Open your body and your spirit to the world. *Receive* the insecurity, the uncertainty, the ambiguity and the emotion. *Receive* the pleasures, the kindness and compassion that is coming your way. *Receive* the totality of your life in whatever form it takes.

Return your attention to your breath…

Zen philosopher Alan Watts once wrote "The truth is revealed by removing things which stand in its light." As you begin to relinquish your attachment to thought, ideas and emotion, you'll begin to feel your breath and spirit more completely. As your cognitive echo chamber quiets down and physical pain begins to fade away, vital sensations and insights will be revealed; you'll begin to feel the full flow of energy through your body.

As you deepen this practice, let go of the "energy sucks" that inhibit your vitality and displace your sense of joy and wonder: resentments, bitterness, anger, blame, hostility, complaint, grievances and expectations. Not only do these attitudes consume our energy, they also obscure our view of the world and inhibit our ability to enjoy the beautiful adventure. The more you relinquish them, the more powerful you'll become.

As your body becomes quiet, you'll become increasingly aware of your innate vitality and the raw experience of being alive. You may well feel as if every cell in your body is participating in the process of breathing, an integrated unity of experience in the simple act of breathing. As you become familiar with this sensation-experience, you'll be able to return to it and refresh your memory of how it feels to be truly alive.

As you further relinquish your attachments and resistance, you may also experience a sense of your own original goodness. As the turmoil ebbs, you'll feel less need to defend yourself against the world. As you soften and stay, you'll begin to see that goodness was really your true nature all along, that everything else was just a shell of rationalization, justification, and protection. All the energy that went into otherizing the world can safely be relinquished; all that's left is a vulnerable, kind human being who simply wants to be happy.

At the same time, you may well be struck by the astounding, baffling, magnificent reality of life. As you let go of familiar conditioning and fully inhabit the present, you will no longer be bound by familiar, habitual perception. Instead, the world will be revealed in its raw form. What remains is what Jewish philosopher and theologian Abraham Heschel (1907–1972) described as "radical amazement." As you relinquish your death grip on familiar interpretations, sensations and story lines, you'll discover an entirely new way to see your everyday world. In turn, this will give you a new aspiration. As Heschel put it, "Our goal should be to get up in the morning and look at the world in a way that takes nothing for granted. Everything is phenomenal; everything is incredible; never treat life casually. To be spiritual is to be amazed."

The retreat is where you are

As our interest in meditation deepens, many of us will go looking for perfect settings and ideal conditions in which to practice. This makes a certain amount of sense. After all, our attention is still fragile, a candle flickering in the wind. We need a quiet setting, free from noise, distraction and disturbances. It's no wonder that many of us seek out retreat centers where we can sink into the experience without interference.

This is all quite sensible, but it's also utopian. And because it's utopian, it's not realistic. Given enough time and money, we may well find the perfect retreat setting, but before long, we'll be compelled to return to a real world of work, people, noise and a thousand distractions. Many of us will give up at this point, excusing ourselves from practice because conditions are sub-optimal. But really, conditions in the world are almost always sub-optimal. If we wait for the ideal time to meditate, we'll never do it. We can't simply jet off to the resort in Mexico or India every time we're feeling the need for quiet contemplation.

So maybe we're barking up the wrong tree entirely. Maybe we're just procrastinating. Maybe our longing for perfect conditions is just an excuse to avoid the struggles of physical engagement or the in-your-face challenge of meditation.

In a sense, conditions are irrelevant. Consider the experience of Fleet Maull. Convicted of a felony offense in 1985, Maull began a serious meditation practice in prison, without question one of the most hostile environments imaginable. This experience was, as Maull puts it, "dharma in hell." But over the course of 14 years, he not only maintained his practice, he found a way to deepen it. On his release in 1999, he returned to outside life and became a powerfully influential social activist and educator. If Maull had simply dreamed of a utopian retreat setting for his practice, he simply would have suffered.

What we need is something that works for us, right here and now, no matter how difficult conditions might be. This means that ultimately, you're going to have to learn how to meditate in less than ideal conditions. As your practice solidifies, you'll want to take on greater challenges: more noise, more distraction, more time pressure. You'll develop the ability to meditate in settings that would normally drive you crazy: workplaces and waiting rooms, hospitals and restaurants, anywhere where there's a place to sit.

Ultimately, the real test is meditation under emotional duress, when we're right in the midst of anxiety and suffering. Your mind is in turmoil. Your love life just crashed, your family and co-workers are going crazy and your career just fell off the map. Driven by anxiety, you really want to do something, anything. Action might drive away the stress and yes, action and physical exercise might well be good choices. But there's only so much of the world that we can act upon, only so much exercise that we can do. And then what?

This will be the time to sit and face the chaos directly.

Even if your mind is screaming.

Even if your entire being is consumed with anger.

Even if you're lost in confusion about what to do next.

Even if the ground beneath your feet is crumbling.

This is your most powerful practice. This is where you will make your best progress. Instead of dreaming about utopian conditions or a utopian life, start using what you've got. The retreat is not on the other side of the mountains or years away in the future. It's right here, right now.

Remember the words of American author and naturalist John Burroughs:

> *The lesson which life constantly repeats is to 'look under your feet.' You are always nearer to the divine and the true sources of your power than you think. The lure of the distant and the difficult is deceptive. The great opportunity is where you are. Do not despise your own place and hour. Every place is under the stars. Every place is the center of the world.*

Lesson 10

Take ownership

I am not what happened to me, I am what I choose to become.

C.G. Jung

There is an expiry date on blaming your parents for steering you
in the wrong direction; the moment you are old enough to take the
wheel, responsibility lies with you.

J.K. Rowling

As we go deeper into our practice, it's essential that we become familiar with a simple geometric shape, a triangle. This triangle is an incredibly powerful tool, one that explains much of what we do in this world and why we so often make fools of ourselves. Even better, it offers us some concrete ideas for gaining a sense of peace, power and creativity.

The triangle in question is called the drama triangle, a psychological and social model of human relationship first described by Stephen Karpman in 1968. The model is often used in psychology and psychotherapy, but it has powerful applications across the entire range of human experience. In fact, once you understand the basic roles and relationships within the triangle, you'll begin to see it almost everywhere you look; drama is a human universal.

There are three basic roles on the triangle: victim, persecutor and rescuer. Each is important, but the trouble often begins with the victim and especially, the "victim orientation." When we act as victims, we cast ourselves as powerless and attribute our unhappiness and suffering to other people, agents and forces. At the second point of the triangle lies the persecutor. This person finds fault and exercises judgment over the victim. He says "I'm OK, you're not OK." At the third position is the rescuer. This character offers to extract the victim from his or her predicament and in turn, "save the day."

Naturally, these roles are fluid and change often; victims may become persecutors or rescuers and so on in wicked spirals of confusion, blame, recrimination and suffering. This is why this set of relationships is often referred to as "the dreaded drama triangle."

At the outset, it's essential to recognize that the drama triangle is about orientations, attitudes and relationships. Obviously, there are authentic victims in this world, people who deserve our attention and compassion. Just as obviously, there are authentic persecutors who deserve justice. But here we're talking about attitudes, identities and outlook. What roles are we claiming in the world? These are questions of perception, agency and responsibility. By reflecting on our roles in the triangle, we can gain a sense of clarity about what we're doing and how to do it better.

The process begins when we take our first steps into adulthood. Things may go well for a time, but sooner or later, we stumble and fall. We get hurt. We fail to get what we desire; we feel unhappy and we suffer. Looking for a way out, many of us simply react to circumstance and claim victimhood. We point a finger of blame: "The *fill in the blank* is wreaking havoc with my life. It's my parents, my genes, my childhood, my job, my boss, my spouse. It's modern culture. It's government policy. It's stress and overwork. It's everything. Everything except for me."

These accusations may well have an element of truth in them, but this is completely beside the point. The real point is our explanation and our orientation. By claiming the role of victim, we shift responsibility away from ourselves and place it somewhere else, usually on other people.

Alternately, we look to be rescued. We seek out sympathetic individuals who will listen to our woes and maybe even work on our behalf to correct the perceived injustice. The rescuer is often a person, but it could just as well be a substance, a process, an experience, or even an idea. Anything that holds the promise of salvation can play the role.

Sometimes these strategies work for a time, but more often our victim orientation simply digs the hole of suffering deeper. By blaming perpetrators for our woes or running in search of rescue, we give away our personal power. Blaming and complaining put us into a descending spiral of reactivity, dysfunction and unhappiness.

Even worse, blame "otherizes" the world, creating a deeper sense of duality and stress. Tragically, this leads to more blame, more broken relationships, more confusion and more suffering.

Many of us have heard this story before and it's easy to assume that victimhood is something reserved for the dysfunctional underbelly of society; alcoholics, drug addicts and criminals come to mind. But victimhood is alive and well at every level of human culture and no one is immune. We may even call it an epidemic in its own right. After all, victimhood is an easy, seductive trap. There's plenty of blame to go around and excuses are always handy: The economy is in recession. Our parents were flawed, our neighborhood was chaotic. Bullies abused us. The school system failed us and the doctors were ineffective. The cops were unjust and the system didn't provide the kind of employment we deserved. That's why complaining has become a national sport, with entire media empires dedicated to round-the-clock finger-pointing. But try as we might, none of it works.

Create forward

If the victim orientation is such a counter-productive dead end, what are we to do with the challenges in our lives? The key, as many spiritual teachers, therapists and coaches have suggested, is to make a shift from the victimhood to a creative orientation. In this, we are called upon to become artists of our own lives, to focus our attention and our energies on the objects and relationships that we'd like to bring into being.

The creative orientation brings both challenges and rewards. First, it calls upon us to exercise full responsibility, accountability, and authenticity. But as we move beyond old habits of blaming, complaining, excuses and wishful thinking, life begins to open up. We become less reactive and more reflective. This becomes a world of opportunity, power, and freedom.

When we adopt a creative practice, we actually change our identity, our sense of who we are. We say "I create, therefore I am." Instead of blaming events in the past or hoping for a rescue in the future, we ask a new set of questions: What can I do today, right this moment, to advance my creation? Where can I exercise control? Where does my power lie?

Most of all, the creative person embraces radical responsibility. This orientation, championed by Fleet Maul, founder of the Prison Mindfulness Institute, means taking complete ownership of our circumstances, our attitudes and our behavior. With this acceptance, we take responsibility for everything in our lives, even the large-scale conditions of entire families, communities, even the entire world itself. Instead of ducking responsibility at every turn, we say "It *is* my job."

This is not to say that we're to blame for climate change, social injustice, poverty and every other blight on the human experience. Rather, we accept conditions as they are and choose to take action in whatever way we can, whenever we can. We may not have political power or financial resources to move mountains, but we can and do take mindful action.

Ultimately, it's all about attitude and orientation. As Fleet Maull reminds us, "circumstances are neutral." Yes, some predicaments are inherently challenging, but no matter the nature of the adversity, we are free to choose our interpretations of events. We are free to choose our stories. We are free to move beyond blame and rescue.

This attitude, by the way, is the defining quality of our most popular heroes, heroines and superheroes, both real and imagined. These people are not complainers, nor are they seduced by rescue agents, substances or ideas. They may well be fighting epic battles against powerful forces of destruction and injustice, but they keep their energy focused on their creative goals. It's hard to imagine Martin Luther King Jr., Nelson Mandela, Mahatma Gandhi or the Dalai Lama blaming, complaining or looking for an easy way out. Circumstances may turn against them, but they adapt on the fly.

Naturally, there's a mindfulness to avoiding victimhood and becoming a creator. This is where we learn to pay closer attention to our thoughts, our emotions and our explanatory style. With practice, you'll become increasingly alert to subtle, incipient acts of blaming, complaining and wishing. You'll be quicker to recognize your abdication of responsibility and your desire for rescue. By paying attention, you'll stay closer to the path of creativity.

You'll also begin to see that primitive victim responses are literally a waste of time. Blaming and complaining, hostility and anger, wishing for rescue: these kinds of mental activity are bad enough in their own right, but they also displace more important qualities and experiences of life. You can't be engaged in joyful, creative action at the same time that you're blaming the world for your unhappiness. When you choose to live on the crux of life, this all becomes so much clearer. You always have a choice: do you want to be a victim or do you want to be happy?

To fully develop this practice, it's essential to know what it is you're trying to create; this calls for some serious reflection. Many of us have been mired in the reactive victim orientation for so long, we may well have forgotten our creative goals entirely. Indeed, many of us may not even believe that creative action is a possibility. So now is the time to get some clarity. As a creator, what exactly are you going after?

Begin this practice by getting over the notion that creativity is for a special class of gifted people called "artists." Rather, creativity is a human universal. It's been in your blood and your bones since the beginning; it's your birthright. Don't get distracted by the challenges posed by adversaries and don't try to escape to some kind of salvation. Instead, get to work. Ask yourself: What kind of life do you want to bring into being? What kind of relationships do you want to create with the world? What kind of qualities are you trying to cultivate? Once you've got this creative goal in focus, you'll have no need for blame or rescue. You'll be too busy doing what needs to be done.

At the outset, radical responsibility may well seem onerous and burdensome. After all, many of us have our hands full as it is; we can scarcely imagine taking on anything more. But in fact, this is precisely where the power lies. It may well be a paradox, but the process works. As you take on more responsibility, you'll become less reactive to external circumstances and agents. In the process, you'll find yourself with more energy, more time and more power.

This is the path of the creative artist; the more you accept challenge into your life, the stronger and more capable you'll become. As the Dalai Lama put it, "When you think everything is someone else's fault, you will suffer a lot. When you realize that everything springs only from yourself, you will learn both peace and joy."

Lesson 11

Beware false tigers

We are more often frightened than hurt; and we suffer more from imagination than from reality.

Lucius Annaeus Seneca

How much stress we experience depends more on how well we
control attention, than on what happens to us.

Mihaly Csikszentmihalyi

If we're going to learn anything in this world, we're going to have to leave the
comfort of the familiar and journey out into the unknown. We're going to have
to explore the boundaries of our capability and squeeze our bodies and spirits for
a little more skill, a little more endurance, a little more strength, a little more understanding. And in this process, we're going to encounter stress, sometimes a lot
of stress.

This is where things get interesting. Stress, as it turns out, is a paradoxical creature
with a dual nature. On one hand, it can degrade our bodies and our lives; it can bring
disease to our brains, our families and our communities. On the other hand, stress
has the potential to improve our personal and professional performance, leading us
to enriched lives of health, joy and exuberance. Understanding the difference can
make an enormous difference in how we experience the world and the trajectory of
our lives.

Stress 2.0

Stress has always been part of the human experience. Even going back to our earliest days in Africa, we've always had to contend with challenges to our lives and
happiness. Hunger, predation, conflict, injury and disease are all part of the animal
condition and in turn, the human condition.

But today, our challenge seems particularly acute. Most of us are quick to describe our lives as stressful, sometimes even desperate. Surely our ancestors wouldn't have faced such an onslaught of time pressure, workplace overload, anxiety, lifestyle disease and ecological angst that we face in today's pressure-cooker world. Has stress always been this pervasive?

In fact, something has changed. Today, our still-prehistoric bodies face a novel and unprecedented set of challenges: noise, chronic economic and workplace demands, sedentary living, strange foods, constantly shifting social relationships, high-stakes bets on careers and an overwhelming avalanche of choices.

The differences between the old and the new are striking in one important way. In primal environments, challenges and stressors were often acute, but at least they were congruent with habitat and the nature of our bodies. The threats that we experienced triggered appropriate physical and hormonal reactions that contributed to survival. Conditions may have been challenging, even brutal, but they always made good physical sense.

In contrast, modern stressors "attack" us more or less at random and in no particular relationship to our physical heritage or habitat. The challenges that we face are increasingly time and place independent: the cell phone rings or the email arrives, not in any relationship to the natural functioning of our bodies or habitat, but well, whenever. This stimulation of our stress response system is arbitrary and our bodies are unprepared for it. Our bodies look for patterns, but in many cases, no patterns exist.

In its modern, toxic form, stress contributes to massive levels of human suffering. It exacerbates most disease states, especially modern "lifestyle diseases" such as heart disease, diabetes, osteoporosis, attention problems and neurological disorders. And even when stress doesn't kill us outright, it robs many of precious years of life quality and exuberance. Anxiety, anhedonia (loss of pleasure) and depression are exacerbated by stress. When we're highly stressed, we also begin to avoid new things that might give us pleasure (neophobia). Life can lose its joy and meaning.

Not only does stress degrade our bodies and spirit, it also degrades our brains and our cognitive powers, with profound downstream consequences. When stress becomes chronic, we become impulsive and make poor decisions. We become increasingly reliant on habit and more resistant to new ideas. We procrastinate and become less creative. We become socially withdrawn and resistant to collaboration and teamwork.

In the process, stress degrades the "neurological assets" of both individuals and organizations. Chronic exposure to stress hormones weakens precious nerve cell connections and the knowledge and experience that's contained within them. This can destroy the value of expensive training programs, memories and skill sets that often take years or decades to establish. Not surprisingly, this process feeds back on itself to create even more stress for everyone. Positions harden, communication weakens and team cohesion dissolves into chaos.

Meet your autonomic nervous system

To meet the challenge of stress in the modern world, it's essential that we understand the autonomic nervous system, the ancient system that controls the basic regulatory functions of our bodies and in turn, our minds and spirits.

The standard explanation always begins with a description of the two main branches: the branch that stimulates emergency action and the fight-flight response is called the sympathetic nervous system, the branch that stimulates healing and tissue repair is called the parasympathetic nervous system.

Conceptually, the system is straightforward. The "action system" stimulates our bodies for vigorous movement such as fighting, climbing or running away. In this process, every organ and tissue in the body is prepared for emergency physical action; heart rate goes up, digestion is suppressed, blood pressure goes up and glucose is released into the bloodstream. Pain is suppressed and immunity is stimulated. In short, the body prepares itself ready for a highly physical encounter with the world. This is the famous fight-flight response.

The repair system essentially does the reverse: Heart rate and blood pressure go down, digestion picks up and nutrients are delivered to the cells that need to be patched up. In short, the body begins to put itself back together in what neuroscientist Robert Sapolsky describes as "long-term rebuilding and development projects" such as growth and reproduction.

In popular culture, this is often described as the "rest and digest" response. Others, more erotically inclined, call it the "feed and breed" response. (When you're really getting relaxed and comfortable, it's time for feasting and sex.) If the sympathetic system is all about running away from "lions and tigers and bears," the parasympathetic system is all about "loving and hot tubs and wine." Oh my!

The basic functions of the autonomic nervous system are easy to grasp, but there's one more vital point to understanding, one that has huge implications for how we choose to live our lives in the modern world. That is, the actions of the two branches are, for the most part, mutually exclusive. Either you turn on the action branch or you turn on the repair-and-restore branch. Your mind-body has to make a choice; you can't run away from the leopard and heal your broken muscles, tendons and ligaments at the same time. At any given moment in time, you're either running or you're healing, but not both.

Over the course of years and decades, this semi-conscious choice determines, in large measure, the trajectory of our health and performance. The more often we amplify our physiology to meet danger (perceived or real), the less time we spend putting our bodies back together. In the long term, this has profound consequences for our bodies, our cognition, even our spirits. In large measure, it's this ratio of autonomic stimulation over the course of our lives that makes the difference between health and disease.

Is the world friendly?

In the long term, our health and performance hinges on the body's semi-conscious choice between action and healing, but this begs a question: How does the autonomic nervous system decide which branch to fire? How do we make the decision whether to go into fight-flight or feed-breed?

The neuroendocrine influences are wildly complex, but in the end, it all comes down to a judgment call made by the deep brain and body. To personalize it, we might say that the autonomic system asks an existential question about the world around it. It asks, "Is this world friendly?"

Our bodies ask this question continuously, throughout the course of every day of our lives. If the answer is "Yes," the autonomic system fires the "rest and digest" response and goes about the business of healing tissue, building organs, and exploring the world with play, learning and creativity. But if the answer is "No," healing and tissue rebuilding projects are put on hold and the body is prepped for physical action.

Clearly, the way we answer this primal question is of vital importance to the way we create our lives. It is fundamental to who we are and how our lives will play out. Whatever our core belief about the nature of our world–be it friendly or unfriendly–will have a marked effect on the autonomic system and can tip the scales in either direction. The good news is that we have a measure of control in this process. We can choose to focus our attention on conflict, danger, hostility and division or we can train our attention on the wonder, beauty, joy and friendliness of the world around us. No matter our genes, our history or our circumstances, we can still make a choice.

This is where our orientation and relationship with the world becomes so crucial. When we adopt a victim orientation, we tell ourselves a story of powerlessness; we say "the world is not friendly." Persecutors and perpetrators are out to get us. We might be rescued by a friend, a substance or an organization, but our essential victimhood remains. Over time, this belief makes our lives even more difficult. By selling ourselves a story of a dangerous and hostile world, we prime our fight-flight system for activation.

This puts us even deeper into a quagmire. Not only do we give away our personal power, we also accelerate the process of physical decay. Our hyper-active fight-flight response floods your system with stress hormones and leaves little or nothing left over for healing and rejuvenation.

But when we adopt a creative orientation, everything changes. We may well struggle to bring our creations to life, but we remain focused on possibility and potential. And in this, the world begins to look a lot friendlier. In turn, our bodies are more likely to relax into "feed and breed," which just makes everything go better.

Hair triggers and negativity bias

Another challenge posed by the autonomic nervous system is its built-in inclination towards vigilance and fast action. If the system was perfectly neutral, our bodies could simply switch back and forth between emergency action and tissue repair as needed. The mechanism would sense a threat, craft an appropriate response and then switch back to rest, relaxation and long-term rebuilding projects.

But in fact, there's a bias in the system, a bias that's been sculpted by millions of years of evolution. We see this bias in the hair-trigger setting of the flight-flight response; it's a lot easier to turn on "fight-flight" than it is to turn on "feed and breed." The system is primed to detect and respond to danger; if conditions are difficult or ambiguous, it will lean towards action. Thus the body's default assumption: "When in doubt, bet on danger and action." In other words, "When in doubt, stress out."

This inclination towards life-saving action makes perfect evolutionary sense. When survival demands a fast response in a physical crisis, the rewards go to individuals whose fight-flight system can step up right away. If it takes a long time to increase your heart rate or send blood to your muscles, you're lunch. Even worse, if you miscalculate and go towards "rest and digest" when the threat is real, your genes are going to wind up in the digestive tract of a carnivore, not in the bodies of your offspring.

For similar reasons, the human mind has a robust negativity bias. Numerous experiments have shown a clear pattern: When faced with scenarios of equally positive or negative outcome, the negative fact or image will grab more of our attention. In the language of psychological research, this means that "the bad is stronger than the good." This is why modern news media is so heavily slanted towards the spectacular and catastrophic; violence and danger grab the lion's share of our attention.

Taken together, our hair-trigger stress response and negativity bias give us a subtle but powerful inclination towards fight-flight and away from healing, tissue repair and physical rebuilding. This creates a real problem when threats are only imaginary or abstract.

Fortunately, we can learn to dampen this inclination with knowledge, experience and training. Our modern brains come equipped with a powerful, if somewhat unreliable inhibitor, a dampening mechanism called the prefrontal cortex. With experience and training, we can train ourselves to moderate the hyperactivity our fear-response system. Specifically, we can control the firing of the amygdala, the deep brain center responsible for vigilance, threat detection and fear. This is why practice and training are so important, especially in high-risk, high-stress environments. As you gain familiarity and experience, you will literally grow new inhibitory neural fibers that keep our hyperactive stress response in check. Once again, practice pays off.

The biggest problem with our hair-trigger response and negativity bias is that they lead us into "false tiger alerts." This effect is compounded by the fact that humans simply aren't very good at distinguishing between fantasy and reality; a real tiger can turn on our stress system, but an imaginary tiger can do almost as well. If we imagine that we're being attacked by these "tigers" day in and day out, over the course of months, years and decades, we'll poison ourselves with cortisol and increase the odds of suffering disease.

In a sense, genuine tigers are easy. They are large, powerful and absolutely danger-ous. If you ever come face-to-face with an actual tiger–especially on open ground in a wild environment–your body will know what to do about it. But when imagination gets into the act, we often generate "false positives." These are images and interpre-tations that seem like threats, but have no actual basis in reality. The problem is that many of us tend to over-identify threats in our world. We set off false tigers alerts every day, sometimes many times each day. Our bodies try and save us, but in most of these cases, the effort is wasted.

Remember, the important thing in stress is not so much the threat itself, but the perceived threat. If you happen to believe that the labrador retriever in your neigh-bor's yard is a threat to your physical welfare, status or identity, then your body will respond as if it is. Obviously, this labrador is a false tiger, but your body doesn't know that. If you do an effective sales job on your body, you can get it to believe almost anything.

And so, we need to step back, again and again. Is this threat really a true tiger? Will a deadline really make you dead? Unlikely. Will being late to a meeting really be the end of the world? Unlikely. Most things work out, one way or the other. Your brain is smart and your body is resilient. Even when you do mess things up, you will find a way forward. In the end, most tigers turn out to be kittens.

Experience is a big asset in this process. When we're young, it's easy to get obsessed with false tigers. With little knowledge and few skills to draw on, we imagine danger in more places. But as you gain experience and competence, you will look back and laugh at your over-active imagination, realizing just how easy it is to fall prey to false predators. Mark Twain said it best: "I'm an old man now, and I have known a great many problems in my life…most of which never happened."

Stress cognition

As we've seen, the autonomic nervous system has powerful effects on the tissue of our bodies, but stress hormones also affect our cognition, our psychology and in turn, our spirit. Here the story is more nuanced, but several patterns play out consistently.

First, stress drives our attention towards the self as a distinct and isolated entity. Obviously, this is as it should be in terms of evolution and immediate survival; when we hear the menacing growl of the predator in the bushes, it's no time for expanded consciousness. My body is in immediate danger and it's time to focus my attention directly upon that fact.

This is clearly adaptive for life-and-death encounters in the bush, but it can also be a real problem in other settings. Attention to the self isolates us from the wider world. As our cognition shrinks, we lose our ability to see big pictures and experience ourselves in integration with people and habitat. This sets up a wicked, vicious cycle: the more we attend to self, the more isolated we feel, the more stress we experience and so on. This is why relaxation, experience and stress education are so powerful; as our attention reaches out beyond self, we become more capable of rapport and integration.

Stress also has a profound effect on our sense of scarcity and abundance. Fear generates a sense of time scarcity, resource scarcity and choice scarcity. We become increasingly aware of limitations of time, space, and most of all, options. In contrast, the feed-breed system stimulates a sense of abundance and surplus: a multitude of creative options open up. We become increasingly aware of possibility.

Under stress, our cognitive field contracts, as it should, to deal with a smaller, more threatening set of challenges. In the process, we naturally become less attentive to nuance and subtlety; when the lion is chasing us, we aren't inclined to take a poet's eye view of the world around us. More likely, we'll fall into a highly decisive, categorical kind of thinking, one that is quick to label things as black or white.

In contrast, our relaxed, parasympathetic mind feels no particular urgency to impose categories on the world. It is content with "gradient thinking," and a systems-eye view of relationship, one that embraces ambiguity, dynamism and complex webs of interconnection. Even better, we experience a sense of "liquidity," and a willingness to change perspective.

The effect is familiar to all of us. Under conditions of relative safety, friendliness and relaxation, our minds and spirits are fluid; we're willing to entertain the prospect of alternative futures, even dramatic personal life change. But as stress intensifies, our minds begin to take a set, our thoughts and spirits begin to harden. As fear and anxiety increase, we narrow the scope of our attention and focus more completely on the one course of action that we believe will lead us to safety.

Of course, both forms of cognition have their place. Under conditions of immediate life threat, stress cognition is often adaptive and life-saving; when the chips are down, decisive action is essential. But in the context of normal, everyday life, stress-cognition makes us increasingly rigid, brittle and even dangerous. Ever-vigilant for threat and hostility, we assume danger and scarcity in everything we see. This leads to a very real kind of blindness; a blindness to abundance, possibility, nuance and gradient thinking, precisely the kind of qualities that we need for creative relationships with the world. In these kinds of conditions, the stressed-out mind becomes a serious liability.

Matters of interpretation

For non-human animals living in wild environments, the stress response is pretty simple: when faced with an authentic threat, turn on the sympathetic nervous system and act accordingly. But with humans, things are far more interesting. The problem begins with our immense capacity for abstraction and speculation. Not only do we have the ability to sense threats directly, we also have the ability to imagine them in ways completely independent of reality–in past, present or future. And so, mind, spirit, story and culture are always getting into the act, interpreting the meaning of events at every turn.

Even the most casual observer of human biology can attest to the effect of the imagination on the real and tangible tissues of the body. Watch an emotionally-charged movie and you can feel the physical effects in your body: your heart might beat faster, you might laugh or cry, your palms might begin to sweat. Read some juicy erotic literature, your body is likely to reflect that passion in some conspicuous ways as well. Symbols and images, entirely abstract and lifeless in themselves, can trigger massive changes that ripple throughout our bodies, minds and spirits.

Act of imagination have very real physiological consequences. Every thought, every mental image, every muse has a downstream physical effect. The things that we think, imagine and believe can be just as powerful as actual physical events. This is why stress researchers are careful to say that the key trigger for the stress response is not a threat to the organism, but rather a "perceived threat to the organism." In other words, belief matters. If you believe some circumstance constitutes a threat to your life or your status, your body will believe it too. If you believe in the safety and friendliness of your world, your body will believe that as well.

This leads us to an even more comprehensive definition of stress. That is, stress is the difference between perceived capability and perceived challenges. If we perceive our capability to be greater than the challenge, it's going to be an easy day. But if we perceive our capability to be inadequate, it's going to be a struggle, no matter the actual nature of our circumstances.

Interpretation is everywhere. Work by June Gruber at Yale University and others showed profoundly different physiological effects depending on one's emotional state. When a stressor was perceived as a *challenge*, subjects showed increased cardiac output, increased diameter of circulatory blood vessels, increased blood flow to the brain, and increased cognitive and physical performance. In contrast, when a stressor was perceived as a *threat*, subjects showed decreased cardiac output, decreased diameter of circulatory vessels, decreased blood flow to the brain, and decreased cognitive and physical performance. Even a subtle shift in interpretation can add up to big physiological and performance consequences.

The lesson here is simple. Be mindful of your relationship and interpretation. How do you feel about your conditions? Does this event feel like a challenge that's within your capability? If so, your body will almost certainly rally to support you and knowing this, you can relax and maybe even enjoy it. But if conditions feel threatening, you must take action. You body will be working against you and your performance will be seriously compromised.

Interpretation is such a powerful driver of human experience and physiology, it even affects our long-term health outcomes. In a popular TED talk , Kelly McGonigal described a study conducted at University of Wisconsin School of Medicine and Public Health. Researchers asked two questions: "How much stress are you under?" and "Do you believe that stress is harmful to your health?" Years later, they compared death records and found a significant difference in mortality: those who believed that "stress is bad for you" were significantly more likely to die than those who held a friendlier view. The authors concluded that "High amounts of stress and the perception that stress impacts health are each associated with poor health and mental health. Individuals who perceived that stress affects their health and reported a large amount of stress had an increased risk of premature death." In other words, the very belief that stress is bad for your health is bad for your health.

Likewise, our relationship with stress is often revealed in common turns of phrase. For example, when reporting on the state of our lives to one another, we often say "I'm under a lot of stress." This is a classic victim orientation; we're blaming an external agent for our unhappiness. "I am under stress" means "stress is over me." Stress is the perpetrator and the cause of my predicament. Stress is doing things to me. Stress is making me upset and unhappy. Naturally, this simple phrase puts us at a disadvantage right from the outset. If this is the nature of our relationship, we're probably in for a negative health and life consequence. We've already given away our power.

We can do better with a creative orientation and statements of responsibility. "I underestimated how long this project was going to take and now I'm scrambling to get my work done on time." "I bit off more than I can chew." Above all, pay attention to the relationship and take responsibility for where you are in life. If you're feeling panicked, take creative action, but don't blame it on stress.

Smart stress

Ultimately, the objective is not to eliminate stress from our lives; our goal is not "stress-proofing." Rather, the goal is to apply the right kind of stress, in the right intensity, for the right duration, at the right time and in the right context. Look for precision, not eradication. Make the stress episodic, proportional, relevant and coherent. If you're a trainer, teacher or coach, your job is to get people into the sweet spot of optimal stress. Fine tune the adversities. Look for the right kind of stress, in the right intensity, for the right duration, at the right moment, in the right context.

Even more important, emphasize the positive. As we've seen, stress offers some extremely powerful, health-enhancing benefits. In moderate doses, it helps us do what we want with our bodies and our lives. It improves our cognition, memory and concentration. It gives us the energy we need to focus on our creative goals. It also serves as a powerful signal when we're approaching the boundary of our comfort zones. In this sense, stress means that you're doing something right.

Stress is not an enemy to be conquered or a foe to be defeated. Rather, stress can be an essential force for growth, learning and health. When applied with intelligence and sensitivity, stress is one of your most powerful allies. So take your attention off the negative. Abandon your stress-phobia. Yes, there are dangers that come with chronic exposure, but these are mostly the product of your over-active imagination. Don't obsess over false tigers. Keep your eyes open for real tigers, but if the coast is clear, relax. The world really is a friendly place.

Lesson 12

Live the beat

Your hand opens and closes, opens and closes. If it were always a fist or always stretched open, you would be paralyzed. Your deepest presence is in every small contracting and expanding, the two as beautifully balanced and coordinated as birds' wings.

Rumi

An artist must possess Nature. He must identify himself with her rhythm, by efforts that will prepare the mastery which will later enable him to express himself in his own language.

Henri Matisse

As human animals living on a rotating planet, we are immersed in rhythm, embedded in oscillations of all varieties. The biosphere, our habitat, our bodies, our tribes and our work are all in constant, rhythmic motion. Sunlight waxes and wanes, seasons come and go, hormones surge and fade, cognition and emotion rise and fall. Our hearts beat, our muscles pump with concentric and eccentric contractions, our breath comes and goes. At every level, life is a verb.

Rhythm is built into our bodies at the deepest molecular level, a heritage that goes back to the very beginning of life on earth, some 3.5 billion years ago. From the earliest moments of life, one of the primary drivers of physiology was the oscillating pattern of light and dark, the circadian rhythm. Even the simplest living organisms show this rhythmic pattern. Recent decades have seen an explosion in research on circadian influences on human physiology, revealing the immense power of light and dark at every level of our biochemistry, metabolism and endocrine function. We are circadian creatures; our bodies are built to pulse.

Given our rhythmic heritage, it comes as no surprise to find oscillating patterns of physiology and behavior throughout the animal kingdom, with every creature dancing to the beat of light, season and habitat. We also see this dance in the lives of our prehistoric ancestors, a pattern anthropologists have called the "Paleolithic rhythm." For millions of years, we have hunted, then rested, venturing out from camp and back again, exploring and then refreshing ourselves, adventuring and then returning. The details of the pattern surely varied, but the oscillation between striving and rest was always a central feature of human life. So too for our children and our pets in today's world. Intuitively, they know the beat: play hard for hours with complete engagement, fall deeply into rest, then repeat. This rhythmic formula is not only ancient, it also promotes development, health, performance and happiness.

The perils of flat-lining

Oscillation is so universal in human and animal life, we immediately become suspicious of any non-rhythmic quality or behavior. In fact, any form of constancy stands out as potentially deviant and dangerous to health. Any attempt to pin life down, to turn living verbs into static nouns, becomes suspect. Unfortunately, this is precisely what we see in the modern world. As artificial light, 24-7 work cycles and crushing workloads have escalated, our natural rhythm has become distorted and in many cases, very nearly obliterated. Our primal sense of oscillation has been replaced by a uniseason of year-round striving, a lifestyle of continuous partial engagement that is neither healthy or rewarding.

To make matters worse, a hypercompetitive, workaholic culture drives us to extremes, constantly pushing us to compromise the optimal oscillation of our lives. Many of us glorify the warrior entrepreneur and corporate workaholic, especially their ability to endure punishing work schedules. They're constantly strategizing, planning, sorting, managing and prioritizing. They're running their prefrontal brains at full capacity in every waking moment, which is to say, they've got no sense of cognitive, somatic or spiritual rhythm. Obviously, this cannot be sustainable. As our striving becomes chronic, the natural rhythmic curve of our daily effort disappears and we become lifestyle "flat-liners."

This monotonous workstyle kills us at both ends of the cycle. We compromise our rest, and as a result, our performance declines, setting us up for inefficiency, accidents, injury, disease and unhappiness. As we cram more and more into our schedules, we become progressively less effective, less productive and less fulfilled. Flat-line living lead to flattened cognition, flattened creativity and a flattened spirit. Anhedonia, depression and cynicism begin to darken our days.

Unfortunately, we are seduced by the fact that, in the short term, flat-lining appears to work. At the beginning, we can get more done if we cut back on sleep and our precious "feed and breed" time. But this puts us on a slippery slope of lifestyle compromise. We start with the best intentions, but before long we feel the pressure of overload. This is when the deal-making and brokering begins: "I'll stay up late." "I'll get up early." "I'll do it on the weekend." "I'll do it on the plane." "I'll make those calls on the road." "I'll do it on my vacation."

This is the beginning of the end. Before long, we're working at every waking moment, eating into our psychophysical reserves and trading in our health for short-term survival. We might get an edge over our competitors if we triage out our recuperation time, but this advantage soon vanishes and reverses itself into increased error, inefficiency, disease and suffering. For long-term flat-liners, the prognosis is not good.

High contrast living

In a world gone mad with constant striving, chronic work and other flat-line disorders, it's essential that find our way back to rhythm. We need to rediscover the highs and lows of our personal, social and cultural energy. We need to breathe the peaks and valleys of our relationships with our bodies and the world.

Here we take inspiration from the world of professional athletics. Experienced coaches know that training works best in deep cycles of effort and rest; the modern trainer advises his athletes to "train hard and rest deep." Challenge the body with highly concentrated striving and effort, then ease the intensity way off into deep relaxation and down time.

This time-honored practice is spectacularly effective because it's aligned with the body's inherent rhythmic nature. Challenge the body's tissues and organs with powerful efforts in hunting, exploration, adventure or play, then return to camp for serious down time, allowing the body to repair itself and grow in anticipation of similar challenges yet to come. Contrast is the key to success; by striving hard and resting deeply, we stimulate the body's powers of adaptation. If you follow this rhythmic swing, you'll develop your capabilities and your resilience.

Of course, professional athletes have it easy; we give them everything they need to support a high-contrast training lifestyle. By paying them handsomely, we set them free to live the ideal rhythm. They don't need to worry about the details of normal life; they can train fiercely, then rest long and hard. Most of us are not so fortunate, but we can still heed the lesson. Even if we're pressured from all sides, we usually have some say in the matter. We can still increase the highs by concentrating deeply on our work and resting more completely in our time off.

So what's the practice? How do we step out of our low-contrast, flat-line lives and get back into our Paleo-animal swing of high performance and deep rest? For many, the immediate challenge is psychological. Many of us believe that if we slow down, even for a minute, our lives will come crashing down in an avalanche of uncompleted tasks. The wolf is at our door, time is short and the bills are coming due. If we relinquish our vigilance, we're going to be in real trouble.

It's completely understandable. But the mistake we make is to equate constant activity with effectiveness. Just because we're chronically active doesn't mean we're moving forward. In fact, the opposite is more likely the case. Vast experience and research in athletics, workplace and performance science tells us that working smarter, not harder, is the key to success.

Clearly, we need to work both ends of the process, moving towards more engagement and more rest. The place to begin is with authentic, genuine, deep rest. Unfortunately, this is alien territory for many. We are so accustomed to chronic activity that we may well have forgotten what authentic rest looks or feels like. We often think of rest as simply "something other than work." It might be TV, movies, hanging out or some other form of activity. In fact, most of us have no idea how to rest.

Authentic rest is a skill and a practice in its own right. It is not an accident, nor is it an opportunistic stroke of good luck that happens to fall into the gaps between chronic action. Rather, it must be intentional, purposeful and yes, mindful. Like exercise, food preparation, medical care and every other essential health-related activity in our lives, we have to make it a priority and set the time aside. To truly rest, we need to monotask it. This means rest and nothing else. Just rest. Resist the urge to sneak in some other activity; allow your entire mind-body-spirit system to come to a place of quiet.

Of course, given the screaming, incessant demands of modern life, rest sounds like a utopian fantasy. Who has time to "do nothing?" we protest. But rest is not nothing; it is essential to who we are and what we can become. Rest is a time of crucial metabolic and psycho-spiritual revitalization. Every tissue of the body is actively being rebuilt: muscle, bone, tendons, blood vessels, neurons and entire organs are undergoing vital reorganization. Cell membranes are restored, proteins are synthesized and neurotransmitters are rebalanced. And, crucial for performance in the modern world, memories are consolidated and frequently-used neural pathways are facilitated. This means learning is enhanced.

Rest is an absolute necessity for health and human function. Without it, our striving and training is wasted. But with rest, our bodies, minds and spirits can sustain high levels of performance throughout our lives: the deeper we go in rest, the higher we can go in action. And it doesn't take that much time, especially in comparison to the other activities that do find time for. Most of us could easily relinquish a few hours of entertainment each month in favor of genuine rejuvenation. Even in the course of a crazy day, a few minutes of repose can make an enormous difference. Just as we can make time for movement snacks, so too can we make time for authentic rest.

Conceptually, most of us now understand the physiological and psychological benefits of rest. We know that rest will give us time to rebuild our bodies and lead us to greater health, performance and resilience in the long run. The real sticking point is our relationship with ourselves and with life in general. That is, many of us refuse to rest because we are addicted to activity. Uncomfortable in the present moment, we force ourselves to stay engaged, compulsively busy, constantly running from the discomfort of the now. It's not that we have so much that we must do; it's that we have a hard time just being.

The art lies in finding comfort in our skins and in our lives as they are. This is an art that comes with practice. Every time we settle into the present moment and give up our relentless, frenetic quest to do more of everything, the process becomes a little bit easier. Every time we allow our bodies and minds to be still, to breathe in the here and now, we become a little more adept and little more peaceful. Rest, in other words, is a muscle.

Once we've moved towards a deeper a pattern of authentic, genuine rest, we're ready to re-engage and immerse ourselves deeper into our training, our work or our practice. But now we're challenged to step it up and increase the intensity of our engagement and this may be a new experience. After all, in our former flat-lined lifestyle, we fell out of the habit of immersion and full engagement. Chronically depleted by arrhythmic living, we learned to hold back, to withdraw some measure of our capability; we got used to coasting. We may have even forgotten what full engagement feels like.

The practice here is to rest deep, then dive back in with maximum focus and complete mind-body participation. When the cycle of energy swings to the upside, re-focus as completely as possible, even if the effort feels weak and futile at the outset. Find a task or activity that you can pour your entire energy into; put your entire heart into it and build your rhythm from there. In this effort, emphasize depth, not duration. A short, but deeply engaged experience will be far more valuable than a longer, shallower effort.

Perhaps the biggest obstacle to staying in rhythm is our personal sense of static identity, any notion of self that pins us down to one particular level of engagement. Many of us tend to associate ourselves with a particular level of focus, striving or rest. Some of us describe ourselves as "hard-chargers" while others are "easy-going." In either case, such identities keep us out of rhythm by linking us to one part of the cycle or another. Far better to have a flexible, rhythmic identity that allows for continuous movement between phases: "I am a dynamic person, and I can move fluidly between periods of focused engagement and complete rest. I am multi-phasic."

No matter what you call yourself, the first rule of navigation holds true: "Know where you are at all times." At any given moment, you should have a sense of where you are on the master rhythm of engagement. Are you at the apex of concentration? Or are you in the deep well of rest? Are you moving towards increased focus, effort and intensity? Or are you relaxing your concentration and moving towards rejuvenation? If you can't answer these questions, you're probably out of rhythm. Once you figure out where you are, you can join the beat.

High contrast learning

Just as we look for a sense of rhythm with our bodies and our health, so too do we look for oscillation in the learning process itself. On the active side of the cycle, we immerse ourselves in complete engagement with smart, high-quality repetitions. We strive for maximum precision, attentional density and motivation. We focus intently on our creative targets, bringing our wandering attention back again and again. On the other side of the cycle, we let our efforts go entirely. We do something completely different. We play, we lounge, we nap and rest.

We might well describe this process as "athletic learning." Just as the smart coach trains her players to "train hard and rest deep," so too does the smart teacher lead her students through deep oscillations of intensive effort and complete relaxation. This teacher advises, "When studying, study really, really hard. When resting, rest deeply." Sadly, this kind of rhythm is fast disappearing from modern educational environments. As homework piles up and the pressure to perform intensifies, oscillation disappears into a half-hearted low-energy chronic engagement with the subject. This becomes, in the words of some educational critics, a *Race to Nowhere*. (the title of a documentary film)

The solution is to work both ends of the cycle with more intensity *and* more rest. When studying, dive in with intensively-focused discipline, then follow with complete abandon. This kind of oscillation would go a long ways towards improving the health, performance and culture of all our educational environments.

Lessons from the drum circle

As we build more contrast into the flow of our lives, we can take instruction and inspiration directly from those who work with rhythm on a regular basis. If you've ever been a beginner in a drum circle, you know how it goes. The advanced drummers get the beat moving, but somehow you just can't get your hands going. Everyone else is right on the beat and they even appear to find it trivially easy. But your arms and hands keep seizing up and your drum sounds like a box of rocks in the back of a pickup truck. You just can't feel it.

Determined to get it right, you push on, assaulting your drum with ever more awkward strikes, hoping that sheer effort can bring you back into alignment with the rest of the group. Sadly, it doesn't work, and you begin to suffer sidelong glances from the drummers on either side of you; you'll be lucky to be invited back next week.

A better approach is to simply stop and listen. This is the power of non-action. Just sit still. Don't do anything. Allow your body to feel the beat, let the rhythm wash over you, then feel it some more. There's no urgency about getting back into the action. Keep listening and feeling it and then, when the time is right, re-enter the rhythm with the simplest, most basic beat that you can perform. A child's beat, even an infant's beat. One strike on the drum head for each measure or so. Stick to the primal basics and stay with this simple form as long as possible. Your simple beat will almost surely fit and will be welcomed into the totality of the circle.

Got the metaphor?

That's right. Begin with nothing. Begin by listening. If you fall out of rhythm, don't despair. Just relax and wait for the next cycle to come around. The next cycle of sound, of touch, of relationship, of communication, of prosperity. Feel the music that flows through the room, through your habitat and through your body. And then, when the time is right, your body will know what to do.

The key, obviously, is practice. Rhythmic engagement is a muscle; it gets stronger with use. We improve our high-contrast living skills by practicing high-contrast living. Do it over and over. When you're climbing to the peak of engagement, focus as hard as possible. But when you're in the valley of rest, allow your body, mind and spirit to simply be. The more you keep to a high-contrast style of living, the more natural it will become.

Ultimately, it's another case of mindfulness in action. Pay attention to the oscillations in your world and your life. Where are the waxings and the wanings? What's the trajectory of the action? If you can feel it, you can play it.

As the saying goes, "play a beat you can repeat." And the more you feel it, the easier it gets.

Lesson 13

Focus your energy

To keep control of passion, one must hold firm the reins of attention.

Baltasar Gracián
The Art of Worldly Wisdom

Do every act of your life as though it were the very last act
of your life.

Marcus Aurelius

Modern life is chaos. We're up to our eyeballs in cognitive overload and surplus information, overwhelmed by things that, according to someone, must be done right away. Stress is eating away at our composure, exacerbated by invasive, always-on technologies that promise convenience but deliver only more tasks that need to be scanned, reviewed, researched and acted upon. Sometimes we manage to keep our heads above water by working harder, but the onslaught continues and our efforts become diluted, our attention fragmented.

To make matters even worse, there's the pesky problem of health and lifestyle overload. If you've ever tried to build your athletic performance or just live a healthy life, you've probably wondered what's truly possible. You've done your homework and learned the fundamentals for developing your vitality and improving your performance but unfortunately, when you take a closer look, you find that things just don't add up. Literally.

Try a back-of-the-envelope calculation: Experts tell us that we need to sleep for a solid eight hours every night. Add another hour for basic hygiene, house cleaning and the like. Maybe an hour or so for food shopping and preparation, another hour for exercise. Add another hour for homework, meditation, reading and enrichment. Another hour or so for positive social time with family and friends. And lest we forget, there's the pesky issue of work and the commute, which adds another 10 hours or so. All of which adds up to a lot more than 24.

And so our dilemma. Mired in a rising tide of overwhelm, most of us realize that we've got to impose some kind of order on the chaos, but what form should it take? Some will lean towards draconian solutions and hard-core discipline in which every single task is programmed, monitored and controlled, but this approach has its own limitations. Strict work-life discipline may keep the chaos at bay for awhile, but it's also brittle and prone to breakage. What are we to do?

Triage

Survival begins with triage. When faced with an avalanche of data and tasks that absolutely must be done right this instant, we've got to make choices. In a sense, we are all ER docs, trying to decide which cases to deal with and which ones we can safely ignore. Physicians practice triage because medical resources are scarce and it's better to concentrate them where they can do the most good.

Similarly, we must be willing to triage the challenges of our lives if we want to remain effective. This is particularly essential in today's hyperkinetic world; if we fail to make decisions about which cases we're willing to attend to, we're going to get swamped. And if we get swamped, things are going to start going downhill fast and we're not going to be much use to anyone.

We triage our lives by dividing our tasks into three categories: those that will go their own way regardless of what we do, those that we can safely ignore without major consequence and those that we can reasonably expect some measure of effectiveness. If you concentrate your effort in the middle, you'll have more control, more time and more opportunities for play and pleasure.

Naturally, success depends on where we draw the line. Some take a radical approach; business advisors sometimes tell young entrepreneurs to "say no to almost everything." In other words, focus exclusively on your core mission and reject the rest. Avoid "mission creep." If it's not on your list of objectives, it doesn't exist.

For the entrepreneur or any person doing creative work, this hard-style approach may well be sound advice. In the early days, it's easy to get excited about the potential and promise of a project. And in this passion, it's easy to take on too much of everything. At first it's exhilarating, but it also leads to increasing anxiety and stress. And unless we step in with decisiveness, it can even lead to systemic failure of the entire endeavor.

The solution is as simple as it is difficult: we must learn to put our energy and resources into our primary mission and reject everything that lies outside and beyond. It will be tempting to stray and fall in love with exciting ideas, hybrids and possibilities that lie at the margin, but the discipline of "No" will concentrate your energy, protect against extreme stress and enhance your chances of success. It's a matter of self-defense.

Of course, this demands that you know what your primary mission really is. Here, reflection and introspection are vital for survival and success. If you don't know your primary mission, then triage and decisiveness have no grounding and no basis for effectiveness. In turn, this can lead to massive, crushing levels of stress. The unexamined life, in other words, can set us up for ineffectiveness and chaos.

Triage is clearly an essential skill in our overheated, overloaded, hyper-caffeinated modern world. Nevertheless, there is danger here as well. When triage is well-executed, it makes us more effective, but when triage becomes compulsive or extreme, it close our minds to the richness, wonder and diversity of the world. As we become hyper-focused on our objectives, our minds begin to exclude new possibilities. This constant narrowing of attention can drive us towards monomania, rigidity and an impoverished sense of life.

Even worse, our extreme focus on triaging *tasks* may well lead to triaging *people* and *experiences*. Obsessed with efficiency, function and execution, we begin to instantly pigeon hole everyone we meet, according to how useful they might happen to be in helping us meet our objectives. "Say no to almost everything" becomes "Say no to almost everyone." Obviously, this is a recipe for personal, social and spiritual disaster. When we classify people according to their utility, we set ourselves up for boredom, shallow relationships and ultimately, loneliness.

As an alternative, some spiritual teachers advocate for a radically inclusive approach to life and counsel us to "say yes to almost everything." This takes us into a world of passion, possibility and boundless options for creativity. Our approach becomes more open-minded and open-hearted. Here we expose ourselves to the exuberance of life and all that it has to offer.

This point of view can be profoundly exhilarating and wildly stimulating, but here too we find limits. Radical inclusivity is a powerful seduction and an essential experience for creativity, but in the extreme, our efforts ultimately become diffuse, vaporous and ultimately, vague. We may well feel one with the world, but if we can't apply our intelligence into focused action, all may well be for naught. Without some degree of focus and yes, triage, we'll never make a difference.

The solution, perhaps, lies in a kind of softer, gentler form of triage. Maintain rigor and discipline in focusing your attention and exercising judgment, but keep some slack in the system. Focus on objectives and eliminate the obvious distractions, but remain open to novelty. Narrow your field of attention when you need to, but once your task is accomplished, open up your mind to the possibilities of life.

Creative limitation

Another powerful strategy for focusing our attention and concentrating our energy is the principle of creative limitation. Here we intentionally narrow our field of play and force ourselves to draw on our resources in a new way. Limits make us dig for more; they squeeze our minds, bodies and spirits for new growth. As Robert McKee put it in *Story*, the classic guide to screenwriting:

> *The principle of Creative Limitation calls for freedom within a circle of obstacles. Talent is like a muscle: without something to push against, it atrophies. So we deliberately put rocks in our path, barriers that inspire. We discipline ourselves as to what to do, while we're boundless as to how to do it.*

Creative limitation brings focus to the entire mind-body-spirit system. When the field of play is too broad, our energy becomes diluted; our attention is spread so thin that nothing is every accomplished. We begin to wander aimlessly, searching for perfection and avoiding difficulty. In contrast, limits will concentrate your energies and force you to draw on resources you might not have even known existed.

We see creative limitation in all kinds of disciplines and art forms. Writers are often called upon to adhere to word limits. TED talks are famously limited to 18 minutes, forcing speakers to condense their ideas into a concise form. Sports are all about performance within limits; you can do whatever you want with your body, as long as you stay within the confines of the rules. Every profession and discipline has its boundaries.

One particularly notable example of creative limitation comes from the world of rock climbing. In the early days of the sport, climbers used a variety of destructive tactics to get up mountains, most notably pitons, metal spikes driven into cracks in the rock. Pitons left ugly scars on the rock and the practice was clearly unsustainable. Early pioneers, most notably Yvon Chouinard, spoke out against this practice and called for "clean climbing" and "natural protection." He proposed one simple limitation: "Don't damage the rock."

At the time, this constraint was little more than an idea, a creative limitation. But the idea caught on and soon became an ethic. Within a few years, innovators developed an entire line of new technology and techniques that opened up the sport to an astonishing level of performance. The limitation made the sport stronger.

We see a similar power of constraint in every art, craft and discipline. Coaches, teachers and trainers are famous for imposing creative limitations on our practices. They tell us to "do it on one foot," "try it with your eyes closed," or "play one chord perfectly and with no effort." By narrowing the boundaries and limiting our options, they force us to dig deeper into our mind-body-spirit capability. This, in fact, may be the very essence of the teacher-coach-trainer's job description; by applying precise, strategic limits to students, athletes and clients, we draw out their latent capabilities.

Of course, many learners are inclined to complain and rebel, at least at the outset. The limitation cramps our style we protest; it's inconvenient, it gets in our way. But of course that's the whole point; it's not supposed to be easy. But if we accept the limitation and stick with it for awhile, things begin to change. Our brains and nervous systems begin to find new pathways and circuits. Neurons begin to grow and connect in new workarounds. Suddenly, the limits that once felt so confining feel like no problem whatsoever.

This is precisely what we see in the modern approach to physical therapy and stroke rehabilitation. In old-school practice, if a patient lost control of an arm, he was simply left to his own devices; conventional wisdom held that full recovery was unlikely. But with the modern approach, therapists may actually limit the mobility of the good arm with a sling, effectively forcing the patient to draw upon remote neurological and psychological resources to work around their limitation. At first, it's a tremendous struggle; it take a lot of psychophysical effort to draw out faint neurological signals and turn them into motor commands. But given enough time and energy, the process works. The brain-body rewires itself.

Our success with creative limitation depends in large measure on our willingness to trust our capacity for physical and psycho-spiritual growth. Artificial constraints may well be annoying and burdensome, but experience tells us that the body is constantly adapting, always looking for solutions, always searching for workarounds. We've adapted to constraints before and now, we can do it again. The body is smart; it's going to find a way. Just give it some reps and some time.

Creative limitation is an almost universal practice our arts and disciplines, but we can also extend the practice into our personal lives. Here, it can take the form of creative black lists, "Things I simply don't do." Most obviously, we begin by placing limits on outrageous acts of bad behavior: adultery, smoking, drunk driving, high-fructose corn syrup, trans fats, hydrogenated oils and "carbage," texting while driving and so on.

Of course, there plenty of things that you might add to your black list, all depending on your personal style, values and inclinations. There are endless possibilities here, but the most important thing is to have an explicit list that sets some guardrails in your life. These self-imposed limits on your behavior will actually decrease your stress in times of chaos, stress and dynamism; these are things you simply won't have to worry about, freeing you up for more challenging tasks.

We can go further. The practice of creative limitation becomes truly interesting and meaningful when we extend it into the social, psychological and spiritual dimensions of our lives. Possibilities include:

No cheap gossip or complaining.

No drive-by-judgment.

No spreading bile or darkness.

In a similar practice, the 18th century Jewish rabbi Nachman of Breslov, once told his followers "It is forbidden to despair." Just imagine the power in this simple limitation. By keeping despair and hopelessness off the table of consciousness, the good rabbi forced his followers to harness other psycho-spiritual resources. This is sound advice for any age, particularly in a world of climate change, habitat destruction and other looming threats to our life.

Similarly, we might well add another item to our list: "Cynicism is forbidden." When faced with the overwhelming challenges of our age and the chaos and sufferings of our personal lives, we rule out certain attitudes. No despair, no cynicism, no blame; these things are simply off the table. These limits force us to shine the light of our attention on creative action, beauty and possibility. They force the mind-body-spirit system to dig deeper into its well, to create. In this respect, limits are allies.

Smart tasking

Triage and creative limitation are powerful practices, but we also need to take a look at how we distribute our attention across the tasks we select. If we're being completely mindful about what we're doing, we'll do one thing at a time, focusing our concentration as completely as possible on to the act in question. Unfortunately, most of us seem to be going in the other direction entirely, spreading our attention out over an increasing number of challenges and activities.

Multi-tasking is a hot topic these days. Almost everyone does it to some degree and many of us believe that it's simply a practical way to get more done. We think we're being efficient, but in actual fact, we're not. A convincing body of neurological research demonstrates that multi-tasking is actually a highly ineffective strategy. In fact, the brain can only attend to one thing at a time. When we try to do two things at once, the brain switches attention rapidly between tasks with lightning speed.

Unfortunately, this high-speed switching comes with a cost: Every time we shift the focus of our attention, we must re-engage with the object or process in question, an act that requires psychophysical energy. As a result, multi-tasking limits our ability to enter into deep engagement with any one thing, which in turn limits how well we can perform. Multi-tasking leads to attentional dilution, poor quality reps and weaker learning. Fast switching of attention eats into our cognitive reserves which in turn leads to errors and exhaustion. Ultimately, it's a lose-lose strategy. As the 1st century BC, writer Publilius Syrus cautioned "To do two things at once is to do neither." Or as the modern version has it: "Multi-tasking: the single best way to screw up both jobs."

Nevertheless, we persist in our delusions. Many job postings advertise for applications who are "good at multi-tasking." And many of us boast about our capabilities, telling our friends "I'm great multi-tasker." But these advertisements and boasts are profoundly out of date and ill-informed. Multi-tasking is an enormous problem that impacts, not just our productivity, but also our social relationships, our health and our happiness. It is no exaggeration to call it an epidemic and a behavioral disease. Over the next few years, multi-tasking and electronic devices may well join the ranks of smoking, trans-fats and high-fructose corn syrup consumption in the pantheon of health-negative behaviors.

Given the compelling evidence that multi-tasking is an inefficient, even dangerous work and lifestyle, we have to ask, "Why do so many of us persist in doing it?" The fundamental problem, as any meditation teacher will tell us, is that we are uncomfortable in the present moment. There's something about our lives, our selves, our bodies or our circumstances that makes us uneasy. We're bored, we're anxious, we're afraid, we're overwhelmed; we can't just sit in the midst of our predicament. Restless, we feel the need to distract ourselves with multiple streams of action. In this sense, multi-tasking is no different than any other form of escapism.

Over time, such compulsive running away from the here and now leads to a habitual pattern of addictive flight from even the slightest present-moment discomfort. We experience incipient boredom, anxiety or confusion, but instead of feeling these feelings for what they are, we layer on additional tasks, hoping for some better experience. But of course, this pattern only makes us less adept at living in the present, which ultimately makes us even more anxious and unhappy. It's a classic vicious cycle.

It's obvious that we have a problem, but the solution is not so clear. Many of us have heard about the virtues of mindfulness training and mono-tasking (also called uni-tasking). Meditation teachers counsel us to pay attention to one thing at a time; the simple qualities of our breath, our bodies, our friends and our habitat. This advice is surely valuable, but can we really practice mono-tasking in a world that demands so much of our attention, all at once?

And when we stop to think about it, we might even wonder if mono-tasking is really a practical strategy for *any* normal life activity. After all, even traditional disciplines demand that we manage multiple tasks simultaneously. Cooking is a perfect example: We wash the vegetables while the water is heating, we slice and chop while the soup simmers. We're doing several things at once, each with its own character and time line for completion. If we were to be absolutely disciplined about singular attention to each individual task, we could never complete a meal.

Similarly, what are we to make of modern challenges such as piloting an aircraft, an act that is nothing if not pure multi-tasking? Even basic aviation calls for split attention and continuous scanning. The pilot must sweep her attention over the sky, look for traffic conflicts, then scan the instrument panel for updates on altitude, airspeed and navigation, as well as communicate with air traffic controllers. Without multi-tasking, modern aviation would be impossible.

And maybe it's not even a problem of modernity. If we think back to ancestral conditions, we might well conclude that hunting and gathering are themselves multi-tasking challenges: you've got to keep your eyes on your prey but at the same time you've got to maintain a wider, more expansive form of attention in order to avoid becoming prey yourself. In fact, some neuroscientists have suggested that the two sides of the brain are constantly multi-tasking in this way: the left side focuses on specific objects of interest while the right side maintains environmental vigilance, keeping it's "eye" on a broader panorama. In this sense, we may be deeply wired for multi-tasking. (See *The Master and his Emissary* by Iain McGilchrist.)

Thus our dilemma: On one hand, it's becoming increasingly clear that excessive multi-tasking dilutes our experience, weakens our concentration, dissolves our intelligence and opens us up to errors of attention and judgment. On the other, a prescription for strict mono-tasking seems unrealistic. So how are we to live?

Perhaps the problem is not multi-tasking itself, but rather the fact that we are increasingly unconscious about what we do; we simply take on additional tasks as they come into our field of experience, automatically and without reflection. In the process, life and work begin to overwhelm us. We take on a little more, then a little more. The mind-body adapts, but our cognitive and spiritual reserve shrinks. We can still manage basic functions, but our performance becomes increasingly precarious; we may well be close to a performance collapse and not even know it.

The end result is that many of us wind up operating at the maximum possible task load all the time. And of course, technology makes it all so much worse. Digital devices hold out the promise of unlimited capacity. We think that we can just keep adding tasks to our lives without cost, but in fact, technology only delays the inevitable. By adding to our task load, we deplete the psychophysical resources that might well be used for more subtle and meaningful aspects of our lives. When we're always maxed out, we've got nothing left over for anyone or anything else.

The art of smart

The solution, as usual, lies in proportion, judgment, skill and of course, beauty. Here we look for intelligent task selection; a coherent body of action in which component tasks and challenges form an integrated whole. For example, the master chef might well juggle dozens of food-related tasks in his kitchen. He's multi-tasking, but all of his tasks are intimately related to one another. His effort is united by a common theme or objective; he rejects tasks that are not related to the actual process of cooking.

So too for any creative art. Look for a unity of purpose. When cooking, cook. When driving, drive. When talking on the phone, talk on the phone. When cleaning your house, clean your house. Resist the impulse to add non-related tasks, even if you can manage them. Even if you do succeed at juggling multiple tasks, you will have broken the spell of unity and integration. Your mind and spirit will be divided. Without a common thread, theme or purpose, it's all just a bunch of stuff to be done. Your effort will have a frantic, desperate quality.

Smart multi-tasking respects an optimal task load; not too much, not too little. The master is vigilant in protecting his attention and maintains a cognitive and spiritual reserve, a capacity that allows him to relax and focus on the skill at hand. Unity of purpose leads to deeper engagement and allows us to participate more completely in what we're doing. The totality of our mind-body-spirit remains integrated and coherent. In contrast, stupid multi-tasking drives us away from flow into a thin, jerky, disconnected and superficial experience; one foot in the task, one foot out, scrambling for control, always on the edge of catastrophe. Obviously, this is a recipe for stress, accidents, injuries and bad decisions.

So how can we know the difference? How do we find the optimal task load? Ultimately, the proof lies in our subjective experience. How does it feel to be operating at this level? Does this combination of tasks feel like an invitation to a deeper, more sustainable engagement with a creative act? Or does it feel like a frantic, desperate scramble that's likely to fall apart in the very next moment? Are you controlling the action? Or is the action controlling you?

It always comes down to understanding ourselves, in context and in motion. Slow down and what you're feeling. Exercise your meta-cognition and be ready to draw the line when the red flags of disintegrated attention appear. Beware of taking on too much. Know which straws are likely to break your attentional back. Do less, but engage more.

Above all, be sensitive to early warnings, especially those that you feels in your body. What does it feel like when your task load shifts from ideal to something slightly more burdensome? Do you feel a shift in your posture, your breathing or your gut? Do you feel a change in the pace or the quality of your thoughts? Does your experience change from challenge to threat?

In the process, stay mindful of aesthetics. A highly integrated task feels skillful and looks beautiful. By taking on too much, we not only increase our neuro-cognitive load, we also erode the look and feel of your experience. Excessive tasking can transform art into frantic, compulsive activity. We may be more productive in some sense, but the things that we ultimately produce will scarcely be worth looking at or remembering.

In the end, the path to sanity and skill lies in the simple rejection of tasks and task loads that go beyond the optimal. In a world gone mad with distraction and chronic juggling, the prime directive of performance and effectiveness is simple: defend your attention. Build a firewall around your most important efforts:

- Just say no to additional tasks that have no relation to your primary challenge.

- Just say no to tasks that will dilute your efforts and cut into your psychophysical reserve.

- Just say no to tasks that will undermine the unity, quality and beauty of your primary quest.

Remember, you are not obligated to manage every single task that enters into your field of experience. Just because the phone rings, doesn't mean you have to answer it. Just because someone hands you an additional project doesn't mean you have to accept it. Just because a flashing light appears on your device doesn't mean you have to click on it. Just because everyone around you is madly juggling a thousand things and spreading their attention indiscriminately doesn't mean you have to do it too.

Your attention is precious, not only to your personal health and effectiveness, but also to your relationships, as well as social and cultural health. Keep a cognitive, spiritual and physical reserve. Maintain coherence and integration. Don't give it away mindlessly. It's too important.

Lesson 14

Wait for the biscuit

A hallmark of being human is restraint.

Laurence Gonzales
Everyday Survival

The secret of all existence is simply to learn to wait.

Robert Heinlein

Stranger in a Strange Land

Consider the following choice: You can have one week in Costa Rica, all expenses paid at the finest luxury resort, right now. The limo will pick you up first thing in the morning and take you right to the airport. Or, if you're willing to wait a year, you can have an entire month in Costa Rica, also fully paid for, also at the finest luxury resort. What'll it be? Can you wait?

If you're sharp, you'll recognize this as an adult version of the famous "marshmallow test." In a now-legendary experiment, social psychologist Walter Mischel gave a series of four-year-old children a simple choice: "You can have one marshmallow now, but if you wait, you can have two." Being a good scientist, he recorded each student's performance and tracked them over the years. The results clearly demonstrated the power of self-control, not just in the mundane choices of day-to-day living, but in the overall trajectory of life success; children who were able to delay gratification went on to succeed in academics, career, health and personal life. Clearly, willpower is vital to how we live and who we might become.

Of course, self control has always been an important part of human success. As our Paleolithic ancestors developed larger brains and more complex social lives, we also gained proficiency in hunting. But hunting calls for self-control and inhibition; you can't simply go charging off into the bush, chasing after game and expect to succeed. You may need to sit still for hours, stalk with great care, or coordinate complex maneuvers with your hunting party. If you can't regulate your impulses, you may well go hungry.

Later, as we entered the age of agriculture, discipline and willpower became even more important to our success. Human time horizons grew longer. We planted crops, expecting to be gratified months later. We built immense monuments that took decades or even generations to complete. The construction of cities, roads, energy systems and modern technology have all relied on our ability to wait.

Today, our need for self-control has become even more pronounced. As the modern world becomes ever more complex, we are called upon to exercise almost heroic levels of self-control in everyday life. An avalanche of innovation has given us incredible new ideas, tools, and media as well as instant food and drink temptations in almost every direction. This adds up to an unprecedented level of distraction and impulse challenge. To make matters even more difficult, we now must sustain our career aspirations for decades, from kindergarten all the way through graduate school and beyond; for modern humans, the marshmallow is many years away. If we're to succeed, we need to hold tight to the reigns of our emotions and our impulses.

Willpower is a muscle

For centuries, teachers, scholars and religious leaders have taught that willpower is simply a matter of character. People with a strong moral fabric have the ability to resist temptation, but others fall short. If people are unable to resist temptation, it's their own fault and discipline must be enforced. Perhaps those who are weak can be redeemed through punishment or manipulation, but in the end, it's mostly about who they are as people. Good people resist temptation; bad people fall for it.

But today, the more sophisticated view holds that willpower is primarily a function of our brains and bodies. Character may still have a role to play, but in general, our ability to inhibit impulse comes down to the interplay between neural circuits, brain structure, hormones and neurotransmitters; it's how we use our brains that makes the difference.

Most important, we now know that self-control is a dynamic capability that's trainable, just like a muscle. This metaphor has been invoked by many, most notably by Roy Baumeister and John Tierney in *Willpower: Rediscovering the Greatest Human Strength* and Kelly McGonigal in *The Willpower Instinct*. Numerous studies demonstrate that active, disciplined training increases our ability to exercise control over behavior. The effect is both specific and general; we can train ourselves to inhibit particular urges and impulses in context, but it's also the case that any kind of training in delayed gratification will strengthen our will.

In a way, the moralists were half-right. People become more self-controlled by practicing self-control; disciplined educational environments tend to promote more disciplined behavior. This is why sports, arts, music and academic training are important parts of a whole-life education. Children who learn these disciplines may or may not use the specific skills in adult life, but their inhibitory powers are transferable to other domains. A child who learns how to delay gratification in school, music class or sports is better positioned to meet the discipline challenges of later life.

One notable example is martial art training for children and young people. Many parents report a dramatic difference in self-control in those children who partic-ipate. It makes sense. The training is basic and is aimed directly at managing the body: "Bow to the mat." "Stand here." "Sit here." "Kick now." "Punch now." "Yell now." Over time, the discipline becomes embodied. Students learn discipline by behaving in a disciplined way. In fact, this may be the real virtue of martial art training. Few of us really need self-defense in the modern world, but all of us need the experience of controlling our behavior and impulses.

Regulate the primate

Our predicament comes into sharper focus when we understand the lopsided, un-balanced nature of forces within our bodies. It's a tenuous relationship: On one hand, the deep body is ancient, fast, powerful and unconscious. Its primary interest is survival; it is constantly vigilant to threats and can take control of the whole system if necessary. On the other hand is our conscious brain, orchestrated by the prefrontal cortex. This system is new and incredibly sophisticated, but also fragile and notoriously unreliable.

In routine daily living, these two systems live in constant dialogue and a occasional harmony. When all goes well, the prefrontal brain inhibits impulses coming from the deep body; it keeps the brakes on. But when stress hits the fan, things can go out of balance in a hurry. The ancient, primal parts of the brain-body begin to assert control. We experience a "reptilian take-over" of our minds and behavior. Even worse, stress hormones begin to erode the function of the prefrontal cortex itself, further limiting our ability to regulate our impulses. In other words, the balance of power begins to shift from new to old. In effect, we travel backwards in evolution to a more primal, reactive state.

If we happen to be in a genuine survival situation, this might well work to our advantage, but such conditions are rare in modern life. More likely, we interpret conditions as threatening–to our status, our position, our identity–and the deep, primal body takes over with high-speed reactivity. Sadly, this reactivity often leads to behavior that is inappropriate, embarrassing and destructive.

In any case, prefrontal inhibition works just like any muscle. It waxes and wanes with our physical health, our disposition, setting and context. It is undoubtedly true that some people have higher levels of self-control to begin with, but even for these individuals, willpower fluctuates.

Sometimes the willpower muscle is well-rested and strong, but other times it loses its vitality. This "depletion hypothesis" tells us that willpower is a limited resource. This presents us with a paradox and a challenge. That is, using our capability makes us more vulnerable to impulse. As Kelly McGonigal put it, "because every act of willpower depletes willpower, using self-control can lead to losing control." This is why willpower lapses are more common late in the day. We might well be paragons of virtue in the morning, but then, after 10 hours of inhibition and self-regulation, we head for the bar and make fools of ourselves.

Unfortunately, many of us fail to appreciate just how much we demand from pre-frontal willpower in our daily lives. Most of us believe that our primary willpower challenge is reigning in our excess consumption of food, drink, intoxicants and lust. If we had just a little more willpower, the thinking goes, we'd lose some weight, get back in shape and feel like an Olympic athlete.

These might well be the classic cases, but we use also our willpower in myriad ways that go far beyond the challenges of carbohydrates, alcohol and sex. As it turns out, most of us put immense demands on our willpower in nearly every minute of the modern day. We use willpower any time we...

- repeatedly call our attention back to some unpleasant task.
- are called upon to rearrange our carefully-crafted plans.
- are forced to remain seated, even though our bodies are craving movement.
- really want to express an opinion, but are silenced by social constraints.
- are working on a deadline, trying to force our performance into a narrow window of time.

In short, most of us in the modern world are running our willpower capability just about as hard as it can go, most of the time. No wonder we break down when the desert cart comes around and our friends tell us it's time for another round.

Care and feeding of the prefrontal cortex

The neurological source of our willpower lies in the prefrontal cortex, a powerful swath of brain tissue that lies just behind the forehead. Sometimes called "the brain's brain," this region is famous for executive functions such as planning, sorting and decision making. The prefrontal cortex has an astonishing array of beneficial functions, but for our purposes, its most important role is to inhibit emotional impulses and in turn, behavior. In the words of Stanford neuroscientist Robert Sapolsky, the prefrontal cortex "makes us do the harder thing."

Unfortunately, the prefrontal cortex is also vulnerable to a number of insults, some external, some self-inflicted. In particular, stress hormones can degrade its connectivity and its ability to perform its inhibitory function. Here we can see the problem of over-work and what might well be described as "chronic fatigue of the prefrontal cortex." As we push ourselves through weeks and months of exhausting mental labor, we squeeze the brain for every last shred of executive function, trying to turn all of our metabolic, psychological and spiritual resources into work products. We pay the cost in the form of degraded connections in the prefrontal cortex; we might even describe this condition as an "overuse injury." We aren't overworking our muscles, but we are overworking vital circuitry and degrading our ability to manage our brains, our bodies and our lives.

Even worse, it's not just a weakening of willpower. Dr. Dan Siegel of the UCLA School of Medicine has identified no less than 9 prefrontal functions including bodily regulation, attuned communication, emotional balance, response flexibility, insight, empathy, fear modulation, intuition and even morality. Clearly, a healthy prefrontal cortex is essential for just about everything we might want to do with our lives.

So, how do care for this precious swath of brain tissue? First–and this is no joke– avoid head trauma. Even minor concussions can threaten prefrontal function. Be mindful of your sporting activity and wear a helmet when appropriate. Second, be mindful of stress. Meditation and other stress-relieving practices are increasingly seen as essential daily "brain hygiene." Third, move your body. Exercise in any form increases blood flow and oxygenation of the prefrontal brain. Finally, positive social relationships will produce a sense of "feeling felt" and generate higher levels of oxytocin, a powerful stress antidote. Sleep and genuine rest are also essential.

As for feeding the system, this is where things get tricky. The prefrontal cortex is an energy hog that uses a disproportionate share of the body's nutritional resources. As Roy Baumeister and John Tierney put it, "it loves glucose." This, of course, explains why we so often crave highly-refined carbohydrates in the modern world. By constantly overclocking our executive brains throughout the day, we become desperate for something fast and easy to digest.

But this poses an obvious challenge. In the short term, we can re-energize our willpower by eating something that's packed with sugar; now our prefrontal brain is happy and ready to get back to work. But in the long term, the news is not good. Those quick energy fixes also produce massive blood sugar spikes and all the complications that go with them. Over time, this leads to insulin resistance, greater inflammation in the body and eventually to Type 2 diabetes. This is the price we pay for chronic work, fueled by fast carbohydrates.

Alcohol also poses a problem. In low doses, it's probably a tonic for the cardiovascular system and general health. But in larger, more sustained doses, it probably reduces the plasticity of the prefrontal cortex. Obviously, this puts us into a wicked spiral of reduced willpower and increased consumption. Finding the optimal dose is essential. That's why some physicians call alcohol "a razor-sharp double-edged sword."

Another obvious solution is to simply stop working so hard. The prefrontal cortex was never meant to work non-stop, all day, every day. Willpower works best as an occasional regulatory tool. By easing back on your chronic labor, you won't feel the desperate need to consume every sugar molecule in sight. At the same time, use your remaining willpower to make better, slower food choices. This means complete meals, high in protein and healthy fats. Slow-burn food will keep your blood sugar from spiking and in turn, keep your brain happy.

Lessons

So what's the practice? How do we increase and sustain our willpower in a world that demands so much? The first lesson is to conserve resources. Trying to exert willpower continuously over every event and situation is a mistake; you'll just get tripped up by some unexpected challenge. Instead, be mindful of the waxing and waning of your willpower capability through the day and over the course of weeks and months. If possible, schedule your willpower challenges for when you're rested and ready to work your prefrontal brain.

Second, recognize and honor depletion events. If you're called upon to exert extraordinary willpower, you're going to need some recovery time. A hyper-focused project at work, a tense meeting, an emotional family encounter: all of these events deplete our resources. If you don't allow for recovery and go straight into another high-pressure challenge, you'll be setting yourself up for failure or worse.

Next, be mindful of the quality of your internal relationship. How do you tell your willpower story? Do you see your willpower as an authoritarian dictator whose sole purpose is to discipline your body's creative desires and impulses? Do you see the relationship as an epic drama, with the forces of reason, purity and virtue pitted against the forces of lust, greed, gluttony and sloth?

If so, you're setting yourself up for an internal conflict and real willpower failure. Paradoxically, this adversarial narrative exaggerates internal tension and depletes the very resources that you would like to conserve. In other words, casting your willpower as an authoritarian force actually makes it more likely that you will fail in your willpower challenges.

The superior approach is to seek an integration, a union of old and new, primal and modern. In this narrative, the relationship is not a war or a battle. Rather, it's a partnership of constant adjustment and regulation. The deep body is not an impulsive, greedy child that must be kept on a short leash and watched over in every second of the day. Likewise, there's no need to think of the prefrontal cortex as a neurological tyrant, ever vigilant to squelch the body's slightest inclination towards pleasure. In fact, once our early training is complete and we learn the proper time and place for inhibition, the process usually takes care of itself.

This brings us to a fascinating set of conclusions about effective living. We know that discipline can be trained and we can benefit from learning self-control; the more we use the prefrontal cortex to inhibit impulsive behavior, the better it gets at doing precisely that. But beyond a certain point, self-control becomes excessively stressful and self-defeating; the whole system can fall apart.

Clearly, there's got to be some slack in our willpower system, a firm kind of discipline, one that holds the line, but not too tightly. One that keeps us away from the worst temptations while still allowing us some room to maneuver. One that regulates the reptile, but still gives us room for pleasure, self-compassion and kindness.

With this in mind, the art lies in keeping a sense of proportion and balance. Maintain a sense of control, but allow some room for interpretation, pleasure and wildness. Run a firm ship; not too tight, not too loose. Regulate your worst behavior with firewalls and real discipline, but give in to life and love. Hold the line as long as you can, but allow yourself to be seduced from time to time. Paradoxically, this will give you precisely what you're looking for, an integrated, disciplined practice with just enough flex to keep your creativity alive.

Above all, practice mindfulness. Willpower is a muscle, but so too is our awareness of our willpower. The more you use it, the stronger it will become.

Lesson 15

Synchronize

The goal of life is to make your heartbeat match the beat of the universe to match your nature with Nature.

Joseph Campbell

Time is what we want most, but what we use worst.

William Penn

Everyone wants to know the ultimate formula for health, performance and happiness, but most of us find ourselves getting distracted along the way. We start with the recommended diet and exercise programs and explore the details of physiology and psychology, always looking for the recipe that will bring us the ultimate in vitality, skill and sex appeal. But sadly, most of us get lost in the weeds and fail to notice the most central issue in all of health and performance training: time.

The inescapable fact is that every single health and performance objective hinges on our ability to immerse ourselves in time-consuming practices such as exercise, food preparation, meditation, smart repetition, positive social experience and contact with the natural world. All of these activities demand time, sometimes big chunks of time. We can try to tweak the process with tighter efficiencies and sophistication, but in the end there is no alternative; the hours have got to come from somewhere.

Obviously, this puts us squarely at odds with our predicament in the modern world, where most of us feel an overpowering sense of temporal poverty. Listening to ourselves, we often hear a sense of desperation; "I have NO TIME for ANYTHING." We talk constantly about being "behind" as if life is nothing but a race. Stressed to the limit, we can scarcely manage our basic life and work functions, much less devote additional time to developing our capabilities for greater health, skill and happiness. We are at our limit. Or so we believe.

Obviously, our condition is not healthy. In fact, we may well describe our modern relationship with time as a kind of "lifestyle inflammation" or a "hurry disease." We live with an assumption of scarcity, no matter our actual conditions. We behave as if life is an emergency; if we slow down or stop what we're doing, catastrophe is inevitable. Unfortunately, the prognosis for this kind of relationship is not good. Our busyness puts us into a vicious circle. It generates errors of sensation, attention and judgment, which puts us further behind the pace of events.

Beautiful pace

So what are we to do about our dysfunctional relationship with time? Are we destined to hurry our lives away in a state of constant busyness and anxiety? Will time simply slip through our fingers, only to disappear into the black hole of remorse and failed opportunities?

Sadly, most of us don't really think much about our relationship with time or take actions that might remedy our problem. Instead, we simply speed up. Most of the time, we're reactive and unconscious. Our knee jerk reaction is simply to stack activities on top of one another and push the pace. We justify this behavior by claiming that we can "get over the hump," but it rarely works. Doing multiple things simultaneously merely spreads our attention more thinly and forces our minds to work faster. And now our sense of urgency actually increases, leading to yet more dilution of our intelligence.

The real problem is that, when it comes to crafting a better relationship with time, most of us don't even know what the goal is. Desperate to catch up, we think that the main objective is to "get a lot done" or "go really fast." But in fact, the goal is not to go fast. Nor is the goal to go slow. Rather, the goal is to synchronize our efforts with our creative goals and the world around us. The objective is to craft a tempo that fits into our setting, context and environment. In other words, the goal is to create a beautiful pace.

It's always a question of harmony. A beautiful pace doesn't push ahead unless circumstance calls for it; it doesn't lag behind unless there's a reason. A beautiful pace is constantly changing and adjusting. The ultimate goal is unity and integration, a merger of our energies with the flow of events. Obviously, going fast when things around us are moving slow is a waste of effort. Similarly, going slow while events are moving fast is a recipe for disaster. In the middle lies effortlessness, pleasure and skill.

Temporal artistry calls upon us to develop a range of skills. We begin by mastering the fundamentals of executive function, things like planning, to-do lists, prioritizing, time estimates, projections, start and stop times. In this practice, we work our prefrontal brains. We track and preview, we map events onto calendars and timelines, always looking for a sense of how things will unfold. There is no mystery to this process: Write things down, do the calculations, track your progress and plot your trajectories. Once you know what's happening in your world, you can speed up or slow down as conditions demand. Even better, you'll have a sense of control. In turn, this will give your body and spirit a chance to relax. Executive labor pays off; the world feels safer and more manageable. You begin to feel a sense of temporal abundance.

Just do less

Of course, there's another solution to our temporal crisis, one that often escapes our notice. That is, we can simply choose to do less. This solution, radical as it may seem, is powerful. Once we scale back our ambitions and cut our to-do lists down to size, things start to loosen up. Our bodies and our minds begin to relax and in the process, we become far more effective at the things we choose to do.

Naturally, this strategy takes guts. In modern culture, the pressure to take on everything is incessant. Doing less is frowned upon and in some settings, even the appearance of being relaxed is discouraged: If your hair's not on fire, you're not one of us. But going against this hyper-active grain is essential; the slowing down has got to begin somewhere.

The beauty of doing less is that it actually creates a deeper sense of temporal affluence and all the benefits that go with it. No longer are we so desperate. We can look around and study the world. We can learn more about conditions. We can be more selective about the actions that we take and in this, we can be far more effective. Our actions become targeted and precise. Doing less means doing better.

While we're at it, we'd do well to stop "the glorification of busy." In today's hyper-kinetic culture, many of us have bought into the assumption that "busy equals important." And of course, we idolize the warrior-entrepreneur who works 100 hours per week, starting companies and changing the world, or the super-Mom who raises a family, also starts a company and runs triathlons in her spare time. If we get really busy, maybe we'll be important too.

But this glorification of busy-important superstars is a distraction that takes us away from our own creative path. It also obscures the fact that by itself, busyness is not a strategy for anything. It's not an intelligent way to get things done. Rather it's an expression of the anxiety and insecurity that we feel inside ourselves. As one meditation teacher put it, "We are not restless because we are busy; we are busy because we are restless." Once we learn how to relax, our busyness will begin to fade away. As a result, we'll be far more powerful in the things that we choose to do.

Here again we find ourselves going back to the drama triangle and the perils of the victim orientation. When we see ourselves as victims of external events, not only do we blame the world for our condition, we also place ourselves at the mercy of the flow of events. We become increasingly reactive and soon we're scrambling to catch up with everything around us. We get swept up in the contagion of other people's activity. Our attention becomes scattered and fragmented. We're late for meetings, we're late for our friends and family, we're late for our lives.

In contrast, the creator takes control of her predicament and in the process, her pace. She knows what she wants to do with her energy and resources and now, she can make choices and establish the pace that works for her. She's active, not reactive. Of course there will always be realities that demand her attention and she may well have to accelerate on occasion to mesh with the flow of other people and processes. But in the main, she is the one who sets the pace.

Naturally, this takes us back to the beginning, to our priorities, our vision and our objectives. What's really important in your life and work? What exactly are you really trying to create? This is no time for vague generalities. As a creator, you must make your targets specific and explicit. By describing exactly what you want to create, you can cut your way through the chaos. An explicit declaration of what's important will give you the ability to triage your tasks and make powerful decisions. Without a sense of what's important, you'll simply try to do it all. Before long, you'll be overtaken by events, overwhelmed and exhausted.

Keep a temporal reserve

No matter what you choose to create, it's essential to maintain a temporal reserve. This is simply a buffer of extra time that you can tap into if circumstances change unexpectedly, which of course, they will. The beauty of this strategy is that temporal reserve gives us a general sense of affluence and abundance. Our sense of "extra time" gives us a mental-cognitive reserve as well as a physical and spiritual reserve. When time is on your side, you're on top of your game, everything just feels easier.

This art begins at the beginning; the place to start is with the opposite of procrastination. That is, front-load the labor, especially those unpleasant tasks that you're most likely to avoid. As soon as possible, dig into the heart of the challenge. Engage early. Immerse yourself in conditions, scout the territory, send out detectives, gather information and do your research. At this point, your action will pay huge dividends. By taking on the lion's share of the effort at the outset, you'll free yourself for a greater sense of ease when things start to heat up. You'll be in a much better position to face the inevitable surprises. Your mind, body and spirit will be relaxed.

We might be inclined to think of temporal reserve as a simple buffer that we can draw upon in emergencies, but it's really a core element for success no matter what happens. Knowing that you have extra time to draw upon, you can focus more intently, think more creatively and pay more attention to the little things that really matter in the long run. Even better, your temporal reserve will free your mind and body for increased sensitivity and a broader vision of your quest. In this process, your body can gather far more information about conditions, information that you can use to maintain or even extend your temporal buffer. Clearly, this is a powerful win-win.

Once you get into the habit of establishing and maintaining a temporal reserve, you'll find your performance improving across the board. In lesson here is clear; no matter your plan, allow more time than you think you need and then add a little more on top of that. As your plan unfolds, stay mindful of your reserve. Every time you transition to a new activity, check your time and allow a little more.

Focus on abundance

As we've seen, our sense of temporal poverty is closely related to a general sense of scarcity. We're frightened. The world, we believe, may not provide what we need. Everywhere we look we see vital systems on the verge of collapse. Resources are tight and diminishing; we must hurry to get our share before it's too late. This perception drives us harder and harder. Individuals, organizations, society and culture; we all feel the urge to go faster; if we wait too long, there may be nothing left.

Our urgency is driven by interpretation, not reality. The world is rich with evidence for any point of view; we see what we choose to see. If we were to focus on abundance rather than scarcity, things would look and feel entirely different. If we focused on the bounty of pleasure, wealth and wonder in our lives, we would instantly slow down and relax. We would feel safe and there would be no need to race.

This is where we have a choice. You can choose to spend your days obsessing over the scarcities, challenges and wicked problems of the world. If you make this choice, you can expect to feel anxious, rushed and desperate for resolution. Life will become an emergency and your time will shrink to almost nothing. Or, you can choose to direct your attention to the beautiful adventure and the fact that we are participants in a glorious and spectacularly bountiful biosphere that is rich beyond our imagining. Human systems and organizations have their problems to be sure, but we are intelligent, resilient and resourceful. People create beauty countless times every day. Art is everywhere. When you keep your eye on this ball, your body will relax and time will open up. This is where you will do your best work.

Live here now

Ultimately, creating a beautiful pace requires a fundamental revision in how we live. If we're going to turn temporal poverty into temporal affluence, we've got to change our relationship with the present moment. Naturally, we all have a tendency to flee forward in time. When faced with the prospect of living with boredom, anxiety, insecurity, fear, confusion, grief, uncertainty, or sadness, we reject the present. We charge ahead into the future, hoping for a better moment along the way. We look for a rescue; perhaps the future will save us from our unhappiness.

But this frantic flight from the present is a non-solution, even an anti-solution. If the present moment is unpleasant, going faster will only generate a faster, more desperate form of unpleasantness. This will only feed our sense of urgency and our perceptions of scarcity.

The only truly viable solution is to inhabit the present, with all its ambiguity and insecurity. So practice getting comfortable with this moment, no matter how restless you may feel. Pay attention to your reactive, mindless lurching into the future. Be mindful of your sense of urgency and your desire for rescue. This practice will challenge you, but it will also dampen your sense of temporal poverty and lead you towards a sense of abundance. In the process, your life will open up to new possibilities and effortless action.

Lesson 16

Improvise

Genius is not a gift, but rather the way one
invents in desperate situations.

Jean-Paul Sartre

You have to have an idea of what you are going to do, but it should be a vague idea.

Pablo Picasso

Heraclitus would be smiling and nodding his head right about now. "You can't step into the same river twice" was true enough in ancient Greece, but now it's true a thousand times over. Dynamism is the rule of the day; the world is changing faster than ever before in history. The pace of cultural innovation is accelerating; every system, organization and process is in transition. We train ourselves in various arts, professions and disciplines, but our knowledge seems outdated before the ink has even dried on our certificates. Solutions that worked this morning seem obsolete by sunset.

Faced with this accelerating current of change, many of us try to hold firm to the solid ground of yesterday's skill sets. We fight against change and do what we can to maintain a grip on familiar forms of security. Sometimes it works, but the river keeps flowing and we're often left without a choice. We have to adapt.

Sadly, many of us have forgotten this art. As children, every single thing we did was improv, but as we grew older, our sense of play began to atrophy. We wanted to appear serious, knowledgeable, and competent. We wanted to look grown-up, so we pretended to know what we were doing. We grew to fear public exposure and the possibility of ridicule. Before long, our sense of improv began to disappear.

Today, improv is a common theme in the arts and the humanities, but in other realms it's often treated like a side-show and a curiosity, suitable for crazy artists, but not for the real challenge of making our way in the world. But what if improv is actually a core competency, a fundamental skill that contributes to success in every realm of human endeavor? It hardly seems far-fetched. Life, after all, is always in motion.

In fact, improv is a central theme in some domains. In the world of athletic training, coaches and trainers often make a distinction between athletes who are *adapted* and those who are *adaptable*. The adapted athlete has learned how to excel in a particular context, in a particular setting, usually a standardized, competitive sport. In contrast, the adaptable athlete demonstrates the ability to improvise in novel situations, on the fly.

This may seem to be a minor distinction, but it's actually crucial, not just in the world of athletics, but for how we live our daily and professional lives. For the spectator, the adapted athlete may appear to be the perfect exemplar of high performance, but there is also weakness here. If the context or setting changes, even just a little, the highly adapted athlete my find himself floundering, injured or surpassed by less well adapted but more adaptable competitors.

This is the problem with standardized sports. Professional athletic competitions are utopian in nature; they take place in an artificial paradise of regulation and constancy. Standardization makes for spectacular match-ups, but as a model for living in a hyper-dynamic world, it's very nearly irrelevant. The modern world is nothing at all like a professional sporting event.

In fact, deep specialization in any art or discipline actually makes us vulnerable to dynamism; we should be extremely wary of taking life lessons from those who are adapted, but not adaptable. As Eric Hoffer, the American social and political philosopher put it, "In times of profound change, the learners inherit the earth, while the learned find themselves beautifully equipped to deal with a world that no longer exists."

So how are we to develop our adaptability and our ability to improvise? The short answer comes from what we already know about training and the nature of the nervous system. That is, we get precisely what we train for. There's no magic to this process; we develop our improv skills by practicing improv. Improv is a muscle; we become more adaptable by practicing adaptability. Instead of practicing rote forms in highly consistent, stereotyped conditions, we deliberately put ourselves in contact with ambiguity, novelty and uncertainty. We mix things up, forcing our mind-body systems to respond and create in the moment.

We can also take inspiration from disciplines like *parkour*, sometimes referred to as "urban free running." Similar in some respects to obstacle course training, parkour practitioners move smoothly and efficiently through their environment, whatever it may happen to be. In natural settings, these *traceurs* run and climb gracefully across hills, ravines, around and through trees, up and over rocks. In urban environments, they maneuver up and down stairs, railings, building and across any other "obstacle" that may present itself. Parkour involves seeing one's environment in a new way, and imagining the potential for movement in every setting.

According to Vincent Thibault, author of *Parkour and the Art du deplacement: Strength, Dignity, Community*, parkour is all about agility, grace, strength, resilience, adaptability and improv. The buildings, stairs, railings and obstacles are real, but they're also metaphors for the rest of our lives. In this respect, parkour is not about "overcoming obstacles," it's about merger in motion. It's about the relationship between our bodies, spirits and the world around as it is.

In a world gone mad with attempts to control almost every aspect of habitat and environment, this is a refreshing and inspiring point of view. Parkour opens new ways of thinking about moving through the world. It inspires us to think and feel more flexibly, to improvise our relationships and our philosophies of life. It every case, the challenge is the same; living with grace, power and fluidity, constantly adjusting our movement and position to suit conditions. Ultimately, this is a profoundly spiritual discipline.

Health opportunism

In the world of health and lifestyle, improv is vital. We all know how the process works: We start with the best of intentions, trying to fit the details of our lives into some kind of program, routine or regimen. We want to be in control of our health, so we organize our food, our exercise sessions, our meditation and our visits with health providers. Everything in its place; all of our various health-promoting activities laid out in the right order at the right time. Some of us even log it all on a spreadsheet.

But it never quite works. In fact, unless you're a professional athlete with a team manager, it hardly works at all. Life is always throwing monkeywrenches into our best-laid plans. You've got a healthy meal all planned out, but someone in the family wants pizza and ice cream. You're all primed to go to the gym, but the boss says you've got to work late. You really want to have a quiet evening in meditation and contemplation, but your spouse wants to see an action-adventure movie.

Things get messy. No matter how rational our calculations, no matter how detailed our spreadsheets, our plans always seem to break down in the face of reality. Local changes are bad enough, but in a hyper-connected world even distant events can force us to abandon our precious and carefully designed plans. We try to fight the chaos, but it never seems to work. Entropy is always having its way with us.

The practice here is to work with what we've got. Be an opportunist. Instead of forcing your will onto the universe, try waiting and watching for opportunities to present themselves. In this way, you become a hunter of experience, scanning the grassland, ready to seize whatever game might happen to come along. After all, you just never know how events might unfold. If an opportunity arises, act.

When you open your imagination, you'll begin to see possibility everywhere. For example, consider your need for physical movement. Even when your schedule is disrupted and you can't get to the gym or studio, there's almost always a handy alternative. Steps and stairs are almost everywhere, in parks and parking lots. Open ground is really all you need for some squats, some skipping and jumping. In this practice, there's no concern about official time and place; it's all about using what's there. As they say in parkour, "The world is my playground." Use what you've got.

Food is another ideal domain for improv. Obviously, some of us like to manage every last molecule that passes our lips; we labor hard on every detail of shopping, selection, comparison and preparation. In moderation, this effort is laudable, but beyond a certain point it becomes a stressful burden and in the extreme, ridiculous. The problem is that out in the messy real world, food availability and quality is unpredictable and often uncontrollable. Who knows what evil lurks in the office luncheon or the school potluck, to say nothing about travel to distant cities and foreign lands?

This uncertainty is never going to go away. Anytime we eat in a community setting, we give up a certain measure of control. But this is not the end of the game. We can always make choices and we can always be alert for opportunity. As nutritional hunters, we lay in wait for the choicest offerings to come our way: the fresh and yummy vegetables, the well-prepared salads and, if so-inclined, the best of the grass-fed meats. It's all out there.

So too are the opportunities for meditation. There's no need to wait for the perfect class or teacher; there are always gaps in the action and space in our days for contemplation. Instead of filling those gaps with mindless busy work or compulsive distraction, you can simply sit down and pay attention to your breath and the activity of your mind. No special setting, time or props are required.

No matter what dimension of health you happen to be interested in, the art of opportunism is always the same. It all begins with situational awareness. What is happening right here, right now? What is possible? Can you reframe this moment from "dead time" or chaos to something more meaningful? Most importantly, get out of whatever pigeon hole you happen to be in and release your attachment to the notion that things must look a certain way.

The enemy is never wrong

The key to success in improv is mind-set or rather, the lack of mind-set. Fluidity of body, mind and spirit are essential. Once we get stuck and begin to fixate on any one condition, expectation or outcome, we make ourselves vulnerable to changing conditions.

This is a common theme in the martial arts, of course. In the *Tao te Ching*, Lao Tzu wrote "The highest good is like water. Because water excels in benefiting the myriad creatures without contending with them and settles where none would like to be, it comes close to the way."

In combat, the goal is to maintain our physical, mental and emotional fluidity. Keep your agility. Maintain your dynamism. Don't assume, don't get wrapped up in any particular point of view. Whatever happens, keep moving.

A wise sensei once reminded us of this fluid approach by teaching "The enemy is never wrong." In other words, the enemy just is. Stop thinking of your opponent as a static object; in fact, he is changing in every instant. Your mind may well rush to judgment about the nature of your adversary, but once you get stuck in evaluation, you'll lose your ability to adapt.

This is a call for adaptability. Your opponent is clever and dynamic; he's always trying to throw a monkeywrench into your positions and strategies. So too for life. In this, our sensei might well say "Conditions are never wrong. Conditions just are."

Similarly, we extend the metaphor to every other relationship we might encounter. Instead of fixating on static qualities or judging the merits of circumstance, we simply accept what comes. Maintain your adaptability. In this spirit, remind yourself "My habitat is never wrong." "My culture is never wrong." "The people around me are never wrong."

On the face of it, these assertions may well seem preposterous. Of course our conditions, institutions, organizations and communities are often less than ideal. Of course the people around us are flawed. But this is beside the point. This point is to not get stuck. By blaming others or our environment, we give away our power. We've framed the problem in a way that almost guarantees stress and even failure. Conditions now control us. We've created defeat before we've even begun.

So get over the rightness and wrongness of your conditions and your adversaries. Start moving and creating.

The art

Improv may well sound like the ultimate in skill and an ideal way to live, but there are some real challenges here. The most obvious is exposure and risk. When we rely exclusively on our wits in the moment, we make ourselves vulnerable to the unknown. When we yield control to our deep bodies, we can't really predict what's going to happen. We might well make fools of ourselves with errors, awkwardness, stupidity, gaffes, inefficiency and waste. When you make stuff up in improv, there's a very real good chance that you're going to blow it at some point. But this is the price we have to pay for authentic creativity. There's always going to be an element of risk.

For improv to work, you must give yourself permission. You must cut yourself loose to produce a lot of material, a lot of ideas and a lot of guesses about what might work. You may be inclined to edit your work at the very instant of creation, inhibiting the flow before it even begins. But for improv to work, you've got to let it go. As Edward DeBono, author of *Lateral Thinking* put it, "The only way to have a good idea is to have a lot of ideas." So teach yourself to generate. Spew. Don't hold back. Embrace the risk and the uncertainty. Remember: no ambiguity, no art, no adventure.

Clearly this practice calls for a special sense of compassion for ourselves as well as a sense of humor. The art lies in relationship and attitude; we need to cut ourselves some slack. In particularly, it's essential to give up our idealism; the quest for perfection chokes off our creativity at the source and in so doing, defeats itself. Better to make peace with our missteps, blunders and awkward moves right now. As Maria Montessori put it, "It is well to cultivate a friendly feeling towards error, to treat it as a companion inseparable from our lives, a something having a purpose." Likewise, psychotherapist Sheldon Kopp "We must give ourselves permission to blunder, to fail, and make fools of ourselves every day for the rest of our lives."

Release yourself. Make up a bunch of stuff. Most of it is going to be worthless, but some of it is going to be beautiful. Repeat the process a few times and you'll have something you can live with. Repeat a thousand times more and you may well end up with a masterpiece. But whatever you do, practice giving up control. Trust your body and trust your training. Your body will deliver. The harder you train, the more you can relax. The harder you train, the more you can trust.

And above all, get over yourself. Self-consciousness is the great improv killer. As soon as you get out of your own way, the movement will begin to flow. As Stephen Nachmanovitch put it in *Free Play: Improvisation in Life and Art* "For art to appear, we have to disappear."

Lesson 17

Find the sweet spot

Everything in excess is opposed by nature.

Hippocrates

Proportion is the heart of beauty.

Ken Follett

The Pillars of the Earth

It's a human universal.

In every culture and tradition, people have pondered the challenges of living and no matter the details, we always seem to find ourselves coming back to the virtues of balance. We recognize dangers of extremity and we look for ways to adjust, moving back and forth on the teeter-totter of life and mastery. The art, it seems, lies in finding the center.

All the great philosophers have made this journey. Goldilocks was typical. On a journey through the woods, she happened across a house with a "Little, Small, Wee Bear, a Middle-sized Bear, and a Great, Huge Bear." She discovered three chairs, three bowls of porridge and three beds, sampled each in succession, each time finding the middle one to be "just right." In modern usage, we use the "Goldilocks principle" to describe any situation which is "just right" in some way. A "Goldilocks planet" is neither too close to nor too far from a star to rule out life, while a "Goldilocks economy" is one that sustains moderate growth and low inflation. Likewise, we would expect that "Goldilocks health" would be something that comes down right in the middle between "hypo" and "hyper."

In ancient Greece, Aristotle described "the golden mean" as the middle between extremes of excess and deficiency. Courage was a prime example; if taken to excess it becomes recklessness, but if deficient is becomes cowardice. Similarly, we find the Roman goddess Lady Justice, the personification of moral judgment in legal systems, frequently pictured carrying a set of scales, implying a balanced approach in resolving disputes. Benjamin Franklin listed moderation as one of "The 13 virtues." Likewise, Jesuit philosopher Baltasar Gracián observed in *The Art of Worldly Wisdom*, "People of great ability keep extremes far apart, so that there is a long distance between them. They always keep in the middle of their caution, so they take time to act."

On the other side of the world, Eastern sages came to similar conclusions. Taoist philosophers taught that there must be a balance between yin and yang and that extremes lead to their opposites. There is always a rising and a falling away; attempts to maximize any one thing always leads to distortion and imbalance somewhere else. Similarly, master swordsman Miyamato Musashi wrote in *The Book of Five Rings* "An elevated spirit is weak and a low spirit is weak." Confucius promoted the Doctrine of the Mean and the guiding principle that one should never act in excess. In Buddhism, Siddhartha Gautama famously described The Middle Way as a path of moderation between the extremes of sensual indulgence and self-mortification. His favorite example was the musical instrument; to play well, the string must be neither too tight or too loose. In every case, the art lies in the center.

A world of sweet spots

As we develop an interest in balance and sweet spots, we begin to see them almost everywhere we look. The classic example is exercise: too little and we suffer the perils of sedentary living and lifestyle disease, too much and we beat ourselves up with over-training and over-use.

In the world of nutrition, we see a similar theme. Beyond the sweet spot, substances that are nutritious in moderate amounts can become profoundly toxic. Protein, carbohydrates, red wine, even water; each can nourish us, but only up to a point. The same principle holds true for food quantity. Food is essential, but digestion is also expensive; if we over-tax the system, we rob metabolic resources from other parts of the body.

We also see a sweet spot in sun exposure and outdoor living. Obviously, sunlight is a powerful driver of Vitamin D production and has a profoundly beneficial effect on our mood, outlook and happiness. But beyond a certain point, these benefits begin to disappear, putting us at risk for heat stroke, dehydration and melanoma.

The same principle holds true in the biomechanical properties of the human body. Every joint has an optimal range of motion. If that range is limited by tight muscles, tendons or ligaments, pain and injury are the result. But if the joint is hyper-mobile, it becomes vulnerable to dislocation; this leads to inefficiencies and pain in other areas.

We also hear about sweet spots in the world of toxicology and environmental health. In complex living systems such as human bodies and habitats, no substance is inherently toxic or polluting; it all depends on the concentration. That's why toxicologists often teach that "the dose makes the poison" and "the dose makes the tonic."

Our experience of psychological engagement and flow shows a similar pattern. When we're underchallenged, we're bored and disengaged. Add the right amount of challenge and we rise to the occasion and become fully absorbed in our work. Increase the challenge too far and we go over the top, into a zone of stress, anxiety, error and exhaustion.

Similarly, there's a sweet spot for risk. Too little and we're bored and uncreative; too much and we subject ourselves to injury and death. So too in the world of social psychology. Tribal affiliation, obedience and conformity are vital elements in building a sense of unity and the ability to do great works in common. But these qualities can backfire. Beyond the tipping point, they lead to mindless groupthink and in the extreme, atrocity.

Meet the inverse U curve

All of our sweet spots show the same kind of pattern over time, a pattern most famously described by the classic inverse-U curve. We see it in every living system and it generally express itself the same way: There's a period of increase in which a process builds on itself. Elements, substances, efforts and ideas combine to produce a growth effect, a bounty or a payoff. This leads into a sweet spot of ideal or optimal function. Further increases in concentration, effort or intensity lead to diminishing returns as we approach a tipping point. This is followed by a reversal of the original benefit as the system begins to degenerate into illness, injury or chaos.

We see the inverse U in almost every encounter we have with life. It is so common in fact that we might well wonder if there is *any* aspect of human and biological life that doesn't conform to it. Time after time, we discover that "more is better" and other ultimate "solutions" always fail when pushed far enough. Extremism, in other words, is almost always a vice.

One of the most obvious examples in human experience is stress. A brief tour of the curve shows a familiar pattern: At the lower left end we're in a state of complete relaxation. There are no threats or time pressure, no anxiety and no worries. This state can be pleasant, but for learning and performance, it's clearly sub-optimal. A wide range of studies have shown conclusively that we actually need stress hormones to function at our best. When researchers remove the adrenal glands from rodents for example, they (the rodents!) no longer pump stress hormones and in turn, become incapable of learning new tasks.

As levels of stress hormones rise, good things start to happen to body, brain, cognition and even spirit. Metabolic fuels are released into the bloodstream to feed our attentive brains and muscular movements we need to perform. At the same time, our brains secrete "neurotrophic factors," chemicals that actually stimulate the growth of new nerve cells, dendrites and synapses.

In this sweet spot, learning feels like an adventure. We're playfully engaged and curious, but also flexible. Our minds become athletic, powerful and agile. Memory is enhanced; detail and meaning are easily stored away for later retrieval. Our attention is focused and engaged; we enter into a state of "flow." We have the energy to pursue strange and wonderful flights of fancy or odd recombinations of unlikely elements. Our sense of humor is up and running. Not only that, our social and emotional intelligence is enhanced. We're attentive and open-minded; other people become welcome participants in our curiosities and projects.

This sweet spot is a wonderful place, but if stress is sustained over long periods, the effect begins to reverse itself. Beyond a certain point, our sweet stress becomes distress and physical and cognitive functions begin to decline. The effects will be subtle at first, but as stress deepens, the fall-off becomes progressively steeper and more destructive, to mind, body, spirit and the totality of our lives.

The erosion of performance begins with energy depletion; we find that it takes increased effort simply to get the same results that we're accustomed to. Our cognitive, psychological and spiritual resources are drained, causing both greater fatigue and greater effort. Memory and learning begin to diminish and it becomes tougher to absorb and recall new facts and material. And now we're spending more and more of our physiological reserves just to stay on top of things: We're "burning up the furniture to heat the house."

At the same time, physical recovery begins to decline. Our bodies are slower to recover from workouts, injury and illness. This leads to decreased physical and psychological resilience, which makes us increasingly vulnerable to all sorts of stressors, even those that we would normally weather without a second thought. Aches and pains seem worse than normal and we begin to worry about the trajectory of our health.

It gets worse. Over time, chronic activation of the stress response inhibits the growth and connectivity of precious neurons and even damages key brain centers involved in learning, memory and impulse control. Key neurotransmitters such as dopamine become depleted, which leads to a loss of pleasure in life. This leaves us less cognitive and emotional energy to investigate new ideas or to drive disciplined training. In turn, learning slows, both in depth and breadth.

Over time, our mood becomes increasingly serious, then grim. We become more conservative and risk-averse, or impulsive. Our social behavior becomes increasingly strained and challenging; we may move towards isolation. And in this process, our sense of play and humor begin to decline, then disappears entirely. We stop laughing. We stop loving life.

Obviously and notoriously, these stress-related performance declines drive us deeper into stress in a vicious cycle. Ineffective performance exposes us to more stress which degrades our performance further and so on. At this point, continued effort may be completely counter-productive; "trying harder" may simply make our situations worse.

Eventually, when stress hormone exposure becomes chronic, we enter the dark world of the extreme right side, a world marked by full-blown states of disease, dysfunction and depression. At this point, stress hormones can actually become neurotoxic, endangering neurons and even killing them outright. Chronic exposure erodes the structure and function of the hippocampus, a crucial brain center involved in explicit, short-term memory and learning. Together, this can lead to a host of neurological disorders ranging from minor attention problems and premature cognitive decline all the way to full-blown dementia.

Even worse, stress hormones also become psychotoxic, leading to anger management problems, impulse control problems and substance abuse, especially alcoholism. High concentrations enhance the sensitivity of the amygdala, a brain center responsible for fear and vigilance. The afflicted individual begins to "catastrophize " his predicament, imagining worst-case scenarios in every direction. And of course, he will behave accordingly, with increasing levels of suspicion and paranoia.

Finally, when the stress stimulus is inescapable and endured over long periods of time, we may also develop a condition called "learned helplessness." In this state, we begin to generalize our lack of control to other circumstances, even to those cases when control is in fact possible. This state is marked by a sense of resignation, apathy and lethargy.

Mindfulness

There's a lot we can learn about life from studying the inverse U. First, no matter what your art or discipline happens to be, it's safe to assume that there's a zone of optima and a sweet spot. No matter what you're dealing with, whether it's substances, effort or experiences, there's almost certainly a similar pattern of increase-tipping point-decrease. You're always *somewhere* on the inverse U.

The trick, of course, is to know where you are. The art lies in being sensitive to the curve and learning how to recognize your position. In some instances, it might be possible to measure your position, but in most real world cases, things get complex in a hurry and calculation becomes a burden. A better barometer is your own body. Feel your position with your gut, your organs, your breath and the activity of your mind. Listen for the subtle signals in your mind-body-spirit that tell you "hypo," "hyper" or "optimal."

Likewise, be alert to beauty and feelings of pleasure. When you're in the sweet spot, things just look right and feel right. This is a place of equanimity and equipoise. You feel calm, but energized. You're powerful, but fluid. You're willing to move forward into challenge, but you're equally willing to remain still and quiet.

Above all, be mindful of tipping points. Your time in the sweet spot is wonderful and you may well be inclined to push matters just a little bit further. With just a little more effort, a little more attention, a little more of everything, you might be tempted to "go to the next level." But beware; in all likelihood, things will flatten out, returns will diminish and before long, the system will reverse itself.

The classic case is stress. Be mindful of these warning signs:

- Anhedonia (loss of pleasure)
- Neophobia (avoidance of new things) and perseveration (repetition of established habit patterns)
- Reduced ambiguity tolerance (black and white thinking)
- Social withdrawal and isolation
- Cognitive distortions, especially over-generalizing and small-picture, short-term thinking
- Physical lethargy, poor sleep quality, decreased resilience
- Irritability, "making mountains out of molehills"
- Catastrophizing; going straight to the worst case scenario
- Decreased sense of humor and play
- Poor concentration and attention span
- Impulsive behaviors, reduced self-control
- Decision resistance and procrastination

Recognizing the tipping point is always a judgment call. Experience will help, as it will increase your sensitivity and your ability to see the trends and trajectories of your efforts.

In any case, beware the enemies of balance, the seductions that pull us out of the sweet spots in our lives. Our brains our impressed by the spectacular, the unusual and the incredible, but these qualities can distract us from the optimal middle. Extremity gets our attention, but it also threatens our balance. Outrageous claims of unlimited anything violate everything we know about how living systems actually work. Attempts to maximize any one quality or dimension will eventually fail when they reach a tipping point. The lesson: beware of extremism in any form.

No matter what happens, keep your eye on the dynamism that's inherent in every system. In particular, be aware of all forms of stasis, especially your own belief in a static identity. To say "I am X" is a commonplace statement, but X is just a static point that ignores the fluidity of the living world. The more strongly we attach our identity to any particular quality, role or activity, the more we remove ourselves from the flux and flow of life. This in turn makes us increasingly vulnerable to winding up outside of the sweet spot.

Remember too that no one ever "achieves" balance in any meaningful way. Even the most highly-trained dancer, poised on one foot, is engaged in a constant, incredibly sophisticated process of sensory-motor adjustment. To the external observer, the posture may appear perfectly stable, but it never really "locks in." No matter how things look in this moment, they will change.

Lesson 18

Carve a new path

As a single footstep will not make a path on the earth, so a single thought will not make a pathway in the mind. To make a deep physical path, we walk again and again. To make a deep mental path, we must think over and over the kind of thoughts we wish to dominate our lives.

Henry David Thoreau

Habit is habit, and not to be flung out of the window by any man, but coaxed downstairs a step at a time.

Mark Twain

Pudd'nhead Wilson's Calendar

As we refine our training with quality reps, dedication and curiosity, our efforts begin to pay off and our skills begin to mature. Things go well at first, but after a few years or decades of training, we come up against the challenges of habit. Behaviors and movements that once served us well may lose their usefulness and may even get in the way of our ability to live the beautiful adventure.

Habits are fascinating creatures that can both empower us and enslave us; understanding how they work is essential to the development of a beautiful practice. First the good news: Habits are fundamental to skill development. In fact, the brain is an incredibly powerful habit-forming organ. At every second of every day, our nervous systems build patterns of sensation and motor activity, always building on what came before, always seeking more efficient ways to process information into adaptive behavior. As we've seen, even the simplest actions, repeated a few times, eases the path for similar, subsequent actions.

Once established, these habits can serve us well. They liberate our attention, allowing us to scan ahead to new challenges and opportunities. In fact, mastery in any art or discipline consists primarily of creating a "body of habit," a set of carefully-constructed sensory-motor routines that can be called up instantly, without having to be reconstructed from scratch. Without habit, there would be no skill, no artistry and no mastery.

Another great thing about habits is that they give us a neuro-cognitive surplus, an excess capacity that we can use however we want. Once our basic skills and behaviors are all wired up, we can simply let those habits run as we turn our attention to other things. This is a truly wonderful thing because it allows us to do more with our bodies and minds. We don't have to re-wire our behaviors every morning; we can simply turn them on when the time is right and let them go.

But of course, the upside is also a downside. As we train ourselves with repetition, we etch patterns of action ever more deeply into our bodies, attention and life experience. If conditions change, these habitual patterns may become a liability, locking our attention and behavior into a non-functional, displeasing pattern. Patterns that once served us well may come to imprison us and limit how far we can grow.

Here it's essential to remember that the plastic brain is largely indifferent to what sort of patterns it records; it has no particular bias towards "good habits" or "bad habits." Experience drives the system; our plasticity is "use dependent." Cells fire together and then wire together and the brain doesn't much care what form those patterns take. This is the beauty of it and also the challenge. With repetition, we can learn anything, functional or not, beautiful or otherwise.

The problem comes with our so-called bad habits, especially those lifestyle behaviors that seem to wreak so much havoc with our bodies and spirit. We eat impulsively, we sloth around for days at a time, we drink too much, we gossip about every little thing, and we feel guilty and uneasy about all of it. In fact, these habits give us a creepy feeling that we're really not in control of our bodies, our behavior or our lives. And the older we get, the more we feel it.

Individual habits are bad enough, but the challenge becomes even more difficult when they become embedded into larger patterns of daily life behavior. As we grow into adulthood, we take the individual habits learned in childhood and link them together in sequence to perform the more complex behaviors we need for our working and personal lives. In effect, we develop a "habit stream" that we play out each day.

It's all so familiar: We wake up, then do the shower-dress-coffee-food-kids-car-drive-work routine. The details don't matter much; it's the fact that these habits fit together in one larger pattern that we play out over and over again. Over time, bigger and bigger chunks of our days become automated and habitual.

The problem is that when we're immersed in a habit stream, we become increasingly mindless; big chunks of our behavior drop from the radar of consciousness. We may free up parts of our awareness for other challenges, but we also become captive to our unconscious behavior. Swept along in the flow of habit, we may even loose our ability to change. Over time, this can lead to ineffectiveness, unhappiness and even catastrophe.

The topography of habit

Habit formation is a landscape, sculpted by water. Every action and every thought is like a drop of water falling onto a patch of earth. Naturally, the water seeks a lower level, going where gravity takes it, forming the beginnings of a rivulet. As drops continue to fall, they tend to follow the same rivulet, digging it slightly deeper with their passage. More showers, more rain, and now the rivulet becomes a stream.

Of course, as every school child knows, the passage of water continues to deepen the stream as it gathers ever more water to itself and eventually forms an entire watershed, a valley and possibly even a canyon. Over the centuries, the land pulls in greater amounts of water, carving deeper and deeper into the earth. In *The Emotional Life of Your Brain*, Richard Davidson used the same metaphor to describe the power of attention to resculpt the terrain of habit: "Mindfulness meditation carves new channels in the streambeds of the mind."

Every moment in our lives is a drop of water; every action and experience deepens a rivulet, a valleys or a canyon in the nervous system. These streams and canyons can save us tremendous labor, but they also become increasingly tyrannical and hard to modify. Unless we take intentional action to the contrary, these ruts, valleys and canyons will set the trajectory of our entire lives.

Unfortunately, some of our habits persist and some of them turn out to be wasteful, ugly, maladaptive or even dangerous. We find ourselves deep in the canyon of repetitive behavior, frustrated by our inability to do what we want with our bodies and our lives. We wish for something better, but it's no easy thing. We try to climb the canyon walls of habit, but if we relax our vigilance, we're swept back downstream, even deeper than before.

Obviously, this is the case for our most notorious "bad habits," but it's also true for more subtle habits of attention, posture, sensation, language, movements, social inclinations and worldview. The further we go into the canyons, the tougher it is to reverse course. This is the shadow side of neuroplasticity.

Create and revise

Given the paradoxical nature of training and habit, it soon becomes obvious that if we want to pursue artistry in any realm, two complementary skills are required: the ability to create habits and the ability to revise them. We need the discipline of precise, accurate reps to etch the appropriate grooves into our mind-body, but we also need the ability to abandon those grooves and create new ones as conditions change.

Musicianship provides the perfect example of this two-handed strategy. On the one hand, the musician must perform disciplined reps in order to develop a habit in the first place; scales, chords and passages are the most important rivulets in his mind-body. But over time, those early skills and grooves, even if well-formed, will need to be fine-tuned or even abandoned in favor of something more appropriate, meaningful or promising. And in this sense, every accomplished musician is primarily in the business of making and breaking habits. Learn, unlearn, re-learn and repeat.

As for creating new habits, this is conceptually easy. All we have to do is repeat some action a few times and the rivulet begins to form. This process is most powerful when accompanied by intense attention, emotion and desire. Of course, no one gets it right the first time. Every human nervous system is probabilistic and fallible. In the struggle to learn, the student tries her best and generates a series of neural guesses, best approximations of cellular activity that will produce the desired result. On our early attempts, we may fire thousands of neurons and synapses in a shotgun effort to wire the right pattern. With guidance, we gradually narrow down the neural pattern until the signal is clear and precise.

But we don't always wire it up the right way and even if we do, sophisticated neural patterns require maintenance and re-minding. The cells may well have "wired together" as desired, but if the circuit goes unused, it will begin to decay, just as an abandoned watercourse will eventually fill in with windblown dust and vegetation. This is why repeated efforts and refreshers are vital. If we want our skills to remain sharp, we need to go back up to the ridge line periodically and mindfully place our water drop in just the right place.

The challenge here is that there's often a substantial psychophysical cost to habit revision. It takes energy to drive our thoughts and behaviors down a new neural watercourse. And if we're depleted in some way, the challenge becomes even more difficult. This is why stress can be a real lose-lose situation. We may well need new habits to escape our predicament and create more beautiful behaviors, but stress eats away at the cognitive-spiritual surplus that we need to re-shape our actions.

So how do we revise our so-called bad habits? The classic advice is to simply allow the pattern in question to go dormant, a tactic that might be called "strategic atrophy." If we can suspend use of the circuitry, even for a short time, it will begin to fade and weaken. In fact, the actual tissue of the circuit will slowly begin to return to its original, pre-habit condition. Synaptic membranes will become less sensitive to their upstream inputs and insulating myelin wrappings around nerve fibers will begin to thin out, slowing the speed of the impulse.

This process takes time and reps, just as it took time and reps to build the circuit in the first place. Likewise, such sustained disuse will require intentional, conscious control and persistence. This, of course, is much easier said than done. Intentional disuse requires sustained, mindful attention, strong desire, constant monitoring and maybe even coaching. You've got to want it, and you've got to keep wanting it over and over again. But ultimately, disuse will succeed: cells that no longer fire together won't stay wired together.

Monkeywrench your habits

The simple act of doing something different can also be powerfully effective in habit revision. In *The As If Principle: The Radically New Approach to Changing Your Life*, psychologist Richard Wiseman describes this as the "Do Something Different" approach. This method simply challenges us to do something, anything, outside our normal daily habit stream. DSD works by promoting attention and mindfulness. Brushing your teeth with your non-dominant hand may not seem like a significant behavioral change, but it does require a touch more attention. Over time, the effect begins to add up: if you do several DSD actions during the course of your day, you'll become more alert and wakeful. In the process, you won't feel so deeply mired in habit. Even better, you'll have a greater sense of control.

In this practice, we monkeywrench our routines, intentionally. The idea here is to introduce some novelty into your established pattern of behavior, something that will challenge your old habits and force you to develop new ones. Travel, new professions, moving to a new city or country, new languages; all of these challenges force us out of ruts and put us in a position to create new ones.

In a way, this approach may well feel semi-crazy. After all, you've worked for years, even decades, to build up a set of workable routines for getting things done. Your behaviors might not be perfectly efficient, but they are working. But if you want to take your performance to the next level, you might have to scramble the mix. Novelty will do just that.

Similarly, crisis and catastrophe will also help to revise your habit repertoire. Like it or not, these events will shake things up and force you to go outside our normal, reactive patterns of living. Accidents and screw ups can also be extremely valuable in this respect. Disease, divorce and dislocation are traumatic, but they can also force us into a new way of looking at the world and in turn, greater mindfulness. You will suffer, but you are resilient. Over time, your body and your brain will create new behaviors and link them together in new, more functional ways, ways that might well serve you better.

Guides, teachers and coaches

Of course, hands-on guidance is another powerful way to revise our habit patterns. Coaches, teachers and mentors stand outside of our habitual patterns and can help us see from a new perspective. They can help us take the necessary time, plan our actions, execute and review. Most importantly, they can monitor our attention and help us get back to our creative focal points when our minds begin to wander.

Solo training efforts, no matter how well-intentioned or focused, tend to weaken over time, as we fall back into the familiar and comfortable. All of us prefer to practice what we're good at and we spend more and more time deepening those grooves instead of expanding out into unexplored terrain. We fall into the habit of habit.

Teachers and coaches know the patterns that are most important for long-term skill development. By directing our attention and action back to these patterns, over and over, they helps us carve new rivulets that are more adaptive and appropriate. In a sense, the teacher is simply the first drop of water on the landscape. By demonstrating the ideal form and describing the ideal watercourse, he leads the water drops of the our experience. As the student follows, he develops habits that are both true and powerful.

Habit revision is a muscle

Ultimately, habit revision is a learnable skill. We get better at revising habit by practicing habit revision. We train this muscle by using it, one habit at a time. Start by revising one simple habit. Pick an easy one. Switch your fork to the other hand, stack the dishes in a different order, rake the leaves to the left instead of the right. Once you've succeeded and the new habit is locked in, try another one. Just like training your body itself, it will keep getting easier.

There are no real tricks to this art. It always gets back to attention; there is no substitute for mindfulness. Keep paying attention to smaller and more subtle aspects of your life. Slow down, do less. Take more pauses in the action. Take more time for the intentional discipline of preview-execute-review. Question your behaviors. Do one thing at a time and resist your tendency to accelerate. Stop layering activities on top of one another.

Along the way, be sure to look towards something bigger. As solitary individuals, our best intentions are often seduced by voices of sloth, gluttony and indulgence. As a soloist, you may well feel powerless to make the changes on your own. But when you couple your experience with something larger, a new sense of power will emerge. Suddenly, modifying your deeply entrenched patterns will feel less onerous. Whether you do it for your children, your families, your community, your team or your country, it makes no difference. You might even do it for the sake of your art, your discipline, the biosphere or for the sake of beauty itself. No matter the specifics, a larger purpose will make your habits seem smaller. Pesky lifestyle habits become less significant when you've got bigger fish to fry.

Without question, the single most important element in habit revision is your relationship with safety and security. Habits, even if they're ineffective or dysfunctional, provide a sense of comfort; they may not serve us well, but at least they're familiar. When times get hard, we can always retreat to the comfortable world of routine. Even though these behaviors may not take us where we want to go, we won't have to face the challenge of the unknown.

Embracing ambiguity is no easy path, of course. As Ed Buryn put it in *Vagabonding in the USA*, a certain measure of courage is required:

> *Routines and habits are the Known, protecting us from the Unknown. Habits tame the raw wilderness of existence into the civilized comforts of everyday life. Unfortunately, as we all know, habits gradually domesticate all the wildness and energy out of life. So much energy gets bound up in routines and habituated patterns, keeping them alive, that your life goes dead instead. Thus, if you want to discover again the wild side of life, you have to leave 'home;' you have to break or dissolve your habits in order to release the energy locked up inside them.*

The fundamental question becomes: What is your relationship with ambiguity and uncertainty? If you're motivated by fear, you're more likely to fall back into the well of security and habit. If you're motivated by wonder, curiosity and the lure of the beautiful adventure, you'll be willing to expose yourself. Get familiar with ambiguity, get comfortable with the fundamental insecurity of life. It'll make all of your habit revisions that much easier

Lesson 19

Widen your circle

We are people through other people.

Bantu description of *ubuntu*

Treat everyone you meet as if they were you.

Doug Dillon

As we all know, the human is an intensely social animal. We like to affiliate, we like to gossip, we like to live and work together, even when we drive each other crazy. But to say that we're social doesn't really capture the true extent of our connectedness. Not only are we social, we're radically social. We're social in ways that extend far beyond our obvious desire for conversation, family, team and community. There's something extremely powerful at work in our social nature, something that borders on the metaphysical.

The social revolution

It's easy to be fooled by appearances. The human body, after all, looks and feels like a stand-alone object. We experience the physical self as a unitary organism, a distinct creature that stands on its own two feet, looking out at the world. You look in the mirror and there it is–you, staring back, looking just like an individual.

That perception, compelling that it may happen to be, is at best a fragmentary glimpse of reality, even an illusion. You, grasshopper, are not really an individual at all. Like it or not, your body is part of a much larger social whole. At this very moment, your body is being influenced and sculpted, for better or for worse, by your friends, your friends' friends, and even more outlandishly, by your friends friends' friends. People you don't even know are influencing your physiology, your behavior and your performance. Incredible as it may seem, your body is not entirely your own.

The emerging disciplines of social neuroscience and interpersonal neurobiology have led us to a surprising, but unavoidable conclusion: The thing that we call "the individual" is really just a fiction of appearance, reinforced by Western culture. What these disciplines now reveal is an ancient, indigenous, relational view of the human body. Just as we are embedded in habitat, we are also embedded in a social ecosystem. We co-create our minds, our bodies and our health. This is not mere metaphor; it is now a well-established fact.

This may well come as a surprise. After all, our bodies look like individual units, tightly wrapped with a protective skin. Openings allow for the passage of solids, liquids and gasses, but otherwise, we feel like a closed system. But in fact, we are incredibly permeable to the social world. The "stuff" of social interaction flows into and out of our bodies constantly: emotions, non-verbal gestures, postures, facial expressions, words, ideas, memes, and most of all stories. In a very real sense, we are open systems.

It starts with emotional contagion, but this is just the beginning. Emotion shapes cognition and the actual physiology of who we are. As soon as we communicate with other people in any form, we make ourselves vulnerable to their moods, their ideas and their inclinations. They sculpt our bodies and our lives, just as we sculpt theirs. It seems astonishing that unknown people, several degrees of separation away from us, could actually be shaping our physical selves, but the reality is now impossible to ignore or deny.

Popular science writers now describe an "interpersonal nervous system" that connects people across space via a "social synapse." Louis Cozolino, author of *The Neuroscience of Human Relationships*, tells us that "the human brain is a social organ" and suggests that it's folly to study human brains in isolation. We are so thoroughly interconnected that it's now tempting to say that, in the living world "there are no single human brains."

The resonance circuit

The fact of social influence and contagion is clear, but how does it actually work? How do our friends friend's friends influence the tissue of our bodies, our thoughts and our behavior? How do we influence theirs? The short answer is that the process is mediated by the body. In other words, our social nature is fundamentally physical. Our bodies are highly sensitive emotion-detection instruments that register social information in the world around us.

In *The Neurobiology of We*, Daniel Siegel describes a "resonance circuit" that mediates the process. In a drastically simplified form, it goes something like this: We observe the movements, postures, eye gaze and micro-expressions of other people's bodies. This information is picked up by mirror neurons in the cortex of the brain and relayed downward into the limbic, emotional centers. From here, emotional information flows deeper into the observer's body where it can be experienced and felt. This gut feeling allows us to actually experience a simulation of what others are experiencing. In turn, this felt experience flows back upwards via the vagus nerve into our brains where it acts on the prefrontal cortex. Ultimately, this affects the way that we regulate our behavior, our bodies and our behavior.

This resonance circuit makes it possible for us to sense, even live, the emotions of those around us. In turn, this has real physical and physiological consequences. With this lived experience, hormones flow, neurotransmitters cascade, the brain rewires itself and behavior changes. Ultimately, our health and fitness go along for the ride.

Naked on the grassland

We might well wonder where our hyper-social nature came from, but when we reflect on our natural history, the picture becomes clear. Just imagine that you're born into the wild grasslands of East Africa, entirely naked to the world. Your skin is soft, your senses untrained, your limbs nearly useless. You are, to put it in the most elemental terms, several pounds of high-quality protein, protein that is constantly craved by the predators and carnivores that prowl nearby. Unless someone intervenes on your behalf, you will almost certainly be consumed before nightfall. You are, to put it in a single word, exposed.

You are well aware of this fact. You can sense the nakedness of your body and the extremity of your predicament. Your new world feels vast, unknown and dangerous. Your nakedness is not just physical; it's psycho-spiritual. Exposure dominates your consciousness.

At this point, you really have only one option for survival: attach to a caregiver and do it fast. Somehow, you've got to get someone to take care of you, someone bigger, stronger and more knowledgeable than yourself. If you can do this, you'll be able to stay alive and maybe even send your genes into the future. Fortunately, Mom is probably on hand and she happens to like your funny face and big eyes. She'll take care of you and with luck, you'll grow up big and strong.

But this is only the first step in survival. Even after you've grown to maturity, your environment is still dangerous and finding food remains a serious business. Dangerous animals are everywhere. Solitary humans are extremely vulnerable. So, you live and hunt with your tribe, a group of perhaps fifty to one hundred individuals.

This tribe is your primary source of safety, survival and life. Not only does your group offer a buffer against exposure, it also embodies the precious knowledge, experience and oral tradition that is vital to understanding habitat, finding food and making your way in the world. Without this knowledge, you are almost sure to perish. And so, develop a deep and abiding interest in the bodies and behaviors of the people around you. You watch what they watch, and pay extremely close attention to what they do and how they behave. In this process, your tribe begins to function as an extended nervous system, helping you learn more about the world around you. It comes as no surprise to find that we are hyper-social to this very day. We are social because our lives depended on it.

Under the influence

As we come to understand the origins and depth of our social nature, several powerful implications begin to come into focus. First, we are always "under the influence" of social living. Even if we live in relative isolation or in very small groups, we are still subject to the flow of emotion and meaning that courses through organizations, communities and the totality of the human population. Our minds, bodies and spirits are constantly being shaped, not just by our immediate friends, but also by remote social forces.

At the same time, the inverse is also true. Our ideas and behaviors are fundamentally influential; almost everything we do, say or think has the potential to shape others: turns of phrase, memes, gestures, behaviors, stories and intentions are all potentially contagious. Everything we do has social consequences: our creativity, attitudes, willpower and attention touch other lives. The people around us will absorb our emotions and attitudes and pass them off to their families and friends, shaping their minds and their bodies in the process. There is no isolated human action; we are creating and being created by one another, all the time.

Ubuntu

Modern discoveries of social neuroscience and interpersonal neurobiology are fascinating, but they really amount to a rediscovery of an ancient social philosophy. This world view shows up in many indigenous cultures, but is most conspicuous in the African philosophy of *ubuntu*. (pronounced uu-Boon-too)

According to *ubuntu*, there exists a common bond between all human beings and it is through this bond that we discover our own human qualities; we affirm our humanity when we acknowledge the humanity of others. Our identity is not independent; it is intimately connected to the life and welfare of the tribe, the family, the community. We define ourselves, not as individuals, but as participants in something larger. As the bushmen of the Kalahari put it, "We are people through other people" and "I am what I am because of who we are."

Ubuntu has deep African origins, but the same theme has been expressed by spiritual leaders through history and across many cultures: Jesus, Buddha, Mohammed, Gandhi, Mandela, Martin Luther King, Jr. and the Dalai Lama have all given us powerful messages of social identity. South African Nobel Laureate Archbishop Desmond Tutu described *ubuntu* this way:

> *It is the essence of being human. It speaks of the fact that my humanity is caught up and is inextricably bound up in yours. I am human because I belong. It speaks about wholeness, it speaks about compassion. A person with Ubuntu is welcoming, hospitable, warm and generous, willing to share. Such people are open and available to others, willing to be vulnerable, affirming of others, do not feel threatened that others are able and good, for they have a proper self-assurance that comes from knowing that they belong in a greater whole. They know that they are diminished when*

*others are humiliated, diminished when others are oppressed, diminished
when others are treated as if they were less than who they are. The quality
of Ubuntu gives people resilience, enabling them to survive and emerge
still human despite all efforts to dehumanize them.*

Given the dangerous and highly exposed life of early humans, it comes as no surprise that many primal people developed a social philosophy of living, one that emphasized the importance of relationship and mutual dependence. But in the developed West, *ubuntu* comes across as an unfamiliar, even alien concept. Instead, our focus is on the value and power of the individual; we say "I am who I am because of who I am" and "We are people through our individual achievements and accomplishments."

In the West, philosophers coin phrases such as "I think, therefore I am," but this focus on the individual would be unimaginable to indigenous people. In the broad context of human history, our individualistic orientation comes across as rare, abnormal, even deviant. Wise men and shamans of native cultures would revise Descartes and say "We are, therefore I am."

In the West, the closest thing we have to *ubuntu* is something we call team spirit, usually promoted in the domain of high school sports and competition. This is close, but it is not true *ubuntu*. In team sports, the implicit understanding is that participants are banding together in order to beat some other team; this reinforces an "us-versus-them" world view. In contrast, there is no one to beat in *ubuntu*. The power of social identity begins and ends with the tribe and the shared enterprise of living.

Sadly, the modern world poses many challenges to our *ubuntu* inclinations. Commerce and capitalism encourage competition at almost every level and individual performance is measured, tracked and incentivized constantly, at school and in the workplace. From an *ubuntu* perspective, this is a kind of madness. In fact, individual performance and achievement are really something of an illusion in the first place. Just as no cell can ever live or thrive without others, and no muscle in the body can ever perform on its own, no person can create without some connection to the social whole. As Paul put it in Corinthians, "The eye cannot say to the hand, "I have no need of you," nor the head to the feet, "I have no need of you."" Radical individuality is, in a very real sense, non-human and even anti-life. The tribe is who we are. "The hurt of one is the hurt of all. The honor of one is the honor of all."

Big ubuntu

Ubuntu provides us with a powerful reference point for a healthy social identity, something that we desperately need at this moment in history. Of course, the roots of this identity were formed many thousands of years ago, when the average human tribe was small and manageable. At that time, it made perfect sense to tie our identity to our local tribe and declare that "we are people through other people."

Not only that, our brains are literally wired for this kind of small group, tribal experience and a modest number of social relationships. There seems to be a cognitive limit to the number of people with whom we can maintain stable social relationships. This limit was first proposed by British anthropologist Robin Dunbar, who found a correlation between primate brain capacity and the size of a species' social group. Dunbar proposed that humans can comfortably maintain up to 150 stable relationships. After that, things start to fall apart.

Today, we are called upon to live a vast social experience. No longer do we wander the grassland as hunted-gatherers. No longer do we depend on a small band of extended family for our survival. Instead we are part of a massively interlinked population of over 7 billion individuals. As a result, survival has a very different look and feel. We may well feel profoundly connected to the people in our families and communities, but can we identify with everyone all at once? Can we develop a sense of big ubuntu that extends to every human on earth, to every sapient being?

The challenge feels immense beyond our normal reckoning. After all, our immediate tribe mates plenty annoying, petty and insufferable as it is. The gossip, the jealousy, the ambition and the maneuvering can be taxing even on a good day. And if local politics are this challenging and stressful, how can we possibly expect to open ourselves up to the suffering, bickering and conflict of the entire human species? Even the thought of it staggers the imagination.

But really, there's no other option. We are all in the same lifeboat and that lifeboat has sprung some substantial leaks. Even worse, our small-scale tribal identity is now becoming a serious liability; we spend so much time fighting one another that we can scarcely recognize the ultimate nature of our predicament, much less bail the water out of the boat. It may even be the case that our local, tribal orientation is precisely what is standing in the way of progress.

The challenge is to widen our circle of attention, concern and compassion to more and more of creation, to extend our sense of "tribe" to include all people, indeed all life. And while our predicament may well be unprecedented, sages and teachers have issued a similar challenge to us throughout our history, one that lies right at the very center of every spiritual tradition. The Bible: "A new commandment I give to you, that you love one another: just as I have loved you." The Quran: "And mankind is naught but a single nation." The Talmud: "Love thy neighbor, he *is* thyself." The Buddha: "Kindness should become the natural way of life, not the exception."

So too, Marcus Aurelius:

Constantly remind yourself, "I am a member of the whole body of conscious things." If you think of yourself as a mere "part," then love for mankind will not well up in your heart; you will look for some reward in every act of kindness and miss the boon which the act itself is offering. Then all your work will be seen as a mere duty and not as the very porthole connecting you with the Universe itself.

And in our modern era, Albert Einstein called for just such a widening sense of tribe in this now-famous passage:

A human being is part of a whole, called by us the Universe, a part limited in time and space. He experiences himself, his thoughts and feelings, as something separated from the rest, a kind of optical delusion of his consciousness. This delusion is a kind of prison for us, restricting us to our personal desires and to affection for a few persons nearest us. Our task must be to free ourselves from this prison by widening our circles of compassion to embrace all living creatures and the whole of nature in its beauty.

Focus on human universals

The challenge is familiar: When we look at the wider social world, it's easy to get distracted by difference. The people on the other side of the river have strange rituals; the people on the other side of the mountains have alien ideas; the people on the other side of the ocean have an unfamiliar culture. By concentrating our attention on these differences, we sharpen the contrast and deepen the duality between us and them.

Instead, we can promote a sense of big ubuntu by focusing on human universals, those features and qualities that we all share. Donald Brown and other anthropologists have done great work on this score, some of which appears in his 1991 book *Human Universals*. According to common estimates, there are sixty-seven human universals, but you don't have to be an anthropologist to guess what they might be. Every human culture includes language, abstract symbolism, art, music, play, food preparation and other activities that we would all recognize no matter where we come from. Everyone sleeps, dreams, wakes, eats, talks, mates, fights and makes up.

But even more important than these basic activities of life is our common experience of simply being alive in this impermanent and mysterious world. No matter where we're from, we all experience a profoundly ambiguous predicament that's filled with uncertainty, joy, happiness, health, disease, injury and loss. Everyone fears death. Everyone fears abandonment and longs for attention and attachment. Everyone wants to learn and achieve a sense of mastery and control. Everyone loves a story and longs for an explanation of why we're here.

We are also united in our shared neurobiology. Every human brain is a kludge, an assembly of neurological and psychological components, assembled over the course of millions of years. Each of us contains multitudes and those multitudes are constantly in flux. We are moved by competing predispositions; we are wired for love and fear, for approach and vigilance. We are vulnerable to traumas that shape our bodies, our nervous systems and our behavior. We all get stressed, anxious and afraid. We all come up with awkward, unskillful responses to our predicaments. We are all extremely fallible. In this sense, it is absurd to expect consistency or rationality from anyone, including ourselves.

In a very fundamental sense, we are all doing the same thing in life. We're trying to be happy. We're trying to be safe. We're trying to satisfy our needs for security, friendship, abundance and love. Our strategies for meeting these needs vary widely and many of them are awkward, misguided and ignorant, but this too is a human universal.

As we focus more intently on human universals, we begin to develop a wider, more inclusive sense of compassion for every person and every living thing. Everyone is living the same predicament as we are. We all build defenses and keep up appearances of confidence, but at the core, we all share the same uncertainties, the same frustrations, the same desires and the same sense of wonder.

Our compassion grows as we observe our own minds and our own experience. As we open ourselves up to our own sufferings, hardships, fears and folly, we begin to understand that these too are shared. We are not alone in our fears, our challenges and our anxieties. Everyone in the world, no matter their appearance, feels these things too.

In this practice, our sense of hyper-individuality fades and we begin to see ourselves as part of a much larger whole, one that contributes immensely to our knowledge and experience. When other people explore the world and learn new things, their experience flows through social networks, revealing important insights about how the world works. In this way, other people act as our eyes and ears, as sensory organs for the entire tribe. In a sense, we each have 7 billion allies who are scanning the universe, gathering information that might well be important; we are all eyes and ears for one another.

Never mind the fact that a large percentage of our 7 billion scouts and allies are wasting their attention on well-traveled paths and trivial amusements. Never mind that many of our scouts are focusing on aspects of the world that are worthless, ugly or violent. What matters is that a great many of our allies are questing towards new knowledge, undiscovered potential, outrageous beauty and new solutions to old problems. These people are making us all smarter and wiser.

Even better, we find that we are no longer so disturbed by the stupidity and ignorance that we see in the world around us. Yes, of course many of us are behaving badly. But what really matters is the fact that many of us are looking at the world in profoundly important and interesting ways. This extends our intelligence, adds to our knowledge, sharpens our attention and deepens our compassion. Our allies make our life richer. They help us to see a bigger, more abundant and beautifully mysterious world than we could ever see on our own.

Practice

At the beginning, big ubuntu may well feel like an unfamiliar, alien concept. We are not accustomed to identifying with the universal human experience. It's easy to fall back into primitive behavior, fear and xenophobia. But as always, it's a matter of practice and the good news is that there are so many opportunities. Every encounter with another person gives us a chance to see our common humanity. Every meeting, however brief, gives us a chance to see ourselves in others.

As with so many of our arts and disciplines, big ubuntu is a matter of retraining our attention. Compassion is a practice, a muscle we develop by feeling the depth and breadth of the human experience. It's also an art of return; returning our attention, over and over again to the focal point of shared universal experience.

Our commonality is clear, but we forget. Our brains are wired for contrast and vigilant for difference; it doesn't take much to trigger our negativity bias and our xenophobia. So we need to be reminded, over and over again, by our teachers and by each other. We need to return our attention to this focal point of human universals.

Remain mindful of what we share in common. That person across the room may look and behave in ways that are completely alien to you. He may even disgust and revolt you, but at the core, that person is living an experience not unlike your own. He wants to be happy, he wants to avoid suffering. His skills aren't always up to the task and his methods may well be awkward, ignorant and counter-productive. But he's trying to get it right. Just like you.

So keep practicing. And above all, be kind to your kind.

Lesson 20

Feed the right wolf

Love is the bridge between you and everything.

Rumi

You learn to speak by speaking, to study by studying, to run by running, to work by working; in just the same way, you learn to love by loving.

Anatole France

We began with the body and the physical. As children, we played every chance we got, running and jumping, riding our bikes and swimming in every pond and lake we could find. Later, as young adults, we began practicing sports and discovered that we could make our bodies faster, stronger and more skillful with training and effort. This was a powerful experience, one that left a lasting impression about our ability to transform ourselves. It was an exciting time, but today we are beginning to discover possibilities that extend far beyond our original imagining. In fact, it turns out that our potential is even more expansive than we thought.

If we've learned anything from the breathtaking advances in health and performance sciences over the last 50 years, it's that *body* is a verb. Physiology is extremely dynamic and plasticity is the buzzword of the day. All systems in the mind-body adapt according to how they're used, every cell and tissue constantly regenerating itself to meet the challenges of life. The nervous system is the most conspicuous example of our plasticity, but now it's possible to generalize this principle to the entire range of human capability, even to matters of love and the heart.

As we've seen, a fundamental principle of training is specificity. The human mind-body-spirit system adapts according to how its challenged. As Aristotle wrote, "We become what we repeatedly do." If we challenge the body to run long distances, climb big mountains or play a musical instrument, our nervous system and epigenetic system does whatever it can to make it happen. We become strong by practicing strength. We become fast by practicing speed. Similarly, we become kind and compassionate by practicing kindness and compassion.

Love capacity

Here we find some intriguing parallels. In the world of athletic training, coaches train their players to sustain their physical effort through long practice sessions and tough games. This raw physical capability is known as "work capacity." Likewise, researchers are now beginning to study the idea of human "love capacity," the ability to extend, receive and experience love in our lives. Here too, we're beginning to discover that we can increase the depth and breadth of our powers through effort, practice and experience.

This notion of love capacity has been described most vividly by Barbara Fredrickson, professor of psychology at the University of North Carolina. Fredrickson began her study of love by looking at the activity of the vagus nerve. The vagus is a powerful player in our health and love experience because it links the brain with the heart, lungs and other major organs. The vagus slows heart rate, enhances digestion, increases insulin production and decreases inflammation. It stimulates healing, recovery and anabolic processes that are essential to all the good things we want to do.

Scientists and physicians measure the activity of the vagus by tracking heart rate in conjunction with breathing; the result is a measure of "vagal tone." Studies have shown that people with high levels of vagal tone tend to exhibit greater psychophysical health, higher mental and motor functioning, and more adaptive behavioral and social performance than those with lower vagal activity. In other words, high vagal tone is a very good thing for our bodies, minds, and relationships.

The really good news is that the vagus is plastic and trainable, just like muscle. By working with sets and reps of loving thought and imagery, we can enhance its power. Fredrickson's research focused on loving-kindness meditation commonly practiced by Buddhist monks; study participants were assigned at random to participate in a modest amount of meditation each week. Her findings:

Within a matter of months, their vagus nerves began to respond more readily to the rhythms of their breathing, emitting more of that healthy arrhythmia that is the fingerprint of high vagal tone. Breath by breath— moment by moment—their capacity for positive resonance matured.

This ability to increase our love capacity may well come as a surprise. After all, most of us are used to believing that love is an exceptional bolt of lighting that strikes us out of the blue; we think of love as a random, special event, not a skill or capability. But we're wrong. Developing a healthy, loving relationship with the world is something that we can learn. It is a practice.

Practice

So how do we build our love capacity and our ability to love the world? Surprisingly perhaps, this is something that is within our control. The key is embodiment, the active living of the capability we wish to develop. In other words, we lead, not with an idea or a wish, but with an action and a doing. If we challenge the body to develop a particular characteristic, our tissue will do its best to follow along. Likewise, if we challenge the mind-body-spirit to love the world more completely, it will figure out a way to do so.

Just as with our physical and athletic training, the practice consists of high quality reps. We practice loving kindness by repeatedly wishing good fortune, healing, prosperity and happiness on other people or the universe at large. In meditation, we might concentrate our attention on "love targets" or on the experience of loving kindness in general. Of course, this experience has little to do with desire, lust, attachment or the receiving of love. Rather, it is about embrace and merger, of dissolving the duality between ourselves and the world.

The practice should be familiar and obvious by now. Our practice becomes a meditation, with love as the creative focal point. Our attention will drift and wander, just as it does with a typical breath meditation. We will become distracted, but we return our attention, over and over, back to this focal point. There is no trick to this art; there is only diligence.

We also build our love capacity with observations and conversations about gratitude, beauty, appreciation and the wonders of our lives. We list the things that we enjoy and appreciate about others, about events and about relationship. This is the polar opposite of complaining; it's a celebration of the beauties of life and the people around us.

In an earlier lesson, we made a distinction between health and medical practices done *to us* and those that are done *by us*. We saw the enormous potential for *by us* practices such as exercise, meditation, dietary choice and other lifestyle modifications. Clearly, love fits into the same category. In other words, love is a *by us* practice. And because it's a *by us* practice, it has the potential to empower us. By taking control of our experience, we become stronger.

Many of us are inclined to think of love as a thing, a noun, an intense feeling of deep affection and a desire to merge. Of course it is. But the more interesting art lies with the active verb, to love. Here we're called upon to participate in a process and a practice. In this sense, love is not something that we possess, receive or loose, but is something that we create. As Madeleine L'Engle put it in *A Wind in the Door*, "Love isn't how you feel. It's what you do."

Naturally, most of us hold hugely romantic visions of love and give it its own special place among life's experiences. We think that it's a matter of chance or divine intervention. One day, we're pierced by cupid's arrow and we fall, smitten by the immensity of the experience. It's just a matter of luck.

This may well be the case on occasion, but love is also a matter of effort, even work. We make love, we create love, we refresh our love with a thousand microscopic efforts of daily practice. We look at things in the light of love, over and over again. Each effort may seem to be a whisper, almost without significance, but taken together, these acts of attention literally change our brains, our relationships and our lives. And so, the question becomes: Do you believe in love at second sight? At millionth sight? Do you believe that love is a continuous creation? If so, let's have dinner sometime soon.

Sadly, many of us get started on the wrong foot. In conventional thinking, we tend to see love as a transaction. Let's make a deal: "I'll love you if you love me." "I'll make myself vulnerable if you make yourself vulnerable." "I'll heap attention and praise on you if you heap attention and praise on me." We calculate our return on investment; we measure our risk and rewards. We become accountants of the heart.

Naturally, this approach is destined to fail. And when it does, we blame each other for failing us; we cast ourselves as victims and in the process, we give away our power. In desperation, we go looking for rescue with new lovers. Or, we become cynical and hardened to the entire experience.

What we need is a completely different approach. For a start, try turning your mind and spirit around. This is where you'll discover something we might describe as a "paradoxical reward system." In this model, the doing is the reward. Giving becomes getting. Love becomes *autotelic*, an activity that's intrinsically rewarding. Loving the world makes us feel good and it improves our health. Here we're reminded of actress Sarah Bernhardt and her observation, "Life begets life. Energy creates energy. It is by spending oneself that one becomes rich."

Of course, we often lapse back into old habits and fears. What if someone defaults on our agreement and our expectations? What if someone doesn't return our favors? What if someone is a free rider on our love? That would be a catastrophe, we say.

But this may be less of a problem than we fear. Obviously, we all want love to come back around to us. Sometimes it does, sometimes it doesn't. People sometimes disappoint us. People sometimes reject us or abandon us. Love is vulnerability; we may well get hurt. Love can be dangerous, but it would be folly to make our love contingent on consequences. The reward is in the giving, not in the receiving. It's the act of loving that nourishes us and this is something that lies entirely within our power at all times. Even when we're suffering, we can still wrap our arms around the totality of life.

Of course, it's easy to focus on love and kindness when conditions are good. When the people around us are friendly and the weather is mild, it's easy to concentrate our attention on the beauty and wonders of the human experience. It's easy to be a fair-weather lover. But this is not enough. To make real changes in our experience, we need to practice when times are tough. Just as the truly committed athlete does his laps in the rain or heads to the dojo at the end of a hard day, so too will the love athlete practice his meditations under the duress of chaos, rejection and despair. Even when challenged by trying circumstance, annoying people, unrelenting stress and social defeat, he returns his focus to love, kindness and the beauty of the world. Just as with physical training, the payoff comes as we persevere in the face of adversity.

We are so quick to give up. Love knocks us down, love fails to deliver, love disappears, love is unreliable. Instead of redoubling our efforts like we would in any other art or discipline, many of us simply give up and resign ourselves to a life of unhappiness.

The problem lies with our limited imagination; our passions are simply too narrow. We love a particular person with a particular look, with a particular attitude, in a particular context. If we happen to discover such a person, it all feels wonderful. But inevitably, change begins. The river of life flows, people and circumstances change, and now our love is challenged. Soon our hearts are broken, but somehow, we still don't learn. We repeat the process; perhaps some other person with a different look and feel will provide what we seek. But our small, specific love is doomed; it's completely vulnerable to the dynamism of life. What we need is something bigger, something more consistent with the nature of life.

So why not just love? Do you really need a person or an object to focus on? Why can't we simply say "I love" without adding a target? If this is possible, then suddenly our typical excuses fall away. Maybe it's enough to simply open our hearts.

The obvious challenge is to love life itself, to romance the totality of our lives, to give an unconditional "yes" to what is, as it is. This includes our suffering, our pain, our confusion and the mystery we all face. We are called upon to love it all, even the insecurity and impermanence that we try so hard to ignore. It's a challenge to be sure, but there is nothing more important. If we stop loving, we stop living.

In the end, it's all practice. Love has little to do with the luck of the draw or the perfect opening line, but rather with countless acts of attention and choice, spread over our lifetimes. We build our love capacity not once, but in every little thing that we say and do. As the Beatles had it in their final song together: "And in the end, the love you take, is equal to the love you make."

Ultimately, it's all about our where we choose to put our energy. A Native American parable puts it perfectly:

> A boy was talking with his grandfather.
>
> "What do you think about the world situation?" he asked.
>
> "I feel like wolves are fighting in my heart. One is full of anger and hatred; the other is full of love, forgiveness, and peace."
>
> "Which one will win?" asked the boy.
>
> To which the grandfather replied, "The one I feed."

Lesson 21

Tell a new story

People think that stories are shaped by people.
In fact, it's the other way around.

Terry Pratchett
Witches Abroad

The crucial thing is the story. For it alone shows the human background and the human suffering. Only at that point can the doctor's therapy begin to operate.

Carl Jung

Once upon at time, in a land far, far away, there lived a people who told no stories. They used words just like most of us, but only for statements of fact, opinion and information. They worked and raised their families, farmed and hunted, built things and went places. They did most of the things that regular people do, but never did they tell stories to one another.

Can you imagine it?

Probably not.

After all, story telling is a human universal. We are a story telling animal. We breathe stories, we eat and drink stories. A culture that told no stories would be almost unimaginable. Without story, life would be not just dull, but sterile.

Stories are often entertaining, but their power goes far beyond mere enjoyment. Stories help us understand the direction of our lives and our culture, they give us a sense of history, context and relationship. And most of all, they give us a sense of meaning and purpose.

We are accustomed to thinking of stories as fully-developed narratives with characters, plot lines, climaxes and conclusions, but these are simply the classic forms. We swim in a sea of stories, a sea that we call culture. We tell stories with our posture, our tone of voice, or just a few words. These micro-stories, spoken thousands of time each day by each of us, shape the larger narratives of our lives.

Many of us suppose that storytelling is a formalized activity that we only engage in around the dinner table or the campfire. We may even believe that storytelling is a dying art. In fact, all humans are storytellers and it's a full-time occupation. Every action, every behavior, every gesture, every word–all carry meanings that go beyond themselves.

The power of story

It's easy to imagine the origins of story. Clustered around the campfire at night, bellies full from a successful hunt, our ancestors gazed into the flames. Our growing brains became curious and began to generate some big questions who we were and how we got here. For the first time in history, we wanted to know why things were the way they were; we hungered for explanation. Thus were born our first yarns and our first myths. "It's like this," we proposed. We danced with our bodies to share our hunting adventures and soon, simple words began to come forth. Our creative powers exploded and every night we came back for more, craving narrative, always hoping to learn how things got to be the way they are.

Story is so deeply embedded in the human experience that it literally shapes the tissue of our bodies. To an astonishing extent, physiology follows narrative. The stories that we hear cause very real changes to our endocrine system and the flow of information within our brains. Some stories trigger stress hormones like adrenaline and cortisol, others promote the flow of oxytocin, the so-called "love hormone." Even in the short term, the effects can be dramatic and in the long-term, the consequences can be profoundly life-altering.

As we've seen, the human stress response can be radically altered by our interpretation of events. In infancy and throughout our lives, the autonomic nervous system continuously asks a very simple question: "Is the world friendly?" The answer, even when it comes in a non-verbal "Yes" or "No" is very much a story. In fact, it is our most primal story, one that sets the trajectory for our physiology, our health, and our relationships.

We now know that stories can have very real effects on the brain itself. In 2013, researchers at Emory University detected actual changes in the brain that come with reading stories. "Stories shape our lives and in some cases help define a person," said neuroscientist Gregory Berns, lead author of the study and the director of Emory's Center for Neuropolicy. The study focused on the lingering neural effects of reading a narrative. "Even though the participants were not actually reading the novel while they were in the scanner, they retained this heightened connectivity," Berns says. "We call that a 'shadow activity,' almost like a muscle memory."

Heightened connectivity was also seen in the central sulcus of the brain, the primary sensory motor region of the brain. Neurons of this region have been associated with making representations of sensation for the body, a phenomenon known as grounded cognition. Just thinking about running, for instance, can activate the neurons associated with the physical act of running.

"The neural changes that we found associated with physical sensation and movement systems suggest that reading a novel can transport you into the body of the protagonist," Berns said. "We already knew that good stories can put you in someone else's shoes in a figurative sense. Now we're seeing that something may also be happening biologically."

The effects of story go all the way to the deepest levels of human physiology and psychology. Placebos and nocebos are not just tricky pills handed out by researchers; these pills always come with a story attached. In turn, these stories shape our expectation and the flow of information in our bodies. These are not rare events either; we are constantly under the influence of belief, guided by story. This is yet one more reason to be mindful of the words and images we consume; the stories that we hear really do make a difference.

Of course, indigenous people and native cultures knew this all along. In his book *Narrative Medicine: The Use of History and Story in the Healing Process*, Lewis Mehl-Madrona MD. describes our original understanding: "In the indigenous worldview, each person is the sum of all the stories that have ever been told (or ever will be) told about him." The beauty of story is that it speaks to both relationships and communities, aspects of the human experience that are largely untouched by modern methods. We literally become what we tell.

Stories are reps

As we dig deeper into the neurobiology of story we come to the profound and surprising realization that stories function just like reps. Repeat a story one time and your mind-body will take note. Repeat a story two times and your mind-body will detect a pattern and prepare an appropriate neuroendocrine response. Repeat a story a hundred times and the narrative will become embedded, not just in your body, but in your very identity. The words and meaning will carve a groove into the terrain of your nervous system and in turn, your life.

In this sense, stories are both "neuro" and "muscular." When we tell stories repeatedly, we actually wire circuits together, in the brain and throughout the body. The more reps we perform, the faster and more permanent the circuit becomes. As neural circuits become more deeply etched, our minds and spirits are transformed. This, of course, is both good news and bad, depending on the quality of the stories we repeatedly tell.

We also begin to realize that early stories are the most powerful. The first stories of our lives form the watercourse for all our subsequent observations, ideas, explanations and relationships. That's why "the hand that rocks the cradle rules the world." The stories that we hear as children set the stage for everything that comes after; these stories literally shape what we see in the world. So too for every story that's told by every coach, trainer, physician and professor on the opening day of training or study. As storytellers, we are more powerful than we suppose. With every repetition, we shape our culture; we are all authors and playwrights of the human experience.

Naturally, this presents us with a double-edged predicament. Good stories, repeated often, give us a sense of safety, security, comfort and transformation. Good stories remind us of our creative potential, our resilience and the power of love. But stories of darkness and cynicism, repeated often, simply drag us into the abyss. Revenge narratives justify our tendency to blame a perpetrator, keeping us locked into a victim orientation and diminished power. With each retelling, we become increasingly committed to negativity. Growth comes to a standstill as every new event gets swept down the deepening chasm of our pre-existing story line. No longer do we tell these stories; these stories begin to tell us.

Clearly, this challenges us to exercise another meta-skill, the ability to revise the stories of our lives and escape the dogma of static, dysfunctional narratives. Liberation comes with relinquishing or editing our outdated narratives. When we change the plot, tone or profile of our characters, we assign new meanings. Tragedy may become comedy. Darkness may be revealed as common human error. Awkwardness may be seen as a human universal, worthy of compassion and forgiveness.

This is some of our most challenging work. After all, we are often fiercely committed to our most cherished narratives and some of us would literally die before changing a story line or explanation. But hard or not, this is where the transformation lies. And we have a choice: either continue to suffer or change our stories.

Stories for our time

Story revision is a powerful tool for personal transformation, but it also offers promise in larger circles of society and culture. Here we begin to think in terms of narrative activism; if we tell better stories, perhaps we can make a real difference in the world at large. In conventional circles, most of us think of activists as those who push a political, legislative or organizational agenda with tools like fund-raising, lobbying and lawsuits. This is all well and good, and we desperately need individuals who do the gritty work of activism, but stories are essential too, perhaps even more powerful than our conventional tools.

Here we find ourselves wondering about the dominant narratives of our modern age and what they mean for our future. How do people explain our predicament to one another? What do they say about cause and effect? Do today's narratives point us towards solutions? Are they reactive or are they creative?

Sadly, there's a lot of darkness coursing through today's stories. Details differ, but the dominant large-scale narrative of our day is "Looming Planetary Catastrophe." Obviously, this story centers on the destruction of the natural world and in turn, the life-support system for all of us. We're all familiar with the details: runaway population growth, climate change, habitat destruction, groundwater and topsoil depletion, widening gap between rich and poor and the uncontrollable growth of powerful technologies. Other names for this story include "ecological overshoot" and "Malthusian catastrophe."

Looming Planetary Catastrophe has inspired a rich genre of apocalyptic scenarios and dystopian futures, most of which end in desperation and darkness. As singer-songwriter Dana Lyons sings it, "We're sailing on a time bomb."

We hear snippets of Looming Planetary Catastrophe sprinkled throughout our everyday conversation:

"We're killing the planet."

"We are the asteroid."

"We're a cancer on the earth."

"We're nothing more than knuckle-dragging primates with powerful and dangerous technology that we don't fully understand."

"We're smart enough to harness powerful energy sources and use them for our short-term self-interest, but we're not smart enough to act for long-term sustainability."

The problem here should be obvious. There is an undeniable reality to this story of ecological melt-down and it's almost certainly true that we are in for immense suffering; large swathes of the biosphere have already been destroyed and many people are unable to meet their most basic needs. Even the best-case projections for climate change are ominous.

Unfortunately however, this "sky is falling" narrative isn't much help to anyone. In the first place, most of us don't respond well to bad news on such an enormous scale. And even when we do respond, it's usually in the wrong direction. When faced with stories of impending doom, many of us simply become depressed, cynical and reactionary. We bury our heads in distraction or addiction. We become stressed, and when we're stressed, our time horizon shrinks to matters of immediate, personal concern; we think more about short term urgencies and less about long-term solutions. Our attention shifts from a sense of abundance to a fear of scarcity.

Obviously, this narrative puts us in a positive feedback cycle of increasing despair. Looming planetary catastrophe are may well be based on scientific fact, but it's not a particularly useful story for inspiring change. The story must be told, but by itself, it leaves us stranded, desperate and ineffective.

Today's growth narratives

It would be foolhardy to ignore the realities of our planetary predicament, but fortunately, there are other stories circulating through our culture, stories that are bursting with potential. These are the modern growth narratives of neuro-optimism, neuroplasticity, training and practice. These stories offer an inspiring counterpoint to Looming Planetary Catastrophe.

As we've seen, our study of education and performance in the 20th century was dominated by a story of innate, static capability. This narrative was served up by a host of story tellers, all offering up some variation on the theme of fixed human aptitude. The official position was simple: "Neurons don't regenerate. Brain cells can only die." This view was rarely questioned; the dogma was taught to millions of people throughout the century. It was mistaken.

In contrast, today's counter-narrative is not only upbeat and optimistic, it's far more accurate, nuanced, and true-to-life. This story is being told by growth advocates across the spectrum of human learning and performance: teachers, scientists, artists, athletic trainers, psychologists, workforce consultants, dance teachers and meditators. More and more people are discovering that human potential is fundamentally open-ended.

Leading the charge is a new generation of neuroscientists. The old dogma of an unchanging brain has been overthrown by the paradigm of neuroplasticity, the understanding that the brain is constantly in flux, learning and rewiring itself. Neuroplasticity has now become a mature, well-established field with a substantial body of proven findings, all pointing to incredible potential for neural and life transformation. This confirms the experience of musicians and athletes the world over; these artists literally live by and for neuroplastic transformation. Likewise, collaborations between meditators and neuroscientists have revealed profound changes in the brain that come with long-term practice.

Reinforcing the story of neuroplasticity and neuro-optimism is Carol Dweck's work on the psychology of growth. In her landmark book *Mindset: The New Psychology of Success*, Dweck begins with a simple question: "What are the consequences of thinking that your intelligence or personality is something that you can develop, as opposed to something that is a fixed, deep-seated trait?"

In her research, Dweck primed groups of students with fixed and growth narratives and compared the outcomes. Those who believed that their capabilities are fixed tended to perform poorly when faced with novel challenges. In contrast, those who believed in their ability to grow were far more resilient and creative. In other words, students who identified themselves as static nouns tended to struggle, but those who saw themselves as living, growing verbs were far more adept at adapting to new conditions.

Dweck suggests that people with a fixed mindset more susceptible to depression and frustration. When challenged, they tend to become defensive and avoid situations that might reveal a weakness or draw them out of their area of supposed giftedness. In contrast, those who hold a growth orientation tend to be far more resilient when faced with novel challenges and setbacks.

These findings may not be entirely surprising, but they are vitally important because they sharpen our awareness of the power of story and belief. As Dweck points out, our mindsets change the meaning of adversity, challenge and failure. "Believing that your qualities are carved in stone–the fixed mindset–creates an urgency to prove yourself over and over." On the other hand, "the growth mindset is based on the belief that your basic qualities are things you can cultivate through your efforts."

The modern growth narrative is also told by researchers who study mastery and expert performance. It has now become obvious that, when it comes to high-level performance, innate talent counts for very little; it's deep, concentrated training that produces results. In every case of apparent talent and "giftedness," we have discovered a history of sustained, highly focused practice. In the grand scope of transforming our bodies, our organizations and our lives, training is what matters. As a useful concept, talent is dead.

As storytellers and narrative activists, the challenge before us is to become fluent in the growth narratives of our time. Obviously, the dark stories of environmental destruction must be taken seriously and we'd be fools to ignore the realities. But for every yang, there must be a yin. It's essential that we tell the growth narratives at every opportunity.

The practice here is clear. Learn the principles of neuroplasticity and the implications of neuro-optimism. Remind your listeners that their brains are constantly re-wiring themselves, and that transformation is possible. Remind them of the simple fact that every moment is a rep. We become what we practice.

Tell the story of mindfulness and the benefits of stable, present-moment attention. Tell your friends about our original goodness that's revealed when we relinquish our resentments, grievances, anger and hostility.

Tell the story of abundance and beauty. Tell the story of human universals, the fact that we all share the same basic needs and desires for love. Remind your listeners that it's within their power to relinquish their victim orientation, adopt the role of a creator and in the process, gain access to a wealth of power. Finally, remind people that this life, no matter its struggles, hardships and sufferings, can also be a beautiful adventure.

These narratives won't directly heal the wounds that we've inflicted on the earth or on each other, but they will increase the health, intelligence and adaptability of millions of people. In turn, these people who can make better, more inspired decisions about the path forward.

Mindful storytelling

Once we recognize the power of story, we begin to approach the practice much more mindfully. Instead of carelessly repeating whatever story comes to mind, or whatever story happens to be circulating though your culture, think twice about the tone, meaning and consequences of your words. Before you open your mouth or put your fingers to the keyboard, even for a simple meme or micro-story, ask some simple questions:

- What's the intent of this story? What will be it's consequences?
- How will it ripple through my family, my community and my culture?
- How will people interpret these words?

- Will my story justify revenge, hatred and violence? Or will it light the way to compassion and forgiveness?

- Will it keep us stuck in reactivity and a victim orientation? Or will it return our attention to some creative focal point?

- Will this story enhance the health, vitality, compassion and creativity of teller, listener and my culture at large?

- Will my story inspire, enlighten or transform?

As we've seen, the ecological perspective tells us that "We can never do merely one thing." Nowhere is this more true than with story. Every narrative has consequences, even if told only to ourselves. So think twice before you speak. Think three times before you write. Your words are powerful.

Lesson 22

Integrate

The mountains, the rivers, the whole earth,
the entire array of phenomena are all oneself.

Musô Soseki

The Destiny of Man is to unite, not to divide. If you keep on dividing you end up as a collection of monkeys throwing nuts at each other out of separate trees.

T.H. White

As your training belt becomes darker, you'll naturally begin to think about putting all your training and experience together into a single whole. This drive towards integration is a popular theme in many disciplines. We hear it in the world of athletic training, where coaches stress the importance of integrated movement and tell their athletes "Lift the weight with your whole body!" We also hear it in the world of psychotherapy, where counselors encourage their patients to adopt integrative narratives that bring their lives together into a single coherent whole. And we even hear it in unlikely places, where strategists in business, law, education, design and public policy advise us to reach for an integrated "systems approach."

Some call for *vertical integration*, a non-Cartesian orientation that seeks to put mind and body back together into a single, unitary whole. Others look for *horizontal integration*, a unity of function between left and right hemispheres of the brain. Still others seek *sensory-motor integration*, the ability to coordinate sensory information with muscular contractions across the body. Of course, we also look for *interpersonal integration* between couples, families, teams and communities. And in the world of therapy, we look for *cognitive integration*. In this domain, we seek to re-integrate isolated neural circuits and memories back into the totality of the person's experience, often through story and narrative.

Naturally, all of these moves towards integration have a strong intuitive appeal. All of us desire to become one; with ourselves, our bodies, our habitats, our communities and the cosmos. Beginning at birth, we experience a compelling drive to attach to a caregiver. Even the word *disintegration* causes us some degree of psychophysical stress. And of course, the word health derives from the root word meaning "whole."

As Carl Jung and other observers of the human condition have observed, we all have a natural, innate drive towards integration; no matter how badly we're injured, distracted, traumatized or dislocated, our bodies and subconscious minds are always seeking a path back to wholeness. So it's no wonder that teachers, trainers, coaches and mental health professionals all across the spectrum are united in this quest to put things together. When you get right down to it, all of us are in the integration business.

Whole-part-whole

No matter the domain, the process of integration is always about getting isolated elements working together. And while each domain requires its own specific strategies, language and techniques, there is nevertheless a common orientation that underlies all of these efforts.

In the first place, the emphasis should be on relationship, not objects. The more we fixate on individual elements, the more we loose sight of the totality of the system in question. In fact, it may well be that individual objects are actually illusions. As Alan Watts put it, "Parts are fictions of language, of the calculus of looking at the world through a net which seems to chop it into bits. Parts exist only for purposes of figuring and describing."

Knowing this, we become hunters and gatherers of relationship and connection, always suspicious about isolated objects, people, ideas and memories. No thing is an island. Each apparent object must connect to something larger in some way, but how? Find the thread. Seek the connection. Knit them into the whole.

There's a method and a rhythm to this process. In the world of athletic training, coach Vern Gambetta describes a model he calls "whole-part-whole." When evaluating an athlete with an injury, he begins by observing the entire body and the biomechanics of the complete system. What's the big picture of the athlete's movement? Forget the specifics for now. Look at the whole thing in motion. Watch how long kinetic chains cooperate to produce movement. Is the movement smooth? Or are there kinks in the flow?

Next, focus closely on the area of pain and injury; look at the small picture. What's going on at the joint in question? Does it move freely? Is it inhibited or protected by the muscles around it? Is there a particular area of pain? Is the pain sharp or dull? How's the range of motion?

At this point the trainer or coach offers a recommendation based on his knowledge and expertise. Once the athlete has performed the prescribed rehabilitation program, we return to the big picture view, zoom back out and a look at how it all comes together. How's the athlete moving now? Are the component parts moving in harmony? Is the system more integrated than before?

Similarly, we can take this whole-part-whole approach to any system or creation we're working with: a physical system, a biological system, a human organization. Big-small-big, then repeat. The beauty of this rhythmic approach is that it forces us to continuously re-evaluate the consequences and systemic effects of our actions. By zooming in and back out again, we gather more information about vital relationships, information that contributes to integration.

This athletic, mobile attention helps us knit together the totality of human experience. John Steinbeck made much the same point in *The Log from the Sea of Cortez*:

> *It is a strange thing that most of the feeling we call religious, most of the mystical outcrying which is one of the most prized and used and desired reactions of our species, is really the understanding and the attempt to say that man is related to the whole thing, related inextricably to all reality, known and unknowable. This is a simple thing to say, but the profound feeling of it made a Jesus, a St. Augustine, a St. Francis, a Roger Bacon, a Charles Darwin, and an Einstein. Each of them in his own tempo and with his own voice discovered and reaffirmed with astonishment the knowledge that all things are one thing and that one thing is all things– plankton, a shimmering phosphorescence on the sea and the spinning planets and an expanding universe, all bound together by the elastic string of time. It is advisable to look from the tide pool to the stars and then back to the tide pool again.*

Medicine wheel

Integration implies balance between elements and in this respect, an ideal model for our practice is the bicycle wheel, especially the old-style wheel with manually-adjustable spokes. Here, the problem is obvious: We seek an integration of the entire system, but all it takes is a single problematic spoke to throw the wheel out of true; shortness or weakness in any one spoke instantly disrupts all the others.

Likewise, the wheel of our lives demands a systemic orientation. As soon as we adjust one spoke, all the other relationships in the wheel are affected, and so we need to have a look at those as well. And now we're looking at the health of the entire system, not just the component parts. This calls for a multidisciplinary view. Over-specialization in any single discipline, art, profession or idea is simply inadequate; we need to see and adjust the wheel in its entirety.

We create and maintain the "spokes" in our lives with our time and in particular, our attention. If our attention is well-distributed across the many dimensions of our health, our communities and our human predicament, the wheel remains true and rolls smoothly. But when our attention is fragmented or concentrated exclusively on a single spoke, the wheel becomes unstable and increasingly vulnerable to trauma and stress.

As the wheel goes out of true, we begin to feel it as a wobble in our lives, our bodies and our communities. We experience stress, pain, anxiety and conflict. At this point, our attention often contracts, making the situation worse. We focus on the defective spokes in our experience and take our eyes off the whole. The solution is to redistribute our attention and not get trapped or stuck on the conflict, the pain or the wobble. Simply fixing one spoke is never enough. We have to keep adjusting the entire system. Keep your eye on the whole.

Of course, everyone seems to have their own model of the wheel of health, each with an implicit message of wholeness:

- The popular wheel of health and wellness has three spokes: *mind, body and spirit.*

- In 1977, George Engel proposed a 3-spoke model of health in the journal *Science*. For Engel, the fundamental elements were biological, psychological and social. This is the famous *biopsychosocial* model

- The 4-H Club model has, of course, 4 spokes: *head, hands, heart* and *health.*

- In his book *Disease Proof,* David Katz described an intriguing 4 spoke model that includes *feet* for exercise, *forks* for nutrition, *fingers* for choice and *forest* for big picture ideas that give our lives meaning.

- In indigenous culture, many native people use a 6 spoke model that includes *mind, body, spirit, land, tribe* and *ancestors.*

- Finally, Buddhism gives us an 8 spoke model that includes *right view, right intention, right speech, right action, right livelihood, right effort, right mindfulness* and *right concentration.*

All of these models are interesting and useful; each reminds us of the need for multiple orientations that fit together in integration. We can argue about the details of particular spokes of course, but the essential point remains. That is, our practice of health is not about any one thing. It's about many things working together in harmony. If one spoke is missing or one is too dominant, the entire system will be at risk.

What are the spokes in the wheel of your life? If you're like most people, you'll list your friends and family, your physical health, your career and your creative focal point. Maybe your wheel has just a few spokes, maybe many. But no matter the number, the practice lies in the distribution of your attention. Where's the excess? Where's the deficit? How do the spokes relate to one another?

For athletes, a common training wheel is often built around 6 spokes: specific event training, general physical conditioning, food, work, rest and sleep, and social time. This pattern works well, especially when the athlete's time and attention is well distributed across all the spokes. But excessive concentration in any one area displaces time and attention away from the others and puts the entire system at risk.

Some obvious questions present themselves: Are you obsessive about a single spoke to the exclusion of others? Is your wheel shaped more like an oval? Would your wheel be stronger if you added more spokes in the form of more relationships, more friends and associates? In any case, be mindful of the whole and make adjustments as necessary to keep it true.

This practice is not always easy. In many circles of modern life, the rewards go to the monomaniacs, those who develop impressive one-dimensional powers at the expense of whole-life balance. You can, if you choose, concentrate your power and resources onto a single spoke of your wheel and gain attention in the process, but over the long term, you'll suffer the consequences. An unbalanced wheel simply doesn't roll very far or for very long. You might want to revise your interest in the spectacular and the hyperbolic.

Systemic wisdom

As we've seen, our interest in integration naturally leads us into the study of whole systems. Unfortunately, most of us are untrained in this art. In fact, many of us are anti-trained. We are educated in specializations; we are taught to focus our intelligence in one place and keep it there for years, even decades. As a consequence, many of us become mono-disciplinarians, paid to look at one thing and one thing only. One spoke at a time, we say. "The totality of the wheel is not a part of my job description."

But this view is no longer functional or even interesting. Specialities have their place but isolation is no longer an option. Mono-disciplinary perspectives are not just dull, but dangerous. The time has come for all of us to take an interest in the whole. The time has come for systemic attention and wisdom, a view most famously described by Gregory Bateson (1904-1980).

In short, systemic wisdom is the voice at the back of the classroom or conference room that asks "What about everything else?" It's the voice of conscience that asks "What about everyone else?" It's a multi-disciplinary, multi-spoke perspective that consistently takes into account the totality of the process, harmonizing our interests with the larger communities that we belong. The focus is always on relationship, interdependence and beauty.

Aldo Leopold famously called for systemic wisdom in *A Sand County Almanac* when he wrote, "A thing is right when it tends to preserve the integrity, stability, and beauty of the biotic community. It is wrong when it tends otherwise."

Similarly, the Lakota people of North America often begin a prayer or ceremony with the phrase *Mitakuye Oyasin* meaning "All my relations." This simple phrase honors the totality of the living world and the unassailable fact of interdependence. When we say *Mitakuye Oyasin,* we keep our attention focused on relationships across the entire system of living beings.

It's a common theme across all native cultures. In her extraordinary book *The Spirit Catches You and You Fall Down*, author Anne Fadiman tells us that the Hmong people use the phrase *hais cuaj txub kaum txub*, which means "to speak of all kinds of things." According to Fadiman,

> *It is often used at the beginning of an oral narrative as a way of reminding the listeners that the world is full of things that may not seem to be connected, but actually are; that no event occurs in isolation; that you can miss a lot by sticking to the point; and that the storyteller is likely to be long-winded.*

Obviously, we could all benefit from this kind of systemic wisdom, in every domain of human experience: in the health of our bodies and minds, in our families and communities, in the workplace, medical care, environmental restoration, in law and government. The ancients obviously had it right.

Be bigger

In the end, the challenge of integration calls upon us to be bigger than we are; it calls us to grow our perspectives and broaden our views. Stop hiding out in isolation. Stop distancing and "otherizing" the unpleasant qualities of the world. After all, when we vote people, ideas and memories "off the island," we're eventually left with a very small, very isolated and dis-integrated place to live. Embrace the human universals, even the ugly ones. Embrace your personal history, even the shameful acts of stupidity.

Whatever the domain, remember that integration is never truly complete. In a highly dynamic and complex world, every element and relationship is constantly in flux; you can never step into the same system twice. Therefore, your practice must be continuous. Every day, indeed every minute of every day, you must make adjustments in the flux and flow of muscular action, sensation, cognition, relationship, story and narrative. Don't get stuck on any one element or any single object. Sweep your attention over the entire system and keep adjusting.

Above all, embrace radical responsibility and take ownership of the entire system. This *is* your job. The ancients have known it for thousands of years, and now it's time to broaden our attention. Individual units have their role to play, but without some sense of systemic mindfulness, we are in real trouble. As Bateson reminded us, there's a heavy price to be paid when we ignore the bigger picture: "Lack of systemic wisdom is always punished. If you fight the ecology of a system, you lose–especially if you 'win.'"

Lesson 23

Lead with your life

The ultimate aim of the quest must be neither release nor ecstasy for oneself, but the wisdom and the power to serve others.

Joseph Campbell

You are not here merely to make a living. You are here in order to enable the world to live more amply, with greater vision, with a finer spirit of hope and achievement. You are here to enrich the world, and you impoverish yourself if you forget the errand.

Woodrow Wilson

Years of training pass, a journey of sweat and striving, reps, revision and resilience. There has been joy and suffering on this path, falls and injury, insights, laughter and creative inspirations. Your beautiful practice has been rich in texture, sensation and story. You have come a long way.

Your belt–now supple to the touch and dark in color–has begun to fray around its edges, revealing the color white, a color not seen around your waist for years. Now you are called *sensei*, one who sees ahead. By virtue of your considerable time on the mat, you are becoming a leader. It is time to step into this role.

Of course, some will imagine that taking such a position is optional, a path that one might choose if he has the right sort of personality or disposition. And many will be content to let others expose themselves to the risks of standing up in front of others, sharing their knowledge and shaping the future. But in your case, standing aside is not an option. Your long experience brings with it an obligation. You've learned some powerful lessons and now it's time to close the circle and return your insights to the community of practice. As one inner-city leader famously put it, "The more you know, the more you owe." It's time to step up; the rest of us are depending on you.

Unfortunately, many would-be leaders get off on the wrong foot by supposing that leadership is all about taking charge, building their stature and amassing power.

But this is a perilous path that is contrary to *ubuntu*, traditional values and systemic wisdom. In fact, the true purpose of leadership, coaching and teaching is to return our experience to the community that gave us life. It's not about maximizing power and control in the world; it's about inspiring transformation. Ralph Nader put it well when he said "I start with the premise that the function of leadership is to produce more leaders, not more followers."

Be the change

At the beginning, many assume that leadership is a top-down, command-and-control process that's exercised by powerful individuals in conspicuous positions of influence. Sometimes this is true, but in actual practice, leadership can come from anywhere at any time. Hyper-social animals don't necessarily take their instruction or inspiration from organizational flow charts or officially-sanctioned individuals; people take their leadership where they find it. Anyone's life can inspire us. Knowledge can come from above or below, left or right. Wielding power might well be useful and even important, but in the end, it's not our position but the way we live that makes us leaders.

This gives us a more expansive view of the process and the art. No longer can we think of leadership as something only to be exercised in rare instances or "leadership opportunities." In a beautiful practice, *every* moment is a leadership opportunity. Every moment is a butterfly moment. We are always exerting some kind of power and influencing people in unknown ways. In this sense, leadership is not a rare or exceptional event; it's a continuous engagement.

As a whole-life practice, leadership calls upon us to embody our teachings, to be the change that we seek to create in the world. The ultimate test is not knowledge itself, but the grounding of that knowledge into our bodies and behavior. Facts, concepts and ideas may well be interesting, but when it comes to making real substantive changes to the way we live, action is the first and most crucial step for everything we might wish to become.

This is precisely the approach advocated by William James, the father of American psychology. James believed that the best approach to transformation was to begin with action, not an idea. As he famously put it, "If you want a quality, act as if you have it already." In other words, start with the doing. Even if you don't feel it or understand it, do what needs to be done. Put your behavior out in front and the rest of your body and your life will follow along.

Whatever the state of your mind or spirit, start with a doing. Start by doing the very thing you wish you could do. Embody it, even if you have to bluff. Even if you are sweating and your stomach is in knots. Even if your mind is rebelling and you feel like a fraud, do the act. Once you do, your body will begin to take the hint. Your physiology and psychology will fall in line behind your new behavior.

A enormous body of research now supports the validity of this "behavior-first" transformational approach: When we change our facial expressions, our emotions go along for the ride. When we walk with long strides, an upright posture and an energetic swing, we begin to feel happier. Work by Amy Cuddy at Harvard, described in her popular TED talk, showed that expansive, high-power postures (arms wide, body proud) produced elevations in testosterone, decreases in cortisol and increased feelings of power and risk tolerance. Low power posers exhibited the opposite effects. When action leads, the body follows.

This principle tells us something very interesting about meditation. Many people report that their meditation sessions are difficult and that their time on the cushion is filled with unwelcome thoughts, images and narratives. Many people conclude that they are "bad meditators" and that the whole thing feels like a colossal waste of time. But teachers urge their students to stick with it, knowing that over time, their practice and experience will settle down.

This makes perfect sense. When we meditate, we behave "as if" we are calm, composed and centered. In the beginning of our training, we may well be bluffing, but adopt the posture and demeanor of a person who is at peace with the world. In this respect, it doesn't much matter how much turmoil you might be feeling. Behavior is leading the action now and the mind-body begins to follow along. By adopting the posture and demeanor of a master, your thoughts and our even your physiology will eventually fall in line with what you're doing. Act like a calm and centered person and you'll eventually become that calm and centered person.

The same holds true for exercise. Beginners who come to exercise for the first time often feel incompetent and out of place. They have no sense of being strong, endurant or agile. But in one very important way, none of that matters. If you can sustain the doing, even for a few weeks or months, your body will get the message. Behave as if you're strong, endurant and agile and your physiology will do everything it can to make that happen.

The same principle holds true in every domain of human experience and performance. Want to be a more organized professional? Start by acting organized. Want to be a calmer and more effective presenter? Start by acting calm and effective. Want to be more creative? Start by creating. Want to become a leader? Start by leading.

In a way, it doesn't matter how we feel. The doing can be completely artificial and even forced. You may well feel like an imposter because in some real sense, you are. You're pushing into new territory, a place you've never been before. It doesn't matter if you're filled with fear or anxiety. A behavior, even a poorly-executed behavior, creates a familiar pathway. An actual experience, even one that's awkward and forced, gives the body something to work with. Your body will get the message.

Choose your creative focal point, then lead with action. Behave the way you want to be. Do the behavior, repeat the behavior, and the skill will follow. After awhile, you won't be bluffing anymore.

Take ownership

Leadership begins with ownership. There simply is no alternative on this score. Leaders do not engage in blame, nor do the seek out rescue. No matter what the challenge or predicament, they choose creation. Leaders take radical responsibility for their circumstances, their creations and their errors. Above all, leaders are not victims.

This is where the real power and the influence lies. Audiences will be hyper-alert to your acceptance or rejection of responsibility and your orientation will be instantly contagious. The moment you engage in blame, people will follow your lead. They'll start complaining about circumstances and externalize causes onto other people, groups or conditions. Obviously, this becomes a vicious spiral.

Fortunately, the inverse is also true. By taking on responsibility, you'll inspire others to do the same. By bringing your own wandering attention back to your creative focal point, again and again, you'll show people a creative orientation. Above all, model mindfulness. Demonstrate to others how the practice works. In this respect, leadership is just another form of meditation.

Similarly, leaders show radical clarity in describing the creative focal point, whatever it may happen to be. Don't be vague. Don't be abstract. Describe your vision with concrete details. The most powerful leaders shine light on the path forward. Paint a vivid picture of how things can be and how to get there from here. Make your vision explicit and fill it with texture and sensation. This is what it will look like; this is how it will feel. Don't let people guess. Show them the detail.

Lead with your ears

At the same time, it's essential to keep your attention focused on setting and context. Some might imagine that leadership is all about saying the right things at the right time, in the right setting, with the right authority. Leadership we believe, is something that comes out of our mouths or maybe our keyboards.

To be sure, we all would do well to sharpen our skills with language, but ultimately, leadership is not so much about what we say as about what we hear. To be effective, we need to know the beat and pulse of the world and the people around us. This can only be done through studying, observing and mindful listening. In this art, we remain receptive, even as we're pressured by the need to act. The more sensitive we are, the more effective we can become. As Carl Jung put it, "You can exert no influence if you are not susceptible to influence."

The lesson here is to lead with the sensitivity of your entire body, not just the gears of cognition. Feel what you feel. Feel the emotional state of your tribe with your skin, your heart and your gut. Let your resonance system do its work. Pay attention to your experience, then act.

Be who you are

Public speaking and leadership are among the most challenging experiences we will ever attempt; it comes as no surprise that many of us do our best to avoid the experience whenever possible. Or, when called upon to lead, we go rigid with defensive, factual and boring presentations. We hide behind podiums, we hide behind data, we hide behind carefully-calculated language. And in the process, nothing changes, nothing moves.

In our fear and anxiety, we also try to avoid exposure by taking on the attributes of others. In short, we try to become other people. We select leaders and role models in our field and copy their behaviors, their attitudes and their speaking styles. But it never works; people can tell when we're playing it safe and hiding out inside someone else's personality. And even if this approach did succeed with audiences, we'd still be left with a feeling of emptiness. Our practice, even if technically perfect, isn't genuine. It's not about engagement and risk; it's about fear and defense. Even worse, our lack of authenticity creates vast amounts of stress as we try to maintain a false front to the world. Hans Selye, the father of modern stress medicine, saw this clearly: "Most of our tensions and frustrations stem from compulsive needs to act the role of someone we are not."

The only viable solution is to be who you are and take a chance. Authenticity and risk are only things that work. Every audience gets this right away. As soon as you try to be someone else or say what you think you're supposed to say, people will feel the disconnect. Artificial words never take hold. Even if you get your words, data and facts all lined up right, you will still miss the mark. The only way to be effective is to relax into your own life and tell our own stories. As the saying goes, "Be yourself; everyone else is already taken."

Lead with curiosity

Likewise, we become effective by sharing our lives and our passions. Knowledge, expertise and conviction can go a long way, but curiosity is always compelling and contagious. You genuine, authentic interest will draw people into the circle of your fascination and wonder. "Look at how amazing this is!" It is your love, not your knowledge that will move people. It is your life, not your facts, that will resonate.

This is precisely what we see in the culture of TED, those incredibly inspiring presentations offered by some of the world's most interesting people. The TED guidelines make it clear:

- Thou shalt dream a great dream, or show forth a wondrous new thing, or share something thou hast never shared before.

- Thou shalt reveal thy curiosity and thy passion.

- Thou shalt tell a story.

- Thou shalt not flaunt thine ego. Be thou vulnerable. Speak of thy failure as well as thy success.

- Thou shalt remember all the while: laughter is good.

In other words, it's all about the content, the material and the process. It's all about the art and the human encounter with the world. It's not about you. It's about showing the path and lighting the way with wonder. As the singer David Crosby put it: "Serve the song, not the self." Lead with your sense of wonder and adventure.

Expose yourself

Ultimately, the essence of leadership is exposure. When you stand up in front of others, you will experience a very real sense of nakedness. This exposure can be exhilarating, but it is often frightening, even terrifying. Some people will follow your lead, but others will take advantage of your exposure and attack your ideas, your judgment or your character. Critics and adversaries will take issue with your actions no matter what you do or how well you do it. This is an occupational hazard of leadership: "the tallest trees catch the most wind."

Even worse, you're going to get it wrong now and again. Just as in any discipline or practice, not all of your leadership reps will hit the sweet spot of perfect execution. Along the way, you will fall short and make a fool of yourself, sometimes in spectacular ways. You'll get your facts wrong, present them awkwardly, bore your audiences or lead them in the wrong direction. Some of your students, readers and listeners will protest your incompetence and your reputation may suffer. This goes with the territory. This is not an easy path.

Once again, you must ask some fundamental questions: What's your relationship with ambiguity and uncertainty? Can you live in a world where two apparently opposite things can both be true? Can you take a stance? Can you expose yourself to the tribe and maintain your composure? Can you navigate a world of divergent opinions and frequent disagreement?

By this point in your training, you will surely understand that leadership, like every other quality of the human mind, body and spirit, is muscular. We become leaders by exposing ourselves to leadership opportunities, over and over again. Of course we will struggle. Of course we will make fools of ourselves. But we are resilient. Our minds, bodies and spirits will grow stronger and more endurant.

Trust your body; it will adapt to the experience and the exposure. Trust you mind and spirit; they will adapt as well. Above all, you must believe in your purpose and have a clear understanding of your creative focal point. People will distract you, sometimes in spectacular, annoying and maddening ways. You must be adept at the art of return. It's all meditation.

Lesson 24

Practice is perfect

Work. Keep digging your well.
Don't think about getting off from work.
Water is there somewhere.
Submit to a daily practice.
Your loyalty to that is a ring on the door.
Keep knocking, and the joy inside
will eventually open a window
and look out to see who's there.

Rumi

The highest truth of life is that the process is the objective.

Vincent Thibault

Parkour and the Art du déplacement: Strength, Dignity and Community

Take a look at your belt.

After years of training and dedication, your experience has begun to show. The fibers are soft and worn, darkened to black, then gray, by countless encounters with the mat. You've taken thousands of falls and rolls; your belt has literally absorbed the dirt of your life experience. Your body has become strong, your mind has become sharp and your spirit has become expansive and resilient. The time has come to reflect on the nature of mastery.

Unfortunately, our language trips us up right at the outset. In common conversation, we often use the word *mastery* to describe skill, power and control *over* objects and processes. The word suggests authority, supremacy and domination. In this sense, the perfect master is one who has total control over his discipline, his body, his mind and his relationships with the world.

But this is an adolescent view of mastery and it clearly takes us down the wrong path. In fact, the supreme accomplishment of the experienced practitioner is a finely-tuned relationship *with* the world and ourselves; in this respect, we would never seek mastery *over* any process, skill or object. Rather, we might learn to exercise mastery *with* a process, skill or object. In this respect, mastery is not a top-down form of command-and-control; it is a kind of intimacy, a merger, a participation and an engagement. Mastery, in other words, is a kind of compassion.

Practice doesn't make perfect

The word mastery also trips us up because it implies an ultimate, flawless and permanent achievement, a noun. Indeed, the old cliché tells us that "Practice makes perfect." In common conversation, we toss this phrase off without thinking, an empty motivator to keep our students and ourselves moving and doing our reps. It is usually spoken by adults to children who lose enthusiasm for their piano practice, their sports or their studies, but we even hear it from experienced coaches, teachers and trainers.

But when we use this phrase, we do a disservice to both the listener and the process. We suggest that mere repetition will deliver all that we seek. We may not be OK now, but if we keep our nose planted on the grindstone, we'll eventually have a flawless set of skills; ultimately, we'll be "perfect." So the story goes.

Of course, some teachers and coaches raise the bar a notch and update their language to say "Perfect practice makes perfect." This idea is more sophisticated because it suggests the power of discipline and attentional density to build superior skills. We are reminded to focus on high-quality execution in every rep, at every stage of the process. The tighter and more mindful our early reps, the further we can go.

This refinement may well be a step in the right direction, but it doesn't really get it right either. In fact, it makes things worse. The problem is that the word *perfection* implies a stable, complete and finished end state. But nervous systems and human lives simply don't work this way. Even our most highly developed skills are temporary; nothing ever truly "locks in." The ruts and grooves in the topography of our brains are constantly eroding, just as wind, dust, and vegetation fill in the gullies and ruts in a natural landscape. To be sustained, our skills must be periodically refreshed. If we stop training, even for a few days or weeks, the synaptic patterns that we've worked so hard to create begin to degrade; cells that no longer fire together don't stay wired together. So, if we're going to be neurologically correct, we might say that "perfect practice makes for temporary perfection."

But even this refinement still leaves us unsatisfied. The emphasis in all these quips is perfection, an idea that carries an enormous load of psychological and cultural baggage, baggage that can sabotage the very notion of a beautiful practice and whole-person development. Is perfection truly what we seek? And if so, why? Is our quest for perfection an authentic human desire, or is it a reflection of some underlying insecurity, a defensive reaction to our earthly predicament? Is it simply a way to defend ourselves from the uncertainties of a temporary and often challenging world? Are we running to something or away from something?

To say that "practice makes perfect" suggests that practice is a means towards an end without flaws. But could we ever arrive at such a place? And if so, then what? Would we be content in our perfection? Of course not.

Practice is perfect

The more sophisticated approach is to put the emphasis back onto practice itself. In this, success is not measured by any particular achievement, but in continued participation, continued attention and continued creativity. The perfection, if we must use such a word, is to be found in the quality of our dedication and experience, not in any end product we might achieve.

As we continue to learn, we discover that there's always more to be done. The art grows right before our eyes, becoming broader and deeper with each passing day. Our practice reveals new possibilities and opportunities for exploration; there's always some new element that we can add, some quality in need of refinement, or some unnecessary thing that can be taken away. The art calls for a little more discipline in some places, a little less in others, a little more creativity here, some new attention there. And it never ends. Our beautiful practice may become mature, but it is never finished. We never quite get there.

This insight dates back all the way to Buddha's legendary moment of awakening under the Bodhi tree. When we hear his story, many of us tend to assume that his enlightenment was sudden, complete and irreversible. In modern language, we might say that the Buddha had a "breakthrough" into a higher state of consciousness. Once he achieved it, all that was left was to go out into the world and share his experience with others. His enlightenment, in other words, was yet another noun.

But this is an enormous misunderstanding. Buddha's insight was precisely the opposite. Far from being a "get it and forget it" proposition, enlightenment is what we'd today call a full-time job, a work-in-progress. That is, we need to wake up over and over again, every day. Enlightenment doesn't happen just once; enlightenment comes when we enter into a practice of doing it continuously. In other words, enlightenment is a verb.

And so, we need to sit under our Bodhi tree again and again. We need to refresh our attention repeatedly, waking up, over and over. Enlightenment comes, not in some blinding flash of light, but in subtle, moment-by-moment acts of attention and re-engagement. We cultivate it; we grow it. Every moment is an opportunity.

In this respect, mastery is not an achievement, nor is it an arrival. It's a life of wandering away and returning to attention, to compassion, to the breath, to our creative focal points. Distractions will continue to pull us, but training and sincerity will turn our attention back to the process, with an ever greater sense of resilience and confidence.

The process is incremental and there is always work to be done. There is no magic. As screenwriter Paddy Chayefsky put it:

> *Artists don't talk about art. Artists talk about work. If you're an artist, whatever you do is going to be art. If you're not an artist, at least you can do a good day's work. It's what you come in every morning to do. It's work. It's never art. Art is for academics. Art is for scholars. Art is for audiences. Art is not for artists.*

Practice is not perfect

Of course, no matter how diligent our efforts, things don't always go as well as we'd like. We might well believe that practice is perfect, but if we're honest, we're forced to admit that in many instances, our practice is not perfect and not very beautiful either. And on some days, it's downright ugly.

Sometimes our practice is difficult and filled with suffering. Sometimes we loose our attention and wakefulness for long periods of time. We miss sessions, get stressed and distracted, avoid challenges, rationalize our bad habits and create some really ugly works. Sometimes we hide from the world in cowardice and lapse into reactive mindlessness. Other times we get trapped in the drama triangle, behaving like victims, blaming the world and praying for a rescue.

It gets worse. When we create these ugly works, we run from that fact as well. And now our problem is compounded. We fail and judge the fact that we have failed. We cover up our errors and try to ignore them; we deny or dismiss our blunders as deviations and an exception from our true nature. We pretend that everything is just fine.

But when we do this, we miss a vital opportunity to experience the growth that lies within our failings, our ignorance and our ugliness. Not only are these things that we can work with, they are often our most fertile grounds for progress. As James Joyce put it, "A man's errors are his portals of discovery." Similarly, Marcus Aurelius, "What stands in the way becomes the way."

The practice lies not just in grudging acceptance of our blunders, but rather in active exploration and embrace. This is a point made with spectacular clarity by Ernest Kurtz and Katherine Ketcham in *The Spirituality of Imperfection: Storytelling and the Search for Meaning*:

> *It is only in the embracing of our torn self, only in the acceptance that there is nothing "wrong" with feeling "torn," that one can hope for whatever healing is available and can thus become as whole as possible. Only those who know darkness can truly appreciate light; only those who acknowledge darkness can even see the light…Our very brokenness allows us to become whole. To experience sadness, despair, tears, and howls of pain demonstrates not some violation or deficit of spirituality but rather the ultimate spirituality of acceptance.*

Likewise, Elizabeth Kubler-Ross,

> *The most beautiful people we have known are those who have known defeat, known suffering, known struggle, known loss, and have found their way out of the depths. These persons have an appreciation, a sensitivity, and an understanding of life that fills them with compassion, gentleness, and a deep loving concern. Beautiful people do not just happen.*

Our suffering, in other words, is not some deviation from an ideal life path or a flaw that needs to be repaired and forgotten. Rather, it is the raw material of our growth and our progress. Don't try to avoid it. Use it.

And so, as your training belt fades from black to white and you reflect on the nature of mastery, has anything changed?

Perhaps so. These things still hurt, to be sure. Practice will not made you invincible or impermeable to suffering. On the contrary, much of your training has gone in precisely the opposite direction, towards greater sensitivity, vulnerability and exposure. In this sense, you might well be surprised to discover that pain, loss and suffering actually hurt more than before. So what have we learned?

As we've seen, our conventional, primitive responses to suffering were all clustered around common tactics of running, hiding, defending and denial. We masked our pain with substances, we took refuge in fundamentalism and extremism, we adopted a victim orientation and blamed everyone around us for our woes. But none of it worked, and most of it backfired.

But now, as we've grown, we've discovered new orientations, strategies and perspectives that can make a subtle but powerful difference. Most of all, we've learned to fully inhabit our lives, to embrace the reality of our circumstances. In this practice, we've come to realize that there may well be such a things as beautiful pain, beautiful suffering and beautiful loss. These things still cause us pain, but they are part of the beautiful adventure, an adventure that we can live with dignity, honor and a sense of equanimity.

Knowing this, your practice now becomes more complete. Pain and suffering still hurt, but your sense of desperation will begin to diminish. And in its place, a sense of potential and possibility will begin to emerge.

So keep your practice and stay mindful of your creative focal point. And remember, it's not the outcome, but the doing that matters. If you're doing it with sincerity and authenticity, it's beautiful.

Lesson 25

The world is our dojo

We're at the point in our evolution that we all have to become conscious. This is a time of revolution. There's no holding back. So I'm about tearing down the monastery walls and seeing the whole world as the monastery, as the practice, as the spiritual temple. What we're all working on is this very being, this very life. This is the temple, it has no walls.

Genpo Roshi

As we've seen, the challenges we face in this modern world are not only immense and often wicked, but also unprecedented. Our primary, life-supporting relationships with body, habitat and people have been stretched almost beyond recognition. We are suffering on a scale that is almost unimaginable.

It's a frightening predicament to be sure, but a new story is taking hold, an optimistic narrative of growth, neuroplasticity and potential. We are entering a new era of experiential learning, where practice will take on an increasingly powerful role in human life.

In conventional practice, we concentrate our efforts at particular times, in particular places. We spend our time in the gym, in studios, workplaces and classrooms. We practice fundamental skills and learn some valuable lessons.

This is all well and good, but now the challenge is to move beyond the confines of formalized programs and structures. The time has come to take your beautiful practice out into the world, no matter where you go.

You know enough to begin. You have practiced long and hard. You have studied and stumbled. You have sweated and struggled. There is plenty more to learn, but that will come in due course. Now is the time to give it away.

The discipline and insights that you've gained in your primary practice can be adapted to any setting. Your understanding of health and learning, your sense of the habitat, rhythm and sensation, your ownership of circumstance and radical responsibility, your sense of *ubuntu* and human universals: these can be applied anywhere. It's all about opportunism and improv, keeping your attention focused on possibility. The opportunity for art lies in every moment and every setting.

Every instant of your life has the potential that you seek. Ideal settings are wonderful, but far from necessary. You can create beauty anywhere. A beautiful breath, a beautiful pause for mindfulness, a beautiful gesture to the world; all of these are possible no matter where you live, work or travel.

So don't wait for perfect conditions. Do your work where you are. No matter what happens, stay engaged. Keep adapting, keep paying attention to body, habitat and people. Show respect for the process. And above all, keep waking up.

In the end, it all comes down to those familiar qualities: training, mindfulness, attention, love and compassion. This is where we started, this is where we finish. This is our beautiful practice.

Selected websites

Charter for Compassion

Center for Investigating Healthy Minds

Jack Kornfield

Dr. Dan Siegel

Mind and Life Institute

The Center for Compassion and Altruism Research and Education

Mindfulnet

Oxford Mindfulness Centre

Prison Mindfulness Institute

Order of Interbeing

Yale Stress Center

University of Massachusetts Center for Mindfulness in Medicine, Health Care, and Society

Reading list

Biology and Human Behavior by Robert Sapolsky, The Teaching Company

Brain Rules by John Medina

Buddha's Brain: The Practical Neuroscience of Happiness, Love and Wisdom by Rick Hanson, Ph.D. and Richard Mendius, MD

Counter Clockwise: Mindful Health and the Power of Possibility by Ellen J. Langer

Deep Survival: Who Live, Who Dies, and Why by Laurence Gonzales

Dharma in Hell: The Prison Writings of Fleet Maull by Fleet Maull

Disease Proof: The Remarkable Truth About What Makes Us Well by David Katz, MD

Effortless Mastery: Liberating the Master Musician Within by Kenny Werner

Emotional Intelligence: Why it Can Matter More than IQ by Daniel Goleman

Everyday Survival: Why Smart People Do Stupid Things by Laurence Gonzales

Flow: The Psychology of Optimal Experience by Mihaly Csikszentmihalyi

Free Play: Improvisation in Life and Art by Stephen Nachmanovitch

Full Catastrophe Living: Using the Wisdom of Your Body and Mind to Face Stress, Pain, and Illness by Jon Kabat-Zinn, Ph.D.

Last Child in the Woods: Saving Our Children from Nature-Deficit Disorder by Richard Louv

Learned Optimism: How to Change Your Mind and Your Life by Martin Seligman

Lifting Depression: A Neuroscientist's Hands-On Approach to Activating Your Brain's Healing Power by Kelly Lambert

Love 2.0: How Our Supreme Emotion Affects Everything We Feel, Think, Do, and Become by Barbara Fredrickson

Made for Each Other: The Biology of the Human-Animal Bond by Meg Daley Olmert

Man's Search for Meaning by Viktor E. Frankl

Mindfulness by Ellen J. Langer

Mindfulness in Plain English by Bhante Gunaratana

Mindset: The New Psychology of Success by Carol Dweck

Mirroring People: The New Science of How We Connect with Others by Marco Iacoboni

Molecules of Emotion: Why You Feel the Way You Feel by Candace Pert

Narrative Medicine: The Use of History and Story in the Healing Process by Lewis Mehl-Madrona

Nerve: Poise Under Pressure, Serenity Under Stress, and the Brave New Science of Fear and Cool by Taylor Clark

Parkour and the Art du deplacement: Strength, Dignity, Community by Vincent Thibault

Pronoia: How the Whole World is Conspiring to Shower You with Blessings by Rob Brezsny

Punished by Rewards: The Trouble with Gold Stars, Incentive Plans, A's, Praise and Other Bribes by Alfie Kohn

Relaxation Revolution by Herbert Benson, M.D. and William Proctor

Social Intelligence: The New Science of Human Relationships by Daniel Goleman

Soft-Wired: How the New Science of Brain Plasticity Can Change Your Life by Michael Merzenich

Spark: The Revolutionary New Science of Exercise and the Brain by John Ratey

Surviving Survival: The Art and Science of Resilience by Laurence Gonzales

Taking the Leap: Freeing Ourselves from Old Habits and Fears by Pema Chodron

Tao Jeet Kune Do by Bruce Lee

The Age of Empathy: Nature's Lessons for a Kinder Society by Frans de Waal

The Aims of Education by Alfred North Whitehead, The Free Press 1957

The Art of Happiness by The Dali Lama

The As if Principle: The Radically New Approach to Changing Your Life by Richard Wiseman

The Emotional Life of Your Brain by Richard Davidson

The Joy of Living by Yongey Mingyur Rinpoche

The Lab Rat Chronicles: A Neuroscientist Reveals Life Lessons from the Planet's Most Successful Mammals by Kelly Lambert

The Mindfulness Revolution Edited by Barry Boyce

The Moral Molecule by Paul Zak

The Neurobiology of "We" by Daniel J. Siegel, M.D.

The Neuroscience of Human Relationships by Louis Cozolino

The Plastic Mind: New Science Reveals Our Extraordinary Potential to Transform Ourselves by Sharon Begley

The Power of Full Engagement by Jim Loehr and Tony Schwartz

The Power of Story by Jim Loehr

The Power of TED (The Empowerment Dynamic) by David Emerald

The Relaxation Response by Herbert Benson, M.D.

The Spirituality of Imperfection: Storytelling and the Search for Meaning by Ernest Kurtz and Katherine Ketcham

Tao Te Ching by Lao Tzu

The Willpower Instinct by Kelly McGonigal

Train Your Mind, Change Your Brain by Sharon Begley

Undoing Perpetual Stress: The Missing Connection Between Depression, Anxiety and 21st Century Illness by Richard O'Connor, Ph.D.

We're All Doing Time: A Guide for Getting Free by Bo Lozoff

When the Body Says No: The Cost of Hidden Stress by Gabor Maté, M.D.

When Things Fall Apart: Heart Advice for Difficult Times by Pema Chodron

Why Zebras Don't Get Ulcers: The Acclaimed Guide to Stress, Stress-Related Diseases and Coping Third Edition by Robert Sapolsky, Henry Holt 2004

Willpower: Rediscovering the Greatest Human Strength by Roy F. Baumeister and John Tierney

Gratitudes and appreciation

Books are an illusion. On superficial inspection, they appear to have been written by a single individual, but the knowledge that appears on the page is actually a living, growing thing, continuously created and refined by an community of interest and practice. No one does it alone.

In this respect, I have been profoundly fortunate. I've been challenged, inspired and supported by special tribe of friends and senseis who have turned the writing of this book into a beautiful experience:

Sam, Beth, Alex and Travis Forencich, Dawni Rae and Alia Joy Shaw, Susan Fahringer and Keith Worman, Kay Turner, James O'Keefe and family, Steve Laskevitch and Carla Fraga, Navin Kulshreshtha, Josh Leeger, Seby Alary, Stuart Brown, Kwame Brown, Colin Pistell, Michael and Tonya Levy, Erwan Le Corre, Edward Drax, Steve Myrland, Tara Wood, Martha Peterson, Corey Jung, David Katz, Fleet Maull, Gary Gray, Lyman Woolens, Kelly Lambert, Vincent Thibault, Skye Nacel, Robert Sapolsky, Andrea Brixey, and the team at En*theos

Continuing your practice

Beautiful Practice® workshops are available for your organization, company, or school. These are full participation, experiential training events that include presentations, team-building, vigorous movement and meditation. The classic training event is a full day workshop, hosted by your organization.

Custom trainings and keynotes are also available.

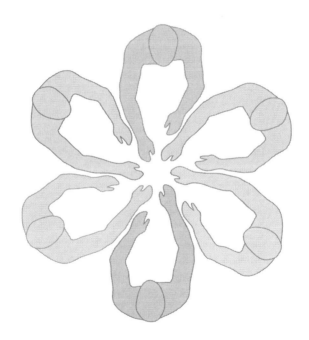

Contact Frank Forencich: frank@exuberantanimal.com

For more information, visit

www.exuberantanimal.com and www.beautiful-practice.com

Frank Forencich

Frank Forencich is an internationally-recognized leader in health and performance education. He earned his B.A. at Stanford University in human biology and neuroscience and has over 30 years teaching experience in martial art and health education.

Frank holds black belt rankings in karate and aikido and has traveled to Africa on several occasions to study human origins and the ancestral environment. He is a regular columnist for Paleo Magazine and a featured teaching partner at En*theos Academy for Optimal Living. In 2012, Frank was named by Experience Life magazine as one of "Five Visionaries leading the charge to better health, and a healthier world."

Also by Frank Forencich:

Exuberant Animal: The Power of Health, Play and Joyful Movement

Change Your Body, Change the World: Reflections on Health and the Human Predicament

Stresscraft: A Whole-Life Approach to Health and Performance

"I have worked with Frank at two major medical meetings. He is a superb public speaker–articulate, extremely knowledgeable and passionate in his presentations. He has a fun and endearing interactive style that is both enlightening and entertaining. I speak at and or attend science and medical programs around the U.S. dozens of times each year and have the chance to see and hear top scientists frequently. Frank Forencich is one of the most effective presenters with whom I have ever worked."

James O'Keefe MD, cardiologist
St. Luke's Cardiovascular Consultants